Bob "Frogfoot" Weller (signature)

GALLEON ALLEY

The 1733 Spanish Treasure Fleet

by Bob "Frogfoot" Weller

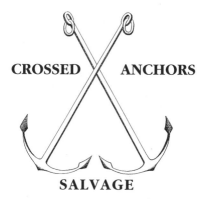

CROSSED ANCHORS

SALVAGE

GALLEON ALLEY
The 1733 Spanish Treasure Fleet

by
Bob "Frogfoot" Weller

Edited by Ernie "Seascribe" Richards
Typesetting by EN RADA Publications

ISBN #1-893758-00-1

Library of Congress Catalog-in-Publication data:
Weller, Robert M.
Galleon Alley

COVER PHOTO: Cannon on "Galleon Alley." By Denis Trelewicz.
BACK COVER PHOTO: Weller Family Album.
COVER LAYOUT: EN RADA Publications.

Other books by Bob "Frogfoot" Weller

"Famous Shipwrecks of the Florida Keys"
ISBN #0-9628359-0-0

"Sunken Treasures on Florida Reefs"
ISBN #0-9628359-1-9

"Galleon Hunt"
ISBN #0-9628359-2-7

"Shipwrecks Near Wabasso Beach"
*ISBN #0-9628359-4-3

"The Dreamweaver"
ISBN #0-9628359-5-1

"Salvaging Spanish Sunken Treasure"
ISBN #0-9628359-9-4

About the author...

Bob got his nickname while serving with the Navy Underwater Demolition Team ONE during the Korean War. He began salvaging Spanish galleons in the Florida Keys in 1960 at a time when the 1733 fleet of Spanish galleons were first being located. It was a time of excitement and reward for those that followed their dreams of sunken treasure, and Bob found more than his share. Since 1978 he has been methodically salvaging the 1715 Spanish treasure fleet, an experience that has allowed him to author books which put the reader "on the bottom" with the salvage crews.

*Co-authored with Ernie "Seascribe" Richards

ACKNOWLEDGMENTS

There are a great many people that made this book possible, friendships collected from the many salvage experiences over the past 40 years. The salvagers that made it possible for everyone to enjoy the recoveries from the 1733 fleet are, Bobby Klein, Marty Meylach, Dr. R. Welberry, Bobby Savage, Jack Steffany, Ray Manieri, Brad Patten, Pat Patterson, Chuck Mitchell, Tim Watkins and his *Buccaneer* crew, Jim Hettel, Carl Ward, Richard MacAllaster, John Berrier, Jimmy Janda, Kip Porter, and Bernie Smith. A special thanks to Don Gurgiola for his help on the "Tres" and "Herrera", and to Jim Clupper at the Islamorada Library for his research. The greatest asset any author has is a researcher in the halls of the Archivo General de las Indias in Seville, Spain, and Jack "Blackjack" Haskins filled those shoes admirably. He is also one of the better salvage divers, having recovered the greatest artifact from the 1733 fleet.

A special moment for those divers no longer with us: Art Sapp; Craig Hamilton, to whom I owe my jump-start in Spanish galleons; Henry Taylor; Duke Long; Bobby Klein; and Richard MacAllaster. They left behind a legacy that will someday play a major role in history as the "Treasure Salvage Years" come to a close. As always, Ernie "Seascribe" Richards waved his literary wand and chased away all the improper English gremlins. When it comes to editing, I'm glad he's in my corner.

Somehow I have to tell you about my cats. I have four of the most spoiled cats in Palm Beach County. But I love them. They have managed to stay under foot, roaming my computer, and curling around my feet or under the lamp near the desk. I have never been alone during these months at my desk, working on books. They have managed to slip a little catnip between the pages. This is our seventh book—the cats and mine together—and I hope you enjoy it as much as we did in "pawting" it all together. *"Frogfoot"*

Margaret "Lady Gold-Diver" Weller, the author's wife, navigator, boon companion, soul mate, and accomplished treasure finder.

Pumpkin, one of the Weller cats.

TYPICAL SPANISH ANCHOR OF 1733 being brought ashore during the "halcyon" years of treasure salvage in the Florida Keys.

TABLE OF CONTENTS

Acknowledgments

Table of Contents

Chapter   **Page**

FOREWORD

"GALLEON ALLEY"

When the Spanish treasure fleet of 1733 was driven ashore along the Florida Keys it left a story behind that has provided the local residents, and visitors as well, a heritage that lends itself to the way of life in the Keys. The 120 miles of "keys," or small islands, that skip westward in a curve from Homestead to Key West are merely the "above water" part of a ridge of coral that extends to seaward as much as five miles, ending in the "dragon's teeth." The dragon's teeth, so called because of the sharp, piercing coral that faces the deep, cobalt blue Gulf Stream, have caught many an unsuspecting sailing vessel navigating northward with the push of the current. When hurricanes aimed their whirling dervishes up the "slot" created by the Bahama Islands on one side, and the Florida Keys on the other, the sailing vessels had no shelter to hide them from the huge waves and great winds that drove them unmercifully onto the dragon's teeth. If they were fortunate to miss the hard reefs offshore, there was no escaping a bilging of their bottoms as they were driven into the shallow water near shore. The skeletons of the hundreds of sailing vessels that lie scattered along the reefs and shallows of the Florida Keys are waymarks of days long past. A way of life passed down, at first, by survivors of these old "freight trains of the sea," and later by those who salvaged the cargoes from these vessels.

Among the many ballast piles marking the final resting places of these vessels are also those representing the Spanish treasure fleets. These are the ballast piles that have added the fantasy and intrigue of treasure lost, of each one's personal hope and dream of finding a treasure of gold doubloons and pieces-of-eight. The one driving incentive is that there is still treasure to be found. Regardless of how often modern salvagers work these wreck sites, they will never find it all. Passengers' baggage scattered for miles along the beaches, in the sands just offshore, and the baggage was filled with the personal possessions of merchants and sea captains who spent many years in the New World in the making of personal fortunes. And they made it. They were carrying it back to Spain when a hurricane ended their dreams of a rich and rewarding life of retirement.

Local residents no longer take notice, but as visitors drive along U.S. Highway #1 between Key Largo and Marathon there is little doubt that they are traveling a corridor of shipwrecks. There is evidence everywhere of the treasure fleet. Huge Spanish anchors lean from concrete pads, or against the sides of dive shops. Cannons are cradled by ballast pile mounts, or coral and concrete monuments, and they grace the fronts of banks, restaurants, dive shops, and motels. Even the Dept. of Transportation in Marathon seems protected behind several mounted cannon facing the highway. There are museums filled with treasure, artifacts, and the romance of sunken galleons.

The galleons are gone—teredo worms and time have done their work—but the anchors and cannons remain, salvaged from the hundreds of ballast piles that mark the final grave sites of these high-masted freight trains of the sea. Many of them have nameplates, each drawing attention to the particular vessel it was salvaged from. Often as not the names of the ships will never be known, lost in archival history. It is here, in the Florida Keys that the salvaging of sunken treasure by modern commercial means really got its start. It is a period of time that will be known in future history as "The Treasure Salvage Years."

One of the significant advantages in writing this book is that it provides, for historical records at least, the names of a few of the galleons driven onto the reefs of the Florida Keys during the July 15, 1733, hurricane. These particular ballast piles then take on some semblance of identification and, of course, each has characteristics all its own. So, if for no other reason, this book will have given these shipwrecks of Old Spain some historical perpetuity. The other objective of this book is to give the modern day salvors who located and worked these sites the credit they deserved for their initative and perseverance in all phases of research, salvage, and preservation. Without them the 1733 sites would have been lost

It is here in the Florida Keys, as one travels down "Galleon Alley," that you actually feel the presence of those years so long ago when the treasures of the New World passed so close by the Keys. If the light from the moon is just right, and the sea has a slight ripple, one often has the feeling that galleons are in sight on the edge of the reefs. And they are probably right.

That's what dreams are made of...

CANNONS ALONG U.S. HIGHWAY #1.
Above: Treasure Village. Iron Cannon and Stone Ballast
from "La Capitana," El Rubí.
Below: Chesapeake Restaurant. Iron Cannon from Herrera.

CANNONS ALONG U.S. HIGHWAY #1.
Above: Caloosa Cove Lodge, M.M. 76. Iron Cannon.

Below: Caloosa Cove Lodge, M.M. 76. Iron Cannon.

CANNONS ALONG U.S. HIGHWAY #1.
Above: Plantation Key Marina. Iron Cannon.

Below: Caloosa Cove Lodge, M.M. 76. Iron Cannon.

CANNONS ALONG U.S. HIGHWAY #1.
Above: Crane Point Hammock Maritime Museum.
Iron Cannon.
Below: Buccaneer Resort, Marathon. Iron Cannon.

SPANISH GALLEON ANCHORS ALONG U.S. HIGHWAY #1.
Above:
Cobra Marina, Snake Creek. Iron Anchor from El Lerri.

Below:
Veterinary Clinic, Upper Matecumbe. Iron Anchor.

SPANISH GALLEON ANCHORS ALONG U.S. HIGHWAY #1. Above: Caloosa Cove Lodge, Lower Matecumbe. Iron Anchor from The "Pillar Dollar Wreck," 1760.

SPANISH GALLEON ANCHORS ALONG U.S. HIGHWAY #1. *Below: Treasure Village, Plantation Key. Iron Anchor from "La Capitana,"* **El Rubí.**

CHAPTER 1: FOLLOW YOUR DREAM

Yes, there is still a fortune in gold and silver lying on the bottom of the ocean along the east and west coasts of Florida. During my 40 years of salvage diving here in Florida the question most asked by enthusiasts of the underwater world has been, **"Is there still anything left to find?"** The answer is a resounding "Yes!" Although there are several groups such as mine actively searching out Spanish galleons here in Florida, no matter how long nor how hard we work at it, there will always be something left. The ocean bottom is a BIG place, and to find something like a gold coin or a piece of jewelry takes an incredible amount of patience and perseverance, as well as the time to cover areas meticulously. Even with technology as we know it today — metal detectors that can locate artifacts twelve to eighteen inches beneath the sand— you have to understand the reefs where the Spanish galleons bilged their bottoms and became a part of our historic past. The reef system has cracks and fissures that make the best possible hiding places, and heavier objects such as gold and silver coins have an uncanny habit of being able to squirrel themselves away.

A good example happened to one of our best salvage divers, John Berrier. We were working the Douglass Beach wreck site of the 1715 *patache "Nieves,"* 2-1/2 miles south of the Fort Pierce inlet. The bottom where John was working consisted of flat coquina, a consolidation of a whitish rock composed of marine shells and white sand, often hundreds of years old. He had a "hit" on his metal detector in the middle of the area, indicating a metal object just below the surface. There were no holes or cracks to be found within several feet of the hit, and the bottom was too hard to just dig through. However, about four feet from the hit he spotted a small break in the bottom, a hole no bigger than three inches. By using a screwdriver he was able to carefully break the coquina layer (which was about 2-1/2 inches thick) from the hole to the area of his hit. It was worth his effort, because the hit turned out to be a gold doubloon dated 1714. The coin had dropped into the hole and, over the years, had worked its way several feet to the spot where John found it.

By most estimates there are somewhere between 4,000 and 5,000 shipwrecks along Florida's coastline. That really is not surprising when you consider the role that the Gulf Stream plays in funneling shipping from the Gulf of Mexico northward along the east coast of Florida. The northward two-knot current is a slingshot that vessels take advantage of. Since the early sixteenth century, travel on this side of the Atlantic was by water. The maze of concrete highways never really materialized until the turn of the last century, and before that the sailing vessel was king. As an example of the traffic along the waterways of the world, England's coastlines are a virtual scrap heap of wreck sites. In just one year, 1864, there were 1,741 vessels sunk along her shores. In 1880 another 1,303 vessels were sunk (Steve Singer: *Shipwrecks of Florida*). But of course not all sunken vessels are treasure wrecks. Here in Florida it is quite possible for a treasure **hunter** to dive a new wreck every week of his salvage career and never recover a single gold or silver treasure coin. But with proper research and guidance he can narrow the odds considerably.

To become a treasure **finder** requires a certain amount of pursuit in the rumor market. Once research identifies the target and the general area, then you have to roll up your sleeves and track down net fishermen and beachcombers who may have recovered something of interest from a "snag" area...or from the beach after a storm. Old newspaper files have provided descriptions of storms and marine disasters. Pawn shops sometimes have artifacts for sale, recovered by lobster fishermen or recreational divers and with a story behind them. The rumors to avoid are the "stories" of treasure galleons in remote places.

Once involved in the search for sunken treasure the salvor will find treasure stories coming out of the woodwork. Sometimes a story has been passed around the rumor table so many times that when it finally gets back to the originator, he believes he is hearing a story of a new wreck site.

Keep this in mind when sifting through the stories of sunken treasure wrecks: In the early sixteenth century the Spanish Main covered the entire Caribbean, and here was an area filled with reefs and shoals in the most unexpected places. In the early years of Spanish exploration a great many vessels were lost, many without survivors, because of the remote reefs the vessels were lost on. Once the enormous flow of gold and silver began from the mines of South America and Mexico it became necessary to find a "safe" route for the Spanish treasure galleons to follow. The harbors of Nombre de Dios (later shifted to Porto Bello in 1595), Cartagena, and Vera Cruz were to become the designated ports to receive the precious metals for transfer to the galleons.

The voyage back to Spain had to be made along a "safe" route, one that was known to be free of hidden reefs and shoals. This route, once located, became known as the *"Carrera de Indias,"* or roadway of the Indies. This became the water highway of the Spanish Sea, one the Spaniards followed without exception. If a galleon captain failed to follow the route and lost his ship —and the king's treasure— he suffered more than did the captain of the *Exxon Valdez* for running his oil tanker on an Alaskan shoal! And it was along this route that storms, hurricanes, or just poor navigation caused the treasure galleons to bilge their bottoms and become a part of archeological history.

When a treasure finder hears rumors of a "treasure" galleon resting among some remote Bahama islands he normally dismisses it, because a treasure galleon would have no reason to be sailing there in the first place. These ballast piles usually turn out to be island traders, with a few iron cannon to ward off the local pirates. The search for treasure galleons begins with the known shipwrecks of the treasure fleets, scattered along the *Carrera de Indias*.

Along the coast of Florida there are a number of known treasure fleet shipwrecks. In 1554 three galleons of the treasure fleet were sunk in a hurricane near Rio Palmas, latitude 26 degrees, 30 minutes. They were tentatively identified as the *Maria del Camino*, 350 tons and under the command of Captain Diaz of the Terra Firma fleet, *San Estevan*, 200 tons and under the command of Captain Mercerno, and *Sancta Maria de Yciar*, 200 tons under the command of Captain Ozosi (Marx: *Spanish Treasure in Florida Waters*). In 1563 *La Madelena*, a Spanish galleon of 250 tons under the command of Captain Cristobal Rodriguez, was driven by a storm onto the reefs of Cape Canaveral. In 1568 the *urca, El Mulato,* and a *nao, Vizcayo,* were lost off Indian River. In 1589 one of Martin Perez de Olesabal's treasure fleet galleons was lost on the reefs of Cape Canaveral (Albert Manucy, *History of Castillo de San Marcos & Fort Matanzas*). In most cases these galleons were lost on the south side of the Cape if sailing during the summer months. In the summer months 95% of the storms are out of the southeast, in the winter time 95% of the storms are out of the northeast.

In 1618 the Honduran *almiranta, San Martín,* was driven ashore near Wabasso Beach. (Weller/Richards: *Shipwrecks Near Wabasso Beach*). This site is presently under the state lease to Treasure Salvors in Sebastian. In 1622 a hurricane sank eight galleons of the treasure fleet under the command of the Marqués de Cadereita. In 1971 Mel Fisher located the anchor of the *Atocha* scatter pattern, and in 1985 he discovered the mother lode. In 1980 his salvage group located and salvaged the *Santa Margarita*, sister ship of the *Atocha,* near the Marquesas Keys ("Frogfoot" Weller: *The Dreamweaver*).

In 1623 the *Espiritu Santo el Mayor*, a large Spanish galleon of 400 tons, was driven ashore somewhere south of Cape Canaveral by a hurricane. Little of her treasure was ever recovered. The *Santissima Trinidad*, another large 600-ton Spanish galleon, sank offshore during the same hurricane, probably in the same area (Marx: *Spanish Treasure in Florida Waters*; Hudson: *Tragedy on the High Seas*). In 1659 the *San Francisco y San Antonio* came ashore near present day Jupiter Inlet. There were 33 survivors (Dr. Eugene Lyon: Research). In 1660 the *San Miguel el Arcangel* was also wrecked close to present day Jupiter Inlet. A great many gold and silver coins, two gold bars, a gold disc, and a 90-pound silver bar have been recovered to date by the Jupiter Wreck, Inc. group.

In 1715 one of the greatest disasters to befall the Spanish treasure fleets occurred along the east coast of Florida. On 30 July a savage hurricane sank the entire fleet of eleven ships. A French frigate, the *Grifón*, had joined the fleet in Havana and was the only ship to survive, arriving in France four weeks after the disaster. Of the five vessels of General Ubilla's *flota*, all were smashed against the reefs from Ft. Pierce Inlet to Sebastian Inlet. The six ships of General Echeverz' *flota* were scattered from Sandy Point just south of Vero Beach, northward as far as Nassau Sound above Jacksonville. One vessel, *El Ciervo,* a French prize vessel captured near Porto Bello, sank in deep water with no survivors. The Spanish were able to salvage over 5,000,000 pesos from the primary galleons, but over a million pesos remained after several years of salvage.

Modern day salvors, including the author, have worked the sites on a regular basis and have recovered some fabulous artifacts. ("Frogfoot" Weller: *Sunken Treasure on Florida Reefs*). Six sites have been identified as 1715 shipwrecks. The *Nieves*, located 2-1/2 miles south of the Ft. Pierce inlet has produced more gold and silver coins than all the other sites combined. It was labeled the "Gold Wreck," and the Treasure Coast of Florida was so named because of the recoveries from this wreck site. The *Urca de Lima*, located a mile north of the Ft. Pierce inlet, became famous in Kip Wagner's book *Pieces of Eight*. It became known as the "Wedge Wreck" because of all the silver wedges being recovered from around her ballast pile. The state of Florida has since designated the *"Urca"* as a state park, and it is now a "see, but don't touch" site.

Echeverz' *almiranta, Rosario*, came ashore at Sandy Point about four miles south of Vero Beach. Her scatter pattern of cannons led to the beach...and then disappeared. About 2,000 silver coins and a gold coin were recovered by the Treasure Salvors group in 1963, but that's where the hunt ends. The *Rosario* is still there to be found, with some very nice gold bars and coins on her manifest.

The *capitana* of Echeverz, the *Carmen*, sank directly offshore from the first green of the Rio Mar Golf Course in Vero Beach. About 900 feet from the beach, and in eighteen feet of water are nineteen of the most photogenic cannons —and two large Spanish anchors— a shutterbug could ever ask for. The ballast pile is there, a large one because the galleon was over 1,000 tons, and the deep sand has given up some great artifacts. Fisher and his Treasure Salvors group worked the site in the late 1960s and recovered 149 gold coins, some gold bars, and two beautiful gold crosses with pearl posts. John Brandon and Kane Fisher have also worked the site more recently, each recovering a number of gold coins. One frustrating aspect of this site is the gold dust. When you fan the sand from the bottom and study the small cracks and fissures, all you see is gold dust! The *Carmen* was carrying a few bags of the golden flakes, and they scattered all over the bottom. Salvor Gene Evans used a barge outfitted with a dredge for several days and recovered enough gold dust to fill a small vial, as well as a piece of gold jewelry, but it was more fun than financially rewarding.

Ubilla's *capitana* sank about five miles north of Vero Beach, and the *Regla* disintegrated when it struck the nearshore reef and scattered northward. Salvors have worked this site for a number of years with some success. Art Hartman has recovered a number of gold and silver coins, as well as a few gold discs. John Brandon has also recovered a number of gold coins and discs, and a few gold bars as well. The author recovered a large number of silver coins and artifacts during the 1984 salvage season. The beach opposite the wreck site is known as "Corrigan's," named for Hugh Corrigan, who used to own the property and who recovered some great artifacts from the beach after storms. In 1984 the now famous "Thanksgiving Storm" struck the area and cut away the sand from Corrigan's. Over 2,000 silver coins and at least sixteen gold coins, as well as a few gold artifacts, were recovered by beachcombers with metal detectors in a single day. When northeastern storms barrel down the coast, the first place beach hunters look today is "Corrigan's."

The "Cabin Wreck" is also a famous site due to Kip Wagner's book *Pieces of Eight*. It was here that he first located silver coins along the beach after a storm. And later, after buying the lone cottage that sat on the beach near where the coins were being picked up, he discovered the pile of cannon just 200 feet out in the water directly in front of the cabin. The rest is history, as Kip and his Real Eight group recovered some great treasures. The wreck site turned out to be Ubilla's *almiranta*, the *San Roman*, and even today the scatter pattern is giving up some fabulous treasure. In 1993 the author's group, Crossed Anchors Salvage, recovered gold earrings and brooches containing 441 diamonds, 21 gold rings, gold toothpicks, and other artifacts. The other wreck sites of the 1715 fleet are still to be located and identified. That's what dreams are made of.

This book is about another fleet of Spanish galleons, the largest to be sunk along the coast of Florida. On July 15, 1733, a hurricane sank or grounded twenty of the 21 ships in General Rodrigo de Torres y Morales' *flota* as it made its way up the Bahama Channel near the Florida Keys. Because it wasn't as vicious a storm as the 1715 hurricane, many of the galleons remained intact, and later several were refloated and sailed back to Havana. The fleet carried 12,286,253 pesos in registered silver coins and bars (plus a considerable amount of unregistered treasure) and, after the salvage was completed, salvagemaster Sanchez Duran was kind enough to leave behind a few thousand silver coins scattered among the ballast piles. This fleet of Spanish galleons has been the source of some of the best treasure hunts in decades. The water in the Florida Keys is, for the most part, gin clear and usually warm. In the late 1950s treasure salvage groups began locating the various wreck sites based on charts drawn by the Spanish salvagers in 1733. By 1966, when the *Populo* was located, most of the sites had been discovered, identified, and to some extent worked by modern day salvagers. Only the *San Fernando* remained to be located.

Today the ballast piles and some ribs and bottom planks remain for the casual visitor to photograph, or yarn ashore after a vacation diving trip to the Keys. And occasionally one finds a silver coin, a lead musket ball, or possibly a brass button to highlight the trip. Sand and time have managed to cover the piles, but a few remain to be seen, a grim reminder of the struggle so many survivors had as the huge waves drove their ships ashore. Treasure is still there and will never be completely recovered.

The passengers' baggage contained some great artifacts representing life in Spain's New World, and this scattered shoreward. Within recent years a gold box, along with several gold rosaries, was recovered on the site of the *San Ignacio* in Coffins Patch near Marathon. Some great treasures have been recovered in isolated pockets between the wreck sites and the shore, and more will be recovered in the future.

This book is for the young at heart, for those that have a desire to "Follow Your Dream" of finding sunken treasure. This book is about the 1733 Spanish Treasure Fleet.

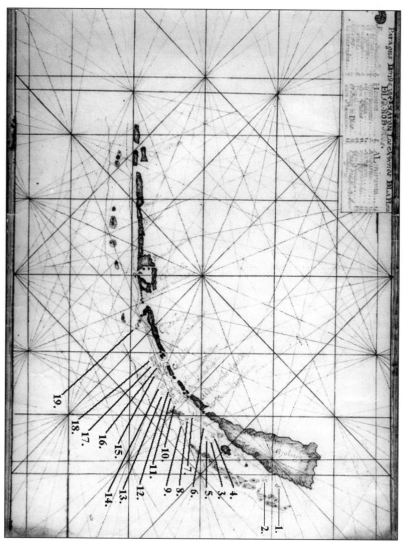

"*Parajes Donde Vararon Los Navios de la Flota del Año 1733.*"
—"Places where the ships of the 1733 Fleet ran aground."

1. *El Pinque Populo*
2. *El Aviso*
3. *El Infante*
4. *San José (San Joseph)*
5. *La Capitana (El Rubí)*
6. *Chavez*
7. *La Balandra*

8. *Herrera*
9. *Tres Puentes*
10. *Murguia*
11. *San Pedro*
12. *El Lerri (El Terri)*
13. *El Poder de Dios*
14. *San Francisco*

15. *La Almiranta*
16. *Las Angustias*
17. *El Sueco de Arizón*
18. *San Fernando*
19. *San Ignacio*

CHAPTER 2: THE 1733 TREASURE FLEET

By the year 1732, when the Treasure Fleet was assembling, the ships had undergone a dramatic change from the image many people have of a "galleon." The old shape of a galleon—with a narrow stern, high and slender aft superstructure, a narrow fo'c'sle and a wide and flat projecting beakhead—had ceased to exist. The galleon was now wider of beam with a sloping deck, and with one, possibly two decks aft. She had a sleeker look with better sailing characteristics. The three decks of cannon were replaced by cargo and passenger spaces. The two lower decks in most cases were continuous, housing the crew, cargo, and ship's stores. There were cannon, but a 60-gun *navio* was considered heavily armed. By now the square rigged sails were beginning to take on the look of a true "Ship of the Line."

The Spanish struggle to keep the English, French, Dutch, and an assortment of pirates from capturing one of their treasure galleons had reached an end. The Spanish struggle was now aimed at maintaining its share of the trade with the New World. The competing countries were selling goods cheaper in the colonies, and they no longer had to "fight it out" with the Spanish galleons to reap a reward of gold and silver. As a result the Treasure Fleets had taken on a new look, the look of a merchant fleet with great cargo capacity—and a few heavily armed *navios* that were primarily consigned to carry the king's treasure back to Spain. The Treasure Fleet system, by 1765, had been successful for 169 years, but competition would end its existence.

It is quite possible that the greatest confusion within the salvage community regarding the 1733 fleet...is the names of the ships involved. Somehow, many years ago, the names of the various ships were published without complete research, and as a result it seems the names were cast in bronze. It is understandable how the confusion could happen, based on many of the ships being referred to in numerous documents by their "nicknames," or by the name of the captain of a particular vessel. If you consider the complete length of the official name of many of the galleons, then you can appreciate the reason for shortening their names. Writing the ship's name in the log could become a laborious chore each day. A simple example of this is the *nao, Nuestra Señora del Rosario San Antonio y San Vicente Ferrer*. Taking a deep breath, the quartermaster simply wrote in the log *El Sueco de Arizón*. As you may have guessed, the owner of the *nao* was Don Jacinto de Arizón. One more confusing point concerning the 1733 fleet: Of the ships in the convoy that left Cádiz for the New World, not all of them were in the fleet struck by the hurricane. Also, several ships joined the group in Havana.

So, to set the records straight, the names of the vessels leaving Cádiz on August 2, 1732, under the command of General Don Rodrigo de Torres y Morales are as follows. From the Archives of Seville, *Indiferente General* 2021, except where noted, with (nicknames) in parentheses:

El Rubí Segundo (El Rubí) — *Capitana*. Its *Maestre de Plata* and *Permisión* and Treasurer of the Squadron, Don Balthesar de la Torre. A Royal Commissioner, Don Alonso Barragan, was appointed to sail with the ship as the king's emissary.

El Gallo Indiano — *Almiranta*. Its *Maestre de Plata* and *Permisión*, Don Bernadino de Maturana.

Nuestra Señora de Balvaneda (El Infante) — *Refuerzo*. Its *Maestre de Permisión*, Don Domingo de Lanz.

El Populo — *Pinque.* Its *Maestre,* Don Juan Eques de Raciones, and of the property of the Royal Hacienda, Don Francisco Ymbernon.

San Phelipe **(El Lerri)** — *Nao* of the Marqués de Cañada. Its *Maestre,* Don Joseph del Villar y Andrade.

El Aviso — Advice Boat, Owner Don Nicolas del Castillo. Its Captain, Don Pedro Arrambide (joined the fleet in Vera Cruz).

San Joseph y las Animas **(San José)**— *Nao,* owner Don Joseph del Duque. Its *Maestre,* Don Cristobal Fernandez Franco.

Nuestra Señora de las Angustias y San Raphael **(Angustias)**— *Nao,* owner José Sanchez Madrid. Its *Maestre,* Francisco Sanchez Madrid.

San Francisco — *Nao,* owner Don Cristobal de Urquijo. Its *Maestre,* Don Cristobal de Urquijo. (Urquijo was actually not the Captain of the *San Francisco* when this ship sank, he was on board the *San Ygnacio.*)

San Ygnacio **(San Ignacio)**— *Nao,* its owner and *Maestre,* Don Cristobal de Urquijo.

Nuestra Señora del Carmen y San Antonio de Padua **(Chavez)**— *Nao,* its owner and *Maestre,* Don Antonio de Chavez.

Nuestra Señora de Belén y San Antonio de Padua **(Herrera)** — *Nao,* its owner and *Maestre,* Don Luis de Herrera.

El Gran Poder de Dios **(Poder)** — *Nao,* its owner and *Maestre,* Francisco Sanchez Madrid.

Nuestra Señora del Rosario, San Antonio, San Vicente Ferrer **(Sueco de Arizón)** — *Nao,* its owner Don Jacinto de Arizón, its *Maestre* Don Juan de Arizón.

San Pedro — *Nao,* its owner Don Gaspar de Larrea Berdugo, its *Maestre* Don Gaspar Lopez de Gonzales.

***Nuestra Señora de los Dolores y Santa Isabel* (Tres Puentes)**— *Nao*, its owner Don Nicolas del Castillo, its *Maestre* Don Antonio Loaysa.

***Nuestra Señora del Rosario y Santo Domingo* (Murgia)**— *Nao*, its owner the heirs of Don Andrés de Murgia, its *Maestre* Don Thomas de Apodaca.

***Nuestra Señora de Los Reyes, San Fernando, y San Francisco de Paula* (San Fernando)**— Its owner Don Francisco de Soto y Posada, its *Maestre* Don Joseph Cabeza. (Marx: 1971, p. 211).

The following two vessels accompanied the fleet to Vera Cruz but did not sail to Havana as part of the treasure fleet:

Nuestra Señora del Rosario, San Francisco Xavier Y Las Animas — *Nao*, its owner and *Maestre* Don Luis Lozano. (Author's note: Possibly under contract to Don Juan Chaurio and consigned to Maracaybo).

***Nuestra Señora del Pilar* (El Lanfranco)** — *Nao*, Property of His Majesty, going under account of the *Consulado* and Commerce, its Captain Don Juan Francisco Liano, its *Maestre* Don Francisco Fanales. The *Pilar* returned to Cádiz alone with mail and fruit from Havana, arriving April 12, 1733.

It could not be called a "rag tag" fleet, although it was comprised of vessels built in many countries, including Italy, England, France, Holland, Germany, Spain, and the American colonies. Sailing from Cádiz on August 2, 1732, the fleet caught the Canary Currents southward to the Cape Verde Islands. Here they made any final preparations or repairs, filled their water casks and larders with fresh water and provisions, and left their final landmarks behind as they headed across the Atlantic relying on the North Equatorial currents and favorable breezes to carry them to the West Indies. They reached the Leeward Islands after a five-week voyage of fairly decent weather, fishing for sharks, and playing games on the weather decks to pass the time of day. During the first week in October the fleet dropped anchor in the protected harbor of Vera Cruz, a stay that would last through the winter and the first six months of the following year.

Vera Cruz was a small, isolated town located on the Mexican coast as it curved westward then northward from the Yucatan Peninsula, an area that would later become the *Golfo de Campeche*. Established by Cortez in 1519, Vera Cruz became the primary port for transferring the gold and silver being mined in Mexico to the galleons that would carry the precious metal back to Spain. Vera Cruz was the closest possible port along the east coast of Mexico to Mexico City, the location of the first mint established in the New World (1535).

A fort was built on the island of San Juan de Ulúa located just offshore for protection, but due to the heat and humidity, it was extremely uncomfortable. As a result the town had few inhabitants until the *feria*, a fair that was held when the galleons dropped anchor in the harbor. The fair provided an opportunity for the merchants to trade their precious metals and local goods to the Spanish for their Old World cargoes. And the fair was a cause for celebration. There were jugglers, prostitutes, and games of chance, and a great deal of spirits flowed during the weeks of the fair. Disease also ran rampant, and during the winter months that the 1733 *flota* lay at anchor there was an epidemic of the "black vomit" (possibly cholera). Eight of the merchants, including two of the children of Arizón, and many soldiers and sailors on board the vessels died. At least fifty other merchants on board had to remain in Vera Cruz due to illness. The fleet had intentions of sailing early in April, to miss the hurricane season, but the silver was late in arriving from Mexico City. Then there was a delay as the "fruit of the land," probably citrus and bananas, were brought aboard. They were certainly close to hurricane season when the vessels weighed anchor on 25 May for the three-week voyage to the harbor at Havana.

The *Carrera de Indias*, or sea road of the Indies, was along the coast of Mexico and what some day would become the coast of Texas and the west coast of Florida. Navigation in 1733 still was not great. The sextant had just been invented and would become a major player in the navigation of the galleons, but in 1733 the *piloto mayor* had only the astrolabe to determine a sun line for latitude...and dead reckoning to find his way from Vera Cruz to Havana. He felt comfortable when the ships remained within sight of land as they hugged the coastline. They always had a good idea about where they were, something the pilots rarely agreed upon when they were at sea for any length of time. Contrary winds delayed the fleet, and scattered them to some extent.

June 16, 17, and 18 saw the ships straggling into Havana Harbor. A new vessel recently built in Havana joined the fleet. She was the *Señor San Joseph*, alias "El Africa." She would become the fourth heavily armed *navio* to protect the homeward bound *flota*, carrying sixty cannon and under the command of Daniel Huboni. She carried no treasure, not having sailed to Vera Cruz nor having European cargo to trade for the silver and gold. The only cargo *El Africa* had when she left Havana Harbor with the fleet was a cargo of tobacco. There are no records of transfer of treasure to *El Africa* from the other fleet vessels in Havana Harbor.

Two other vessels would join the fleet on the trip up the coast of Florida. *El Floridano* was probably a nickname, as were "*Fragata de Florida*" and "*Fragata Situada*" (supply ship). There are no records of what she carried on board for her trip to St. Augustine, but in all probability it included a small payload, food supplies and building materials. The second vessel was "*La Balandrita*", a nickname, and in dispatches she was referred to as "the *balandra* that was going to Florida." She carried 256 barrels of flour, which would become one of the staples that would keep the shipwreck survivors alive.

By July 13 the ships had been refitted and loaded with additional cargo and passengers. Cuban tobacco was a much sought after commodity back in Spain, and every square foot of space was stuffed with the dried leaves and strings. Sugar was also a money cargo, and hogsheads from the local sugar mills somehow found room aboard the vessels. General Rodrigo de Torres was careful to observe the conjunction of the moon when it occurred on July 11...and "the strong turbulent effects for two days afterward." He recognized that they were well into the hurricane season, but the king, as usual, was in desperate need of this "Royal Fifth," his share of the 12,289,453 pesos in registered treasure aboard the galleons. There actually was more than this amount on board the fleet. There was considerable "worked silver," as well as gold items that, when made into jewelry or tableware, were not taxed. And in 1733 *sin registrada*, or contraband, was a way of life. As it turned out, that would later become an embarrassment to the various merchants caught with their "hands in the cookie jar." On the early morning tide of July 13, 1733, the twenty-one ships under the command of Rodrigo de Torres y Morales hauled anchor and made their way out of Havana Harbor...into the maws of their worst nightmare.

CHAPTER 3: THE HURRICANE

It was a time to become fidgety. They were already well into the humid month of July, and the ominous threat of a *huracán* was on his mind as General Don Rodrigo de Torres made hurried preparations for his *flota* to depart Havana Harbor for the perilous trip back to Spain. He and his head pilot, Don Rodrigo de Guerrero, had observed the conjunction of the moon on the eleventh, noting favorable winds and its strong turbulent effects for two days afterwards. The decision was made to sail the morning of the thirteenth with the outgoing tide. Unknown to de Torres, a week before, far out in the Atlantic, an area of pressure had developed into a whirling dervish aimed at the string of islands along the Spanish Sea. By the time the storm had reached the Leeward Islands it had become a full blown hurricane, packing over 100-mile-an-hour winds.

By July tenth its center had passed a short distance east of Montserrat and Nevis, leveling homes and driving many of the ships in the harbor ashore. Thirty of the thirty-six windmills on Montserrat were blown down, destroying many of the sugar boiling houses. Picking up speed it crossed St. Christopher, destroying windmills and sending the frigate *Fane* into the rocks at Spanishtown. The *Fly-boat, Nassau, Stapleton*, and the *Ancient Briton* all were driven ashore and sunk at Basseterre on St. Christopher. Captain Wright, on his ship from Philadelphia, was caught entering the harbor and driven onto the rocks at Bel-Tache. It was now a very concentrated but dangerous hurricane. As her winds increased, so did her forward speed, and by the eleventh of July she had crossed Anegada Passage and took aim on Puerto Rico and Santo Domingo. The greatest damage inflicted on Santo Domingo was that "all the cocoa trees were uprooted" (Shepard letter, 1831). On the morning of the thirteenth, as de Torres' fleet was making preparations for getting underway, the hurricane struck the Caicos Islands 550 miles southeast of Havana Harbor, entering the Florida Straits during the night of the fourteenth. By the fifteenth it was 100 miles southwest of Key West.

The vessels in de Torres *flota* were ready for the six to eight weeks' sea journey back to Cádiz. Their holds were loaded with cargo and fruits of the land, as well as the great wealth of silver and gold carried by the three major war vessels. By 7:30 the morning of the thirteenth de Torres' *capitana, El Rubí* cleared the entrance to Havana Harbor, amid the waving of flags and booming of ceremonial cannons, as the fleet passed under the shadow of El Morro castle. They had hopes of picking up the Gulf Stream before nightfall. Rodrigo's diary of the events after that relate as follows. (*Indiferente General* 57-De Torres Diary, 1733)

"This is a diary of what occurred during my unfortunate mishap —On the 25th of May [1733] we left Vera Cruz, having been delayed the 15th, 16th, and 17th by lateness of the arrival of the silver and, afterwards, the other fruits of the land.

"Contrary winds delayed my crossing to La Havana until the 25th, 26th, and 27th of June when I saw anchored here all the ships of my Flota and the cargoes and fruits of the land were loaded in good time and I was ready to sail on the 13th of July.

"At 7:30 of the morning of this day I left the port with little wind from the southeast, the horizons were clear, and one hour afterward I was at the head awaiting the other ships to come outside. At this time I took advantage of the wait in taking in the launch and to tie down the anchors in their place. Afterward, I sent the boat to the ship of Therry and to the Advice Ship to pick up 12 sailors which I had given them.

"Since my ship was to windward of the others, I crossed over in front of them to pick up my boat which I reached a little after 11:00 A.M. I then stowed it within and by now I saw the 19 ships of my Flota, including one Balandra and one Fragata which were destined for Florida [San Augustín]. At 12:00 I trimmed the sails, being now 2 leagues from port, North-South with it and with a strong breeze from the ENE.

"At 3:00 P.M. I changed course to the SE which I maintained until 6:30 when I tacked 1 and 1/2 leagues from land. We were now two leagues from Jaruco and 12 from Havana with the bow to the north and 1/4 north which we maintained all the rest of the night, trimming the sails accordingly to maintain myself with the rest of the ships.

"July 14th. From daybreak we put on more sail in order to see the cayos at the mouth of the Canal of the Bahamas, and at 10 A.M. we saw the land. At 12:00 I recognized this to be the Cayos to the west of the Vacas. At this hour I changed course with the bow to the SE, being about 2 leagues from them. At 3:00 P.M. I changed course again with the bow now to the north, the winds persisting from the ENE with veiled horizons. At 6:00 P.M. the west point of the Key of Vaca bore to the NNW. I tacked with the bow to the ESE and at this time the Florida Fragata arrived off me.

"I continued on this tack and always saw to it that my farol [light] was shining [for the rest of the fleet to follow.] At 7:00 P.M. I took a reef in the main sails, the wind now freshening from the NNW and with the accompanying rise in the seas. I took another reef at 8:00 P.M. and at 9:30 P.M. I furled the topsails, there now being more wind and now from the north. I furled the secondary sails [gallants] over the mast head caps because the other ships were to the leeward of me.

"July 15th. By 2:00 A.M. I had reefed in the others except the two main sails due to the steadily rising winds. Since it was a clear night the ship withstood it well, without torment, the expressed appearance being that we were governing towards the east. At 5:30 A.M. having now 11 ships [in sight], I placed the signs for making the tack to turn around [go back to Havana]. To execute this I furled the main sail; trimming the fore sails we put the bow to the west. By 6:00 A.M. much wind came upon us, forcing us to furl the main sail and to continue with the expressed fore sails until 9:00 A.M. when the sky and horizons became obscured and the ship was not able to follow its course.

"For having arrived at Cayo Largo and Cabeza de los Martires [head of the Martires], I fell off to leeward with the fore sail and two spars, governing towards the south, but the heavy wind and seas did not permit us to govern the ship well with the bow toward the east, and on the starboard side with the forecastle below the water almost capsizing the vessel. To be more secure we resolved to change our tack to port. We fought the storm thus all day until 10:00 P.M. when we attempted to tack to port to ride more securely, bracing the fore sail all around with all the preventer braces and preventer sheets. Aided by the wall of this strength we ran to the south until 11:00 P.M. at which time the sea was so great, and the wind impetuous, forming one great inundation, the wind rising with fierceness producing steep seas."

[The hurricane at this time was passing between Cuba and the tip of Florida.]

"The ship was now unmanageable with the bow toward the east, and with the starboard rail and fore castle under water the ship was now in danger of capsizing for being unable to right itself, while at the same time taking many blows from the sea to windward. It appeared to the head pilot, Don Rodrigo de Guerrero, to the ship's captain, and to some other officials that it was necessary to cut away the main mast, which they did. This carried over to the mizzen mast, while at the same time the top mast of the fore mast fell away, depriving us of all masts. This action served to right the ship somewhat. The wind finally tore away all the fore sails, even though they were well secured, and the yard arm fell away into the sea.

"We remained this way, helpless in the seas, unable to do more than keep up the work on the pumps and to lighten the between decks spaces of cargo."

By the evening of the 16th the hurricane had crossed very near Pinar del Rio Province in western Cuba and headed off into the Yucatan Passage leaving behind a trail of destruction, and twenty of the ships of de Torres sunk or grounded along the Florida Keys.

References:

1. *Armada Española* by Fernando Duro, 1900, V1, 489.

2. *Relación de la Salida de la Flota perdida, del jefe de escuadra Don Rodrigo de Torres, caballero del hábito de San Juan,* Academia de Historia (Madrid, Spain) 1900. V1, 243.

3. *Hurricanes of the Caribbean and Adjacent Regions 1492-1800,* José Carlos Millás, Academy of Arts and Sciences of the Americas, Miami, Fl. 1968. (Contains Shepard letter, 1831.)

CHAPTER 4: SALVAGING THE TREASURE
The Spanish salvage efforts of 1733-34

It was the day following the departure from Havana of General Torres' *flota*. It had been a gala occasion while the treasure fleet lay anchored in the harbor; the constant whirl of social events and great parties that were sure to be yarned ashore when the fleet arrived back in Cádiz. The ladies of Havana wanted to be assured that only the best impressions would be relayed back to their friends, family, and social groups, so every effort was made to entertain at the highest levels. And now the streets seemed empty, echoing only shouts of rowdy sailors on liberty and the bustle of cargo being loaded at the docks. The dusty hillside trails which just a few days before were filled with mule-drawn wagons loaded with hogsheads of sugar, or bundles of tobacco leaf, were now silent.

With the coming of darkness a new sound filled the streets of Havana, the sound of rising wind and pelting rain. The Marqués de Cavesas, governor of Havana, had a sodden feeling that a hurricane was imminent, and his thoughts immediately turned to the *flota* of Rodrigo de Torres somewhere in the middle of the Bahama Channel. By the morning of July 15, 1733, his fears were confirmed. The rain now "flew like arrows" as the wind reached hurricane force. Roofs were demolished and "many cocoa trees uprooted." Because the harbor was well protected, the few ships remaining at anchor escaped damage as the hurricane passed northeast of the Cuban mainland and crossed the low lying islands of the southern Bahamas. By the following day the hurricane had passed over the western end of Cuba (near today's Pinar del Rio Province) and into the Gulf of Mexico. (*Hurricanes of the Caribbean and Adjacent Regions 1492-1800*, José Carlos Millás; *The Deadliest Atlantic Tropical Cyclones, 1492-1994*, NOAA Tech. Memo NWS NHC-47)

The Governor of Havana was certain the hurricane had caught the king's treasure fleet in the Bahama Channel, and when the wind died down three days later, on the nineteenth, he dispatched a *balandra* (a one-masted sloop) to "discover amongst the islands whether or not the *flota* had come to damage." Before the *balandra* could return, the governor's fears were confirmed. On the fourteenth of July Don Nicolas Arechavaleta sailed from Havana for the port of Porto Bello in his *balandra* and, having been caught in the storm, managed to make it back to Matanzas, where he stayed until the eighteenth when the weather cleared. Continuing on with his voyage —by divine providence— he saw, and recognized, off the beaches of the *cayos* up to twelve large ships grounded. Being a merciful man, he returned to Havana to give this notice to the governor, without being able to get close to any of the grounded ships. They were identified as the ships of Rodrigo de Torres.

"Without waiting for a reply from the balandra which I dispatched on the 19th, on the 22nd I promptly prepared 9 balandras [including Arechavaleta's *balandra*] with provisions, divers, munitions, gunners, a company of Grenadiers with all its officials, and the shipbuilder Don Juan Acosta. I gave them instructions for the securing of treasure which is to be remitted to this Plaza, and principally from the English city of Providence which, when learning of this will approach with some wreckers."

[The letter was signed and dated 18 August, 1733, Havana.]

Although the hurricane had not totally destroyed the ships of the fleet (in fact most of them had only grounded in shallow water), the distance between the ships made it difficult to assist each other when it came to sharing provisions that had not been damaged by seawater. The first steps to be taken were to set up *reales* (salvage camps) where the survivors could be brought together for shelter, and as a distribution point to ration out food and supplies for survival.

There were a number of *reales* established along the various keys, usually in the vicinity of several shipwrecks so that their efforts could be pooled together. A total of twelve leagues (about 36 miles) was estimated by the Spanish between the first to the last *real*. The first major salvage camp was established on Matecumbe El Viejo (Old Matecumbe), and on some salvagers' maps Mata Cumbe Grande (same key). We call Old Matecumbe "Upper Matecumbe" today, and Upper Matecumbe and Islamorada are one and the same. This later name was given to the key by Mary and Nora, daughters of William Krone who became chief construction engineer for Henry Flagler's railroad which bridged the string of keys. (*Yesterday's Florida Keys*, Windhorn/ Langley).

The survivors from the *El Infante* and the *Balandrita* first attempted construction of a *real* on Cayo Tavona (Tavernier Key), but the horse flies were so bad they moved their camp to Old Matecumbe, where the survivors of the *capitana* had constructed their *real* on the north end of the island. Another camp was located on Indian Key, where the cargo and cannon were off-loaded from the *Murguia* so it could be floated out to deeper water. Survivors of the *San Pedro* and *El Lerri* would use this *real* as well.

A salvage camp was established on Long Key to support the passengers and crew of the *San Francisco* and the *almiranta*. The last *real*, a temporary one, was constructed on Grassy Key (Cayos de Vacas) for survivors of the *San Fernando*, *Angustias*, and the *Sueco de Arizón*.

The next order of business was to bring together the supplies of water and food until help could arrive from Havana. In a letter written by the Governor of Havana, the Marqués de Cavesas, dated 18 August 1733:

"From the cited 22nd I have not stopped providing supplies, divers, and armed ships of war, without reserving any of what was found in this port. The provision of water has been the most need, all of the Flota being short of this. It was necessary to fill all the ship's casks & barrels, and to employ barrel makers and squid catchers, besides buying bottles to ease this great necessity. This is due to the fact that from the voices that break forth in the rising number of people that comprise the camps of the ships, there was no other [cry] than water, water, water"

The ships that were not flooded to their upper decks provided some supplies to the *reales*. The *Murguia* was completely salvaged, as was the *Poder de Dios*. The *Chavez* provided its supplies to de Torres' main camp, and the *Sueco de Arizón*'s supplies went to the *real* on Long Key. The *Balandrita*, the *balandra* that was going to Florida (St. Augustine), was carrying 256 barrels of flour. She remained afloat, close inshore near the north end of Mata Cumbe Grande (opposite today's Whale Harbor) after the hurricane, her barrels of flour intact.

"One Balandra sailed in convoy with the said Flota. It was dismasted and badly worn, finding shelter between two keys.

All of its people were saved along with 256 barrels of flour which aided in keeping the shipwreck survivors alive."
[19 August 1733, *Escribano real de Torres*]

The *aviso* was located dismasted but afloat, and with some supplies, at the head of the Martires. Its launch was discovered in one of the canals of Key Largo. Both the launch, and the *aviso*, were towed to the *real* of de Torres, and the *aviso* was later re-masted and used to carry fresh water to the various *reales* that stretched from Matecumbe Grande to Cayo Vaca. As the rescue ships arrived from Havana they began transporting the survivors, along with whatever treasure had been recovered at that point, back to Havana.

"The Knight Commander outlined his plan to them (the officials), which would sustain the people, commence salvage operations, and maintain security of it." His next order of business was to commence salvage operations.

"This prompt aid and the 40 divers which were sent in these rescue ships was the major alleviation of those that were shipwrecked. The first thing done was to commence the underwater search [*buceo*] which was executed with all effort, salvaging all the treasure from the Capitana, Almiranta, & Refuerzo [*El Infante*]."
[Letter dated 19 August, 1733 by Juan Thomas de la Herrera and Diego Ángulo]

To institute the salvage operation, various jobs were appointed the fleet deputies in a general council of commerce meeting held at the *real* of Rodrigo de Torres. The first Deputy, Don Juan Feliz de Andrade, and Don Julian de Monsalve, were to pick up the wealth and other things gathered at the *reales*, and go with Don Juan Clemente Sanchez Duran to Havana, "conveying the best correspondence to the Governor and Royal Officials of this port that the Deputies are knowledgeable in the general needs of all the *reales* such as how to best benefit the lives and work on these wrecked ships."

The third deputy Don Antonio Joseph de Herrera, accompanied by Don Joseph Diaz de Guitian, "shall remain in the Real of the Capitana to receive and inventory the wealth and other things which are carried to it, such as those coming from the Patache, Navio of Duque, Chaves,

Tres Puentes, and the one of Herrera, keeping a clear account." It was decided that a separate account would be kept of the things remitted by the launch and boats by one person named for each of the wrecked ships, along with general rules for transporting it.

The second Deputy, Don Pedro de Cordova, would assist in the real of the *almiranta*, along with Don Alonso Balcarcel and Don Francisco de la Razabal. It was decided that Don Antonio Navarro would supervise the off-loading of the *Murguia* and the *San Pedro*. Don Pedro de Iriarte and Don Manuel Gabriel de Céspedes would supervise the off-loading of the *navio Terri* (*El Lerri*) and the *Gran Poder de Dios*. Don Juan Valentín de Villaneuva and Don Gerónimo de Ariscum would supervise the off-loading of the *navios Nuestra Señora de los Reyes y San Fernando*, the *Rosario* of *Arizón*, and the *Angustias* of Sanchez Madrid. They would also be responsible for scouting the beaches close to where the ship of Urquijo wrecked and to pick up whatever things the sea happened to bring in.

Because the *reales* were so far apart one of the boats was armed and put under the command of Don Gonzalo Blanquito to scout the various *navios* (sunken ships) on a daily basis, taking the report to the *real* of the *capitana* from each, and relaying any orders from the *real* to each ship's crew. To thwart the attempts of would-be pirates on the grounded *navios*, the *balandra* of Arechavaleta (taking him a long time to get his ship back) was placed under the command of Lieutenant of Fragata, Don Martín de Funes, which was to be maintained within sight of the *capitana* and *patache* at all times.

The cost of the salvage operation was going to be high, the salvage vessels, supplies and crews from Havana would not work for free. Don Joseph Diaz Guitian was named as the accountant that would attend to money drafts, inspecting the various invoices for supplies and services, and "paying for the imports of the aforementioned Don Mathias Bustillo to whom is entered the support of the letters of payment for the wealth which is entered into his power." "Four boxes of silver coins from the wealth of the treasury were entered into the master of silver and treasurer of this Flota, Don Balthesar de la Torre, which will pay for the furnishings and crews of the three expressed Navios used in the salvage to the respect of 20 Reales per man per day." (Good *per diem* for the time.) The treasury also paid some of the naval personnel, infantry, armory officials, and passengers from 50 to 250 pesos each, depending upon their pay and work in the Indies trade. Some passengers were paid 300, 400, and 500 or more pesos if they were carrying dispatches (permits) for the carrying of money back to Spain.

Finally, the security of the *reales* was addressed.

"For the security of the Real of the Capitana the Commander (Torres) ordered the Naval Captain Don Nicolas Alvares de Losada to construct two forts of four cannon each. This was done in accordance with good military art, and from the front of these they were able to command any route the enemy might choose"

[19 August 1733; *Escribano de Real Rodrigo de Torres*]

The well depression of the fort constructed for the *real* of the *capitana* today is located on the north end of Islamorada, on Christian School land.

The brigantine *El Juan* was also armed with ten cannon and 80 men, under the command of the Official of Orders Don Joseph de San Vicente, to convoy the silver from the *reales* to Havana. As quickly as they could, they began to bring ashore the treasure from each of the sunken ships. On July 23 the salvage of treasure from the *capitana* began, and by 4 August 1,100 boxes of silver coins had been recovered and put ashore. On August 10 the number of boxes of silver coins recovered from the *capitana* had risen to 1,910. Only 30 boxes of registered silver coins remained to be recovered. By August 4 a total of 1,525 boxes of silver coins were salvaged from the *almiranta*. On August 7 the salvage of silver got underway on the *El Infante* and was completed two days later. Of the 186 boxes of registered silver coins on board, 185 were recovered. (Apparently part of the last box was recovered as well.) By September 25 another 13 boxes of silver were recovered from the *capitana* for a total recovery of 1,923, leaving just 17 boxes of silver somewhere within the wreckage. Four of those boxes were recovered before the salvage was discontinued. At 3,000 coins per box, that's 39,000 coins still lying somewhere on the site of *El Rubí*. Another 284 boxes of silver came up from the hull of the *almiranta*, completing their registry of boxes of silver.

In a letter written by Don Rodrigo de Torres y Morales on January 5, 1734, (AGI Mexico 2977 - 9):

> "Here remains all the silver according to the registry and justified. The missing three trunks of the Capitana and the 30,151 pesos from some other accounts balance that we have missed somewhere that on board broke, and others that came in abundance, and in the Almiranta we found the bars that were missing. And in the trunks of accounts balance finding less than 20,441 pesos, and in the Infante of the same nature, well understood that all His Majesty was lacking one bar and 1000 pesos of one of the trunks, and the rest of particulars."

Of the boxes of silver on the remaining ships of the *flota*, no record has been located regarding their salvage, but it is considered likely that because the ships were sunk in fairly shallow water, that most of the silver was recovered. The two exceptions to this are the *San Ignacio*, and the *San José*. From the *San Ignacio* 54,000 pesos of silver coins were recovered, and with only 12,000 on their official registry it is quite possible the salvage consisted of *talegas* (sacks) of coins that were hidden some where aboard ship. On board the *San José* much of what was recovered was in contraband (*sin registrada*). On the official registry was 30,435 pesos in silver coins and bullion. When 236,247 pesos in silver coin was recovered, several merchants aboard admitted to the contraband and offered to pay the *derechos dobles* (double taxation) for its return.

The *capitana* was carrying 592 slabs of copper from the mines of Cuba. These would have been used for ship's fittings and utensils back in Spain. The divers were able to bring up 584 of the slabs, leaving eight unrecovered. The *almiranta* was listed on her manifest as carrying 517 slabs of copper in 30-pound(+) ingots. Only 438 were recovered. These were the only two vessels officially carrying copper.

The boxes of fabricated silver had more of a tendency to break up and scatter or float away as the ships grounded against the reefs, not being as heavy as the boxes of coins that usually remained near the ballast. From the *capitana* the salvage divers recovered 48 boxes of fabricated silver, and 25 boxes from the *almiranta*. From the *El Infante* a total of four boxes were brought up, and from the *San Ignacio* only two. A total of 153 bars of silver were recovered.

A mark of silver equals 8 ounces, the usual way to list fabricated artifacts of silver. If taxes were to be paid on the fabricated silver being carried back to Spain by the passengers, they would been taxed by weight. The manifest listed the following *marcos* (marks) of silver: "Capitana - 699 marcos. Almiranta - 2,579 marcos. El Infante - 643 marcos. Herrera - 359 marcos. Angustias - 605 marcos. Poder de Dios - 139 marcos. San Ignacio - 696 marcos." No record is available of the worked silver recovered other than that already listed.

On the official manifest of the ships leaving Vera Cruz, a total of 12,286,253 pesos in boxes of coins and silver bars were registered. (Original manifest; Haskins, / *Shipwrecks of the Western Hemisphere*, Marx.)

Very little gold was carried on board the *capitana* and *almiranta*, the only ships that would have been designated to carry gold. The *capitana* had a manifest of 3,200 pesos in gold coins, and 104 *castellanos* of worked gold. The *almiranta* also carried 3,200 pesos in gold coins and 196 *castellanos* of worked gold.

(A *castellano* is 1/50th of a mark, and a mark equals 8 ounces).

Authors note: At least two gold coins were recovered from the *El Infante*, 28 gold coins from the *San José* which were reported to the state of Florida offices, an undetermined number from the *capitana*, two from the *Angustias*, and two from the *San Ignacio*, all by modern salvors. Probably someone's pocket change.

A total of 670 cannon were recovered during the salvage operation, all of which were taken to Havana. There still remained a few cannon on each site when modern salvage began in the late 1950s. They were all iron, bronze cannon having been discontinued in the early 1700s. (AGI *Contratación* 5147)

Recoveries of silver coins by the Spanish amounted to 12,281,500 pesos in boxes of coins from the *capitana, almiranta,* and the *El Infante,* and adding to that the 236,247 pesos in contraband recovered from the *San José* and the 54,000 pesos from the *San Ignacio,* the total of 12,571,747 pesos was well over the register on the manifest. Some boxes of coins were recovered from the other sunken ships, quite an embarrassment to General Rodrigo de Torres to admit to the king that so much contraband aboard his ships had escaped his notice.

As an interesting finale to de Torres' adventures: He embarked on one of the salvage vessels for his return to Havana on August 9. On the thirteenth at 2:00 o'clock in the morning the lookout spotted two strange vessels approaching to the eastward. One seemed closer than the other, and lay to until the second vessel caught up. Once they were able to get to leeward of de Torres' vessel they fired two shots to leeward, which were answered, and the chase began. About fifteen minutes later the two vessels fired another cannon round that went over the de Torres vessel. Somehow de Torres caught the wind and was able to escape in the darkness. By daylight they found themselves "Too much into the stream, and at noon time found themselves to the northward of where we first departed. Water and provisions growing short it was concluded to put for South Carolina, but the wind favouring us from the NE'ward got in with the land in Lat. 25:00 when the Admiral went in person and sent us off water. The 18th arrived safe in the Havana." (Letter by Edward McIver, 17 September 1733)

For the most part, the Spanish continued salvage work on the 1733 *flota* through 1734, and when they felt they had recovered all that could be taken from the hulls, they burned them to the waterline. This was done to salvage the iron fittings from the hull, and to dampen the enthusiasm of privateers who flocked around the sunken ships like flies around a honey pot. Although the salvage was considered a more than complete success, coins and artifacts remain in and around the ballast piles. Passengers baggage scattered for miles towards shore, baggage containing the wealth they had accumulated from years of hard work in the New World.

The treasure is there, covered and uncovered by the sands of time, sifted by storms and hurricanes that sweep across the shallow waters of the Keys, waiting for someone lucky enough to be swimming over the right place at the right time.

Cannon from the* San José *of 1733.

CHAPTER 5: *SIN REGISTRADA*
(Not Registered)

In Spanish, *sin registrada* is an old expression meaning "not registered," and to the average layman and finder of sunken treasure, this is the contraband that he is likely to find on a shipwreck site. We use the term quite often when we discuss what might still be left to recover once a ship has been salvaged by the Spanish. In the past this was a dubious quantity, believing that the Spanish merchants, on threat of severe punishment, would never attempt to smuggle silver or gold through customs when the galleon arrived at Cádiz. Many documents have come to light dispersing any thought that all Spanish merchants were honest and above board. Now it's a case of "how much, and where did they hide it?"

I personally have been involved in the recovery of *sin registrada*. On the 1733 *capitana*, *El Rubí*, we found large silver screws that had been screwed into the wood that probably was a bulkhead on board ship. Obviously, once the customs people had left the ship after its arrival in Cádiz, they would have been removed, probably melted down (each weighed one ounce), and each screw had the equivalent value of a piece-of-eight! On the *capitana* of the 1715 fleet, *Regla*, one of the divers recovered a **gold** spike about six inches long and weighing close to six ounces. It probably was used in holding two planks together and painted over, again until customs officials left the ship. I have to admit that when I first saw this spike I believed it was just a shiny bronze spike, but I was proven wrong after the analysis.

I find it hard to believe that such large items, such as an anchor or cannon, were cast in silver or gold to fool the customs officials. And there never existed a "gold 3,000-pound table" or a "solid gold Madonna" (Potter: *Treasure Divers Guide*, p. 134 / Tippin: *In Search of the Golden Madonna*), although they made great story lines. The serious treasure salvager has to understand that the gold mined in New Spain was carefully monitored, and that in any particular year if a ton or so of gold turned up short there would be the several mining managers held accountable. And can you imagine the effort it would take for someone to try bringing aboard ship, and hide, a table or statue that weighed in at over a ton? So the merchants used more subtle methods of contraband.

Often they hid silver or gold coins in the ballast of the vessel. The last place a custom official would want to look for contraband would be in the ballast below the hold of the ship. After a single voyage this area is contaminated with the results of the sea sickness of many passengers, as well as the urine and feces of those unwilling to brave going to the "head" up in the bowsprit when the ship was rolling from side to side or bouncing up and down in bad weather. After a few sea voyages, when the ship was careened for cleaning, the ballast was completely removed and washed down, as well as the inner hull cleaned and disinfected. My group "Royal Fifth," in 1966 recovered a large number of silver coins, as well as twelve "Pillar Dollars," under the ballast of the *Sueco de Arizón*.

If a passenger were caught in Cádiz with treasure not registered, it became necessary for him to pay "*derechos dobles,*" or double taxes. And if caught he became the object of future searches of his personal possessions on other fleets he may ship merchandise. If the ship were to sink prior to reaching her destination, and salvagers were to recover the *sin registrada*, it could not be claimed by the owner because it "never existed." As we will see, if this happened there would be a rush by the merchants, or various owners, to declare the contraband. In the 1733 fleet disaster there are good examples of this.

In a letter from Alonso Herrera de Barragan, the King's Royal Commissioner, written to Francisco de Varras y Valdes, President, Consulado de Cádiz on 25 September 1733, written at the *real* of the *capitana* located on Matecumbe Grande (Islamorada):

> "At the *real* of the Capitana the deputies on hand represented to the Commander Don Rodrigues de Torres and to me, in confidence, that certain individuals of this commerce had lost certain partidas [parcels] of pesos in the merchant ships which had been entered sin registrada [not registered] to be delayed and preserved for cases such as this for entry in other ports.

> "If they be allowed to register this they will give dispositions to its cost of salvage and that they represent that they have not donated it, and that we don't know where these partidas are, nor whose owners they are, nor is it for certain it has even been salvaged because this wealth wasn't lost since they offered it to us.

"We do represent to his Majesty that it is vouchsafed, not
misleading them and that under this all partidas will be
salvaged, but it will be necessary for them to pay double taxes
on the partidas [*derechos dobles*] and that the divers will gain
from them the dress at the tent of the country where we reside
to incorporate them with the other treasure [sort out and identify
the partidas when they are salvaged.] In this belief they executed
it and they have gathered in the aforementioned tent the partidas
of 236,247 pesos being the major part salvaged from the navio
San Joseph y las Animas, giving me part of this. The presence
of my order designated who remains to collect these and other
things of whatever wealth."

When the *Ignacio* disintegrated into Coffins Patch, all except fourteen
people on board lost their lives. Her captain, Don Christobal Urquijo,
was not one of the fortunate survivors. As it turned out, he was bringing
home to Spain all his accumulated wealth, and because he was the captain
of the vessel he had a better opportunity to smuggle his wealth back
through customs without paying the 20% tax. The end result was his
widow became destitute, and through a lawyer petitioned the king for
relief:

[*Indiferente General* 2300 - 1733 *Flota*]
Petition to his Excellency for Josepha Forti:

"Excellency Sir;

"For Donna Josepha Forti, citizen of this city of Cádiz, widow
of Don Christobal Urquijo, Lieutenant of Navio of the Royal
Armada and Captain of those ships named San Francisco and
San Ignacio whose property was navigated to New Spain under
convoy with the Flota of Commander Don Rodrigo de Torres.
With the kindly rendition, he said that they had loaded the two
ships with different valuables which were registered with the
Principal Accountantship of the Royal House of Trade of the
Indies for the account and risk of the husband of the petitioner,
which amount appearing in them was 80,000 pesos, which
comprised the total of his wealth. [The unregistered treasure

was recovered by the salvagers and brought to Cádiz.]

"Having applied to his Majesty with memoranda it is resolved not to make a determination until the arrival of the sailors who conducted the wealth, or the wealth from the salvage effort proceeds from the San Ignacio which was one of those that wrecked in the loss of the Flota, and within which was drowned her husband who lost 40,000 pesos effectively that he carried for his account, and two boxes of worked silver of his use, and 14,500 pesos which he was given at Vera Cruz by Don Pedro Sanchez de Santa Maria to give in the city of Cádiz to Don Joseph Duque, all without registry. [Sounds like El Duque and Urquijo were collaborating to smuggle contraband back to Spain.]

"Undoubtedly the total was more than 200,000 pesos, leaving the petitioner [because of the fatal occurrence] in a very deplorable state of misery and poverty with two young daughters. As their guardian and overseer, because of this lack of goods, she is unable to feed and educate them, and because neither she, nor her daughters, are responsible for the motives of them it appears to be an injustice.

"I appeal to your lordship to provide by your High Grace which is accustomed to the justice of such misery as entered here, and to be able to abide of the money and worked silver that came which was salvaged in the presently arriving ship, that from the San Ignacio the 54,000 pesos of Plata Doble and two boxes of worked silver, paying double taxation to his Majesty as is usually done in such cases.

"In this the petitioner and her daughters deserve of the nobility of Your Lordship."

There are many instances where passengers, to escape taxation, had their wealth fashioned into silver tableware, or jewelry, and then declared these items as having been in their possession when they traveled to the New World from Spain. Keeping in mind that the Spanish merchants and officials came to New Spain to make their fortune, after many years of hard work they were traveling back to Spain with the fortunes they had made as part of their personal baggage. Silver plates, candelabra, gold or silver forks and spoons, gilded silver pitchers and bowls, jewelry, and of course the usual gold discs, bars, and coins, were among the baggage that washed overboard and floated off as the ship sank. A treasure **finder** carefully searches the shoreward reaches of the site for reefs that baggage would possibly hang up on.

Treasure is where you find it!

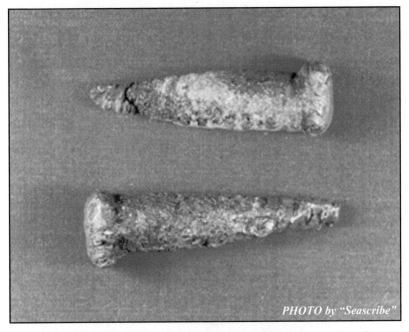

PHOTO by "Seascribe"

SIN REGISTRADA! Unregistered Silver ingeniously disguised as 1-1/2-inch, 1-ounce Screws!

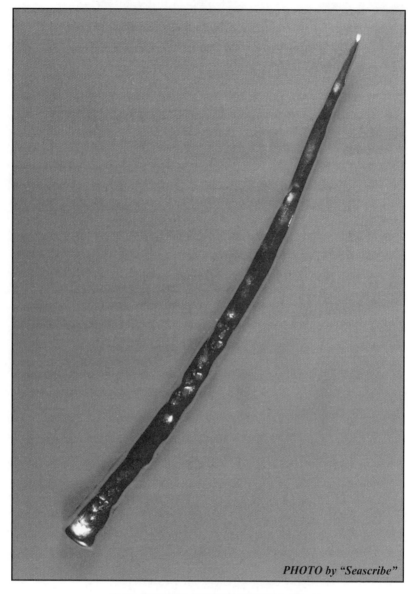

PHOTO by "Seascribe"

...AND MORE SIN REGISTRADA!
A long Gold Nail (Spike), painted and pounded into a plank to be removed at home in Spain!

CHAPTER 6: "FROGFOOT"

It was one of those Saturdays in July, 1960, where any land bound activity was too hot. The day called for some serious underwater exploring down in the Florida Keys, and Harry "Big Splash" Wiseman and I were like free spirits, skimming across an ocean flat as a pancake, with underwater visibility somewhere around 200 feet. Standing on the bow of my 16-foot Mohawk outboard boat I could make out every reef and sand pocket within a hundred feet as we worked our way towards Molasses Reef about five miles seaward of Key Largo. It was one of those days you felt as if you owned the whole ocean, and we were to find out later that there were days you had to fight for every inch. But this day belonged to us, and we had shipwrecks on our mind. Gray smudges in the center of sand pockets often meant a wreck site, and I scanned every pocket as Harry maneuvered the boat in a zigzag pattern heading seaward.

I had graduated from the University of Delaware in 1957, a tenure during which Dr. Harry Wiseman had helped me master the fundamentals of Civil Engineering, and when I accepted a job with Honeywell in Florida, Harry also made a teaching move to the University of Miami. It meant that we could both follow our dreams of sunken treasure and old Spanish galleons. We never intended that this would be any more than a weekend hobby, something to escape the telephones and traffic. That was before we found our first gold on the *El Infante*.

The ocean deepened to a cobalt blue as we rounded the offshore side of Molasses Reef. The bottom was barely visible, and I knew it had to be close to 80 feet deep, too deep for the diving we had in mind. Wrecks happen because the vessel hit a reef, so Harry angled my boat *Frogfoot* closer to the line of reefs that appeared like a brown line stretching to the south. The water was so clear over the reefs that the depth fooled you. What appeared to be only three or four feet was actually almost ten feet, and fish were everywhere. It was like showtime: big fish, little fish, striped fish, spotted fish. I had Harry throttle back so we could both enjoy the show.

For awhile we almost forgot about wreck sites and sunken treasure. It was the curious mound of square cut rocks lying about 600 feet to the east of the red nun buoy inside Conch Reef that jolted us out of our reverie. "Harry...wreck site!"

Harry and I had located a number of wreck sites, mostly modern, along the reefs of the Upper Keys, and as we settled to the bottom with SCUBA tanks on our backs we could tell this was probably a late 1800s shipwreck. The stones were cut along regular lines and weighed anywhere from 200 pounds to as much as a ton or more. After scouting the pile for the better part of an hour we concluded it was probably a barge, or converted vessel, carrying cut stones for a church or possibly Fort Jefferson in the Tortugas. The only artifacts we were able to uncover were several bronze spikes and some copper sheathing, and the excitement was provided by a large green moray eel that came out of nowhere to establish riparian rights to this particular pile of rocks. It all ended when we heard the sound of an outboard motor nearby and saw the shadow of a boat drifting towards *Frogfoot*.

When we surfaced, the officer in a Marine Patrol uniform waved, friendly enough for us to feel we hadn't done anything wrong. "Finding anything?" "Just bronze spikes and a few unwelcome sea urchins," I replied. "The guys down on Little Conch Reef are finding a few silver coins. Thought you'd like to know." I nodded, "Thanks, we appreciate that." Before he disappeared northward we had our anchor up and were full throttling it the 3/4 mile or so south to where three boats lay anchored a few yards apart. In one of the 18-foot outboards a diver was just hauling himself in over the stern. We dropped anchor about 100 feet away and I swam over to introduce myself.

Craig Hamilton was a slight but muscularly built diver, about my age, who had an easy smile and a great twinkle in his eyes. "Come on board and have a cup of coffee." I shook hands and waved an arm in the direction of Big Splash, snorkeling over the edge of the reef. "That's Dr. Harry Wiseman from the University of Miami." I explained the reason we were there. "Marine Patrol said you were finding a few silver coins." Craig shook his head, "I'll have to learn to keep my mouth shut. When you say something to the Marine Patrol it's like advertising in the newspapers." I found out later that he really didn't mind newcomers if they were serious salvagers, but "Weekenders...uugghh!" Up until that time Harry and I were...uugghh weekenders! He pulled a Tupperware container out of the boat box and opened the lid. In it were several small blackened shapes. "We're picking up a few cob coins." I didn't know a cob coin from a corn cob, but I wasn't about to let Craig know it. Gesturing down at the huge ballast pile directly below his boat I asked, "What wreck is this?" "It's the *El Infante*, one of the Spanish 1733 ships. Not much on her, pretty well salvaged by the Spanish, but it's a fun dive and not too deep."

We chatted awhile, and he suggested that if I were real serious about salvaging treasure, I should drop by his house and he would show me some of the things they were bringing up. As it turned out we were neighbors in South Miami. I thanked him and slid over the side to take my first look at the wreck site that some day would become the most visited shipwreck in the Florida Keys. I was not disappointed.

In 1960 the ballast pile was still well-formed, about forty feet wide and close to 120 feet long. In some places the ballast stones reached four to five feet high, and wooden bottom timbers showed on both sides as well as large athwartship members on the north end, which was the stern. Some ballast was scattered toward shore, up a small slope that ended in white sand stretching several acres shoreward. Here the water was twelve feet deep. Over the wreck site the depth was closer to sixteen feet, and gradually deepening seaward, so that 100 yards to the east the water was thirty feet deep. To the north, the reef became fairly rugged, and to the south was a series of reefs with deep sand between. Down the reefs to the south several hundred yards we were to locate the bow anchor of the *Infante* years later, both flukes missing, torn away as the ship was driven over the reefs by the July 15, 1733, hurricane. Later that day, as Harry and I were looking over the reef seaward of the *Infante*, we located the scatter pattern of another wreck. As it turned out, this was the H.M.S. *Fly*, a British Frigate that sank on Little Conch Reef in August, 1805. It was the only day we explored this site, recovering a glass prism from Captain Pellew's skylight, and a bronze door hinge.

I took Craig up on his offer, and several days later I found myself browsing through his shelves of artifacts, treasure he had accumulated over ten years of salvage diving. Things that I had only dreamed of he seemed to take for granted as he pointed out flintlock pistols, boarding cutlasses, clay figurines, pottery bowls, a silver chain with a hinged reliquary dangling on one end, bronze and silver buckles, buttons, conglomerates of straight pins, cannon balls, and a cigar box full of silver coins. He did have two gold coins that he would eventually let me see, but that would be weeks later. What captured my imagination were the "Pillar Dollars." He explained the story behind them, that they were the first round silver coins ever made in the Mexico City mint, and that one of them dated 1732 had been auctioned off at Christensen's for $2,400. I was impressed.

For the next six months Craig took me under his wing showing me what equipment to buy and where to buy it. I had never used a hookah rig,.an air compressor driven by a gasoline engine that pumped air down to the diver all day long. The 40-cfm compressor he used as an air lift, the rig used to vacuum the sand off the bottom, was an air-conditioner compressor used by Eastern Air Lines commercial airplanes. He shared with me the information gleaned from an old chart the Spanish salvagers had made of the 1733 wreck sites. In 1960 only three of the shipwrecks of 1733 had been located. I didn't know it then but I was becoming a part of the salvage scene that would eventually locate and identify the entire 1733 Spanish *Flota*. It would provide me with some of the greatest diving experiences I would ever remember...the "good ole days."

I was into underwater movies, an ambition that was prompted by a Christmas gift of a 16 MM camera in an underwater case. Telling friends and guests that I had some footage of sunken shipwrecks proved more enticing than the usual footage of our last vacation north somewhere with the kids. And so it happened that on my first diving trip with Craig, I wound up on the end of a camera as he prepared to "go to work" with an air lift. "I'll cut a line on the bottom with the air lift, and when you get done with taking your underwater thing, then use the other air lift and work the north side of the line. O.K.?" I nodded agreement, went over the side, and was busy filming away as he splashed above me and drifted down to the sand that stretched northward from the stern of the ballast pile. There was a myriad of fish, and the old *Infante* timbers made a great backdrop that had my full attention.

It wasn't long before sand and shells were spewing out the end of his 15-foot-long, 3-inch-diameter air lift, most of it right on top of me. That wasn't so disconcerting until he suddenly dropped his air lift, reached into the small hole he had burrowed to hard bottom, and held something up for me to see...and smiled. I swam over to take a look and did a double take on one of the nicest gold crosses with four green emeralds I had ever seen. The original cross, actually an earring, had held seven stones, but three of them were somehow lost in the sand. As soon as I had a good glimpse of the cross he headed for the boat, with me right behind. I dropped my camera in the stern of the boat, grabbed the other airlift, and before long both Craig and I were "pumping sand."

Less than an hour into my first commercial salvage effort, I uncovered a GOLD RING! It was a rather small ring, with a design that had been etched with silver. The silver was nothing more than blackened lines within the grooves of the design, but it was my first gold. Craig, from fifteen feet away, shook his head and kept pumping as I took my prize up to the boat. By the time I was back on the bottom Craig had a surprise for me. He waved it in front of me before I could pick up my airlift. It was another gold-cross earring with three rubies of the original seven stones still there; there were three emeralds and four rubies still snuggled somewhere in the white sand that marked the

SALVAGER Craig Hamilton proudly shows off the pair of golden earrings that he recovered from the remains of the 1733 **refuerzo, El Infante.**

stern of the *Infante.* I searched this area for fifteen years after that and recovered only one of the emeralds.

The day of surprises wasn't over yet. Towards the end of the day Craig had drifted over to the sloping embankment that stretched shoreward. It seemed there wasn't much there except dead staghorn coral. Before long he was swimming towards me with a 12-inch piece of the coral in his hand. It formed a perfect slingshot, and in the crotch was a round silver coin. He aimed it at me, pulled back on the imaginary rubber sling, and let me have it! In the boat we took a good look at the coin. It was a perfectly round eight-*real* coin dated 1731, apparently what would later be called a "royal," a coin that was used to "prove" the die. It was a very valuable coin, worth much more than either Craig or myself ever imagined.

Craig and I made other diving trips to the *Infante*, and as both our salvage careers separated we stayed in touch. As he worked the *San Pedro* a year or so later, he called and led me out to the ballast pile near Indian Key. We remained friends until I moved to West Palm Beach in 1970. I was distressed to learn from his step-daughter in 1986 that he had committed suicide. I will never understand a loss like that. The salvage community lost a great shining star.

After my initial work with Craig, Harry Wiseman and I were more zeroed in on what we wanted to do and how we wanted to do it. By the end of 1960 we had a hookah rig that would allow us to remain on the bottom all day long and an airlift for each of us that moved sand at an easy pace to let us recover artifacts. And somewhere along the way we added a suction dredge for those shallow water sites where an airlift would stick out of the water too far to be effective. We soon began finding artifacts as well as coins.

Gold religious medallion and gold ring recovered by the author on the El Infante.

We were back on the *El Infante*, again working near the stern section, when I recovered one of the nicest gold rings I have ever seen. It was a double-banded gold wedding ring. The inside band was solid, and around the outside a second band of gold rosettes was crimped and gold-soldered so that the inner band was visible. It had been flattened, crushed by ballast stones, but it was all there. Bob Page, a friend of mine, and the salvage community, lived in New York where a jeweler was able to restore the ring. It was one of my prized possessions until it was stolen from a museum case in West Palm Beach where it was on exhibit. Harry was also recovering some nice artifacts, including a section of gold chain, bronze powder flask, and a bag of silver coins. Between the two large athwartship timbers in the stern, separated by less than four inches, I spotted the edge of something golden, snuggled in amongst the shells and sand that filled the void. It was about twelve inches deep, and with a coat hanger I was able to maneuver this beautiful gold religious medallion out of the pocket and safely in hand. It had the image of St. Anne on one side, and St. Josep on the other. I still have the medallion today.

A typical log entry during our diving summer on *El Infante*:

"July 2, 1961. Have been diving consecutive weekends for the past 6 weeks on the Infante. Today, in company with Harry Wiseman, my sons Bobby and Rick, Jim Tull, and Moe Wiseman on board Frogfoot. Lall Baines and Jay Ford, and two others from the Pratt & Whitney Company, on board another boat. We located a large formation of coral, tar, and cannon balls. Broke out of the formation approx. 25 cannon balls, and hoisted the remainder aboard Frogfoot. While breaking up this formation on the bottom Harry found a gold plated button, conical in shape, and with a fastener loop on the back. Later, while breaking up the formation we brought aboard the boat, another copper plated button, identical to the other, was found, also a copper shoe buckle and two human joints with parts of fossilized tendons still attached. A total of 34 cannon balls were found in this formation. I took 50 feet of underwater movies, and on the way back to Lowe's Marina we stopped off at Rodriguez Key and I filmed another 30 feet of a Barracuda attacking a fish we had strung out on a fishing line."

Over the next few years we escorted a number of our friends and family, including my three sons, to the large ballast mound that lies so near the edge of the Gulf Stream, and they have all come away with the same exhilaration, a Christmas-every-day kind of feeling that we have experienced. The *Infante* has given Harry and me some great memories, of days when the dream of salvaging a Spanish sunken galleon was realistic and alive—of the "good ole days."

***Earl Benson, Eldred Jones, and Bob Weller ready to board the author's 16-foot boat* "Frogfoot."**

***Author (Facing Page) working the ballast pile of the ship* El Infante.**

Author (above): "Here we have a couple of cannons on the bottom...looks more like a pot of ferns!"

Dr. Harry "Big Splash" Wiseman (facing page, top), author's professor at the University of Delaware, and later a diving partner on the 1733 Spanish treasure fleet wrecks.

Author and "Big Splash" Wiseman (facing page, bottom) mug it up for the camera aboard **The Frogfoot.**

***Author Bob "Frogfoot" Weller salvaging a commercial
charter boat sunk by a hurricane in the
Florida Keys.***

CHAPTER 7: *EL AFRICA*
Señor San Joseph
(*Contratación* 5102 - 1733 *Flota*)

The *San Joseph* had been recently constructed in the Havana shipyards and commissioned to carry 60 cannon. Her first commanding officer was Captain Huboni, a name that the English would later misspell badly. The vessel was completed in time to join the 1733 *flota* of Don Rodrigo de Torres in Havana for the voyage back to Spain, but with a cargo of tobacco. The *Africa* did not travel to Vera Cruz and did not participate in the *feria*, where silver and gold was exchanged for the merchandise carried from Europe. There was no treasure on board *El Africa*.

When the treasure fleet assembled outside the harbor of Havana the *El Africa Brillante* ("Triaca Producida de un Veneno") was assigned to the far western side of the *flota*. As one of the four armed *navios* of de Torres, it was her job to help keep the potential pirate vessels, and other armed vessels, from intercepting the merchant ships being escorted up the Bahama Canal. By the end of the first day the *flota* was well into the Gulf Stream and proceeding up the Canal when the first hint of a hurricane was the huge ground swells that precede a storm. By the late afternoon of the second day the sun was blotted out by the storm clouds, and as the winds began to whip the waves into frenzied whitecaps, the ships of the fleet lost sight of each other. They were on their own, each to fight the battle to stay afloat and survive.

The *El Africa* did survive, entering the bay at Cádiz on September 25, 1733. The Lieutenant of the ship, Don Francisco Perez de Claras, as well as the ship's notary, Don Antonio Prieto, declared the following (*Indiferente General* 1987—1733 *Flota*):

> "The Flota left under the command of Don Rodrigo de Torres on the 25th of May from Vera Cruz. They entered into the port of Havana on the 24th, 25th, and 26th of June where they remained until the 13th of July when they left the expressed port of the Havana. The Flota was comprised of 19 ships; 5 of his Majesty's named El Rubí, El Gallo, El Infante, El Africa, and El Pinque Populo; 13 merchant ships, and the Advice ship of the council. [Did not include the two "string-along" Florida

ships, the *fragata* and the *balandrita.*] They proceeded to the entrance of the Canal of the Bahamas and on the night of the 14th there came upon them a storm out of the north of such qualities that at 2 A.M. this ship [*El Africa*] was forced to run before it, without having seen any other ship of the convoy since midnight. At 11 A.M. of the next day, and within two hours, they lost the main mid mast and mizzen top mast. At 6 P.M. the wind came upon them very strong from the south which lasted all the following night. At daybreak on the 16th it started to calm. By jury rigging the fore mast sail they made their way to Key Largo where the currents were less severe and they anchored with two anchors in 40 brazas [220 feet] of water.

"At this site they discovered on the 17th two lost ships, and after awhile they were able to launch a boat to the water to go out and reconnoiter them. The ships were found to be the pink of His Majesty named El Populo, and the advice ship of the council whose people they picked up around it on the said day, and the following day, and conducted them on board their ship [*El Africa.*] Immediately they started jury rigging the ship to be able to resume their navigation.

"On the 24th of July they made sail from the mentioned site of Key Largo and proceeded on their voyage to Spain. On the 16th of August the wind came upon them very strong from the east, obliging them to run before it with the fore sail. Returning to resume their course, they found themselves short of supplies with the additional people of the Pink and Aviso, and all the calm periods.

"Next they saw the Isle of Fayal and arrived to it on the 7th of this month [September] where they took on some provisions and they left this port on the 14th, continuing on their journey to this bay [Cádiz.] Although they saw at some distance a few strange ships they did not speak to them for the reason of not wanting to delay their navigation. They were unable to give more information than what has already been expressed. The only addition to this is that while at the Isle of Fayal a registry ship arrived from the Canary Isles which had come from Caracas, and they said they had suffered through a bad storm on the 16th of August and they gave notice that at Caracas two more registry consignments were ready of the company of Guipuscoana, all of which were ready to sail in July.

"The cargo with which this ship [*El Africa*] carried was comprised of 4782 bags and sacks of tobacco powder, string, and leaf for the account of Your Excellency in accordance with a note manifested for me by the ship's notary. No letters came in this ship and only I have added the 3 adjacent letters for Your Excellency, and that is as much of this occurrence as I am able to impart for the Royal intelligence of his Majesty.

"Our Señor grant to Your Excellency as many years as he desires.

"Cádiz, 25 September 1733

Francisco de Varas y Valdez

To: Excellency Señor Don Joseph Patino"

In a letter written by General Rodrigo de Torres on January 5, 1734, (AGI Mexico 2977 pg. 9) he said:

"I have learned the pleasant news of the arrival on the 24th of September in Cádiz of the ship El Africa commanded by Don Daniel Huboni with the two crews of the Pinque and Aviso"

Captain Huboni finally did manage to carry some of the 1733 treasure back to Spain. On January 12, 1734, the *El Africa* left Cádiz for Havana as the *almiranta* of a *flota* to carry back to Spain the silver recovered from the 1733 wreck sites. (Contract Inventory 2909A):

"Huboni, on El Africa, returned to Cádiz with some of the treasure in June 1735."

SALVAGER MARTIN MEYLACH *examines the Main*
Anchor from "El Infante", **Nuestra Señora de Balvaneda,**
shortly after its recovery. PHOTO *by Chuck Mitchell.*

CHAPTER 8: *EL POPULO*
Nuestra Señora del Populo
Alias: *"El Pinque"*

The veiled secrecy of the modern day salvage is the real story behind *El Populo*. How four novice divers first searched for the *Populo* ballast pile, found it, then worked for almost two years salvaging this virgin wreck site until other, more professional salvage divers had zeroed in on the final resting place of their shipwreck. It's a success story in many ways, about divers like most of us that travel to the Keys in search for treasure, and for the very few that actually realize their dream come true.

El Populo was one of King Philip's ships, a smaller type of vessel called a pink (*pinque*) that was used as a *guerra* or war scout ship, as well as a trading vessel. She had a narrow stern with a deck that rose gracefully aft. Most pinks were lightly armed with eight to twelve cannon, and a gross tonnage of normally 150 to 250 tons. Not much is known in particular about the *Populo*, except that the king assigned her to Rodrigo de Torres' 1732 plate fleet.

(*Indiferente General* 2021 - 1733 *Flota*):

> "Below are listed the ships that will comprise the Flota for the present year 1732, which will make the voyage to New Spain under the command of Chief of Squadron Don Rodrigo de Torres—[under the heading, "For His Majesty"]— El Pinque named El Populo - Its Maestre de Raciones, and the property of the Royal Hacienda Don Francisco Ymbernon."

When the *flota* reached Vera Cruz the *Populo* traded primarily for cochineal, indigo, hides, brasilwood, a few boxes of gifts, (probably K'ang Hsi porcelain) and citrus. There was no registered treasure brought aboard *El Populo*. With sailors and merchants shopping, and on liberty in Vera Cruz, a few silver coins would have been picked up. There certainly would have been an interest in obtaining a few of the "new" Pillar Dollars. During the 2-1/2 weeks the *flota* lay in Havana Harbor, more strings and bales of tobacco were brought aboard, filling every space not already occupied by cargo or passengers. When Rodrigo de Torres brought his ships past the El Morro fortress and formed up in a convoy, *El Populo* was near the head of the van sailing close to the *capitana*. As hurricane force winds struck the galleons near the mouth of the Bahama Canal, because the *Populo* was a fairly high-sided light vessel, it was driven northward nearly 35 miles ahead of the heavier galleons. The *aviso*, an even smaller vessel sailing close by, was driven almost as far.

Captain Raciones had dropped the bow anchors as his ship passed through the reefs into shallow water. It was a minor miracle that *El Populo* missed the numerous reefs that lay close to the surface where she was driven shoreward. But somehow she survived, holding fast on her anchors and bucking the wind-driven waves. For a short time it appeared as though the ship had survived the hurricane. Then the wind changed as the hurricane passed to the west, and suddenly *El Populo* began a wide circle swing on her anchors. The captain and his crew must have sensed their luck was changing, but it happened so quickly they could do nothing to avoid the reefs that surrounded them. Suddenly the ship struck a coral head, then sprung free and continued swinging on the arc of her anchors. But her hull had been ruptured, and now ballast stones tumbled from a gaping hole in her bottom. As *Populo* began to fill with water she struck hard against another reef 200 yards to the east, much larger than the first. It was more than the gallant little vessel could withstand, and it slid to the bottom in 31 feet of water, its poop deck and part of the main deck remaining above the surface. The captain and the entire crew were able to scramble to the stern and no lives were lost, but the entire cargo, and personal possessions, were a total loss.

The *aviso* was also driven through the same maze of reefs that rimmed the Gulf Stream, and now lay at anchor about one mile to the south of *Populo*. Although without masts and rudder she remained afloat, and her captain and crew also survived. The *aviso* longboat managed to weather the hurricane, and when the wind subsided the captain and crew rowed over to the *Populo* and took aboard the survivors of that vessel. They could see land about four miles distant (Old Rhodes Key), and together they rowed ashore to find assistance and determine where exactly they were located. The Indians of the Keys were friendly to the Spanish, however, they still strongly disliked the English. In the meantime *El Africa*, the newly constructed galleon that had joined the fleet in Havana, had also survived the winds and waves of the hurricane and now lay with two anchors in 40 *brazas* of water (220'). Lookouts spotted the advice boat lying at anchor inside the reefs, and when the winds finally subsided they lowered their longboat and rowed in to investigate. Finding no one on board, they rowed to the *Populo* which they found submerged a mile further to the north. Again, finding no one on board, they rowed closer to shore and found both crews there. Taking them out to *El Africa*, Captain Huboni then made the necessary repairs to his own vessel, and soon he had his galleon under sail on its way back to Spain. They arrived there on September 24, 1733.

By the fall of 1966, after six active years of search and recovery by professional salvage groups, eleven of the 1733 Spanish treasure fleet shipwreck sites had been located and some salvage work completed. The press and TV coverage made headline news as treasure was recovered from the ships the divers had nicknamed *"El Infante,"* *"Capitana,"* *"Chaves,"* *"Herrera,"* *"Tres Puentes,"* *"San Pedro,"* *"El Lerri,"* *"San Francisco,"* *"Almiranta,"* *"Sueco,"* and *"San Ignacio."* *El Africa*, *Murguia*, *Gran Poder de Dios*, the *aviso*, and the *balandrita* were known to have survived the hurricane. The *Murguia* and *Poder* returned to Cádiz in 1734, and the *aviso* and *balandrita* in all probability remained in service in the West Indies. As far as the Spanish salvagers knew, the *situada* had sunk in deep water and had not tried to locate her. There remained only four shipwreck sites to locate, the *"Populo,"* *"San José,"* *"Angustias,"* and *"San Fernando."*

By 1966 the state of Florida had cast a blanket of restrictions over the salvage community. With only ten state agents available, they limited the leases to ten sites. The agents remained aboard the salvage boats as they worked those sites, observing that all recoveries were properly logged and immediately dispatched to Tallahassee for "preservation." A fee was charged for each lease, and charts of work accomplished — along with a daily log of activities— were submitted. "Big Brother" was in their back pocket. Outside the three mile limit the state had no jurisdiction. Here the Federal Government still controlled international waters, and they had not, as yet, become a factor in the salvage of shipwrecks. The two wreck sites that seemed to lay outside the three mile limit were the *Populo*, which probably sank near Pacific Reef, and the *San José* which lay somewhere off Tavernier Island. The rush was on to locate these two sites.

The charts of the Spanish were fairly accurate, once you were able to separate out the various keys and identify them, but still it was a big ocean. Beyond the three mile limit, and nearly out of sight of land, there were few landmarks to guide the hunt. The reefs are the best road maps, but when the surface of the ocean is choppy or the water is wrapped in a blanket of murky visibility, even these are not of much help. Day after day the salvage boats were out, towing swimmers behind on a rope while they searched the bottom. Some of the salvagers had access to small aircraft, and they were seen circling the reefs looking for the telltale smudge of gray that would indicate a possible ballast pile. Some salvagers had magnetometers, the sensors towed behind the boat that could detect large metal masses as much as fifteen feet below the sand. But day after day the search seemed fruitless. The finding of the *Populo* was not accomplished by one of the professional salvage groups. The *Populo* was located by a group of four divers with little or no salvage experience. But what they lacked in experience, they more than made up for in dogged determination. This is their story.

September 1, 1966

Carl Frederick was well aware of the various recoveries on the 1733 wreck sites and was moved like most at the photos of treasure being brought to the surface. He had done some research of his own and was aware that the *Populo* had not been located as yet. He lived in South Miami and, as far as he could determine, the *Populo* had to have sunk almost directly opposite Black Caesar's Creek, the channel between Biscayne Bay and the islands at the head of the Keys. One of his co-workers at Air International in Miami was an electronics superstar by the name of Lee Harding. Lee had worked up the circuit board for an underwater metal detector and was anxious to try it out on a wreck site. Carl Ward was a Miami Beach policeman that had been diving galleon sites in the Florida Keys for about a year. Bob McKay was an airline jockey for Eastern Air Lines, with time on his hands between flights and a desire to search for treasure on old Spanish galleons.

It was a compatible group that found themselves aboard a 19-foot outboard boat searching the reefs beyond Black Caesar's Creek. There was a glass window built into the bottom of the boat, and each would take a turn stretched out on the floorboards, peering through the window at the bottom unfolding below them. If one looked at the bottom more than fifteen minutes at a time he wound up with a headache, so they worked the glass window in shifts. After several weeks they had seen a lot of fish, a lot of reefs, and a lot of sandy bottom, but nothing resembling a ballast pile. They did often see large sharks cruising through the reefs as they passed over, and they often speculated *who* would go over the side in the event they actually did locate something of interest.

It was at a time when frustration was beginning to set in, when they began to wonder if they could actually see the ballast pile without a magnetometer. It was a sun-filled day, water flat calm and crystal clear, and they had just begun to skirt a large reef to seaward when they all spotted the ballast pile at once! This particular reef rose sharply to within fifteen feet of the surface, and at the base they could see the unmistakable pile of ballast stones. Alongside, in the sand, they could also see the outlines of two large cannon. They circled the shoreward side of the reef and saw that the bottom sloped away into sand. Then it was time to anchor up and take a look. Soon they were all in the water, their adrenaline pumping as they checked over the pile. It was like mounting up and riding off in all directions! Each found different things to shout about as they popped to the surface. "Hey, you should see what I've got over here!" —and then swimming back to the bottom. There were iron fittings covering the ballast pile...and some unusual conglomerates that would later turn out to contain cannon balls.

After an hour or so they were all back in the boat, and it was an exciting time for them. They had been searching for the *Populo*, and it was quite possible they had found her. That was certainly an accomplishment. Then they had to laugh at themselves. "You know, we spent all this time looking for the *Populo*, and now that we may have found her...we have no equipment to salvage her!" They took stock in what they did have to work with. There was the 19-foot boat with a suspect motor, a 3-inch suction dredge, and enough SCUBA tanks to keep them on the bottom for about two hours each day. They also recognized that other salvage groups would be watching, and if their wreck site were discovered, the jig was up. It would be fair game for anyone to move in on them. Their opportunity to work this virgin wreck site existed only as long as their ability to keep its location a secret. They took good bearings on the landmarks they could recognize, including Pacific Reef Light, which stood about one mile to the southeast, bearing 68 degrees. Then it was back to their homes where they made plans to begin the salvage.

It was a week later before they could return to the site, a week of speculation that if it were the *Populo, how much* treasure did she still have on her. It was a week of many phone calls, and preparation, of making sure the outboard engine had an overhaul, and that the suction hose for the dredge had proper fittings. Little things that made the anticipation that much more exciting. Then it was through Black Caesar's Creek and out to the reefs behind Pacific Light. That day was unforgettable. The water had turned a bit murky and the surface had a bit of chop on it, so the bottom was barely visible thirty feet below. They couldn't use the glass window, so it meant towing a diver behind the boat on the end of a line. It meant acting like a trolling piece of bait for the large sharks they remembered seeing when they were looking for their wreck site. After over an hour, lining up the ranges they had marked down, they still hadn't been able to locate the shipwreck.

About the time their excitement had abated somewhat, they located the reef, and then the ballast pile. With air tanks on they scouted the pile from one end to the other. The pile lay north to south against the face of the reef and was about 70 feet long and 30 feet wide. The reef rose at least ten feet above them, and on the north end lay deep gray silt and mud. On the south end, where the two cannon lay, white sand stretched out into a bottom of eel grass. Another half moon reef lay several hundred yards shoreward. They located three more seven-foot cannons in the ballast pile, one of them much shorter than the others. The entire ballast pile lay in a patch of white sand a hundred feet in diameter. The reef that helped to hide the site for so many years was no more than 150 feet long.

Before leaving the location that day they decided to raise the smaller of the cannon on top of the ballast pile. It took a lot of struggling to get it up in the boat, even though it was no more than 3-1/2 feet long. The next day their excitement mounted even higher when they chipped away the coral encrustation and discovered their cannon was *bronze!* It had some distinctive markings that would later help to identify their wreck site as the *Populo*. Their immediate reaction was that bronze cannons usually meant a treasure wreck, and they were certain that treasure lay somewhere in the pile of ballast. Now it meant even more secrecy in keeping their wreck site from other salvagers. No markers would be used, and a lookout would always remain topside to warn of approaching boats.

From that point on, often entire days of operations would be shut down because a fishing boat had anchored no more than a hundred yards away, and the divers would sit with fishing poles over the side...without bait. Trips to the site were more often made during the week when fewer boats were working off the outer reefs. When aircraft circled overhead, the dredge was shut down, the hoses disconnected and thrown over the side. Once a lobster fisherman became suspicious that these new divers might be raiding his traps and circled them for most of one day, while he kept his eye on them. They sat through it all, and soon their 19-foot boat became a part of the everyday activity.

As they dug into the ballast pile, and the recoveries seemed different almost every day, their families grew closer together, each as excited as the next in what was being recovered. At first their efforts paid off with buckets full of cannon balls, grape shot, and lead musket balls. Enough to have them dub their site "The Cannon Ball Wreck." Every once in awhile an unusual artifact would be uncovered by the dredge. The first was a seven inch silver plate with hallmarks of "N" and "O" on the bottom. Then a scattering of blue and white porcelain shards, pieces of K'ang Hsi cups and saucers that had been brought over from China on the Manila Galleons. There were buckets full of olive jar shards, the utility containers of all the Spanish fleet. The iron fittings that covered the ballast were difficult to sledge-hammer apart, the metal long since a part of the coral concretion.

Initially their objective was to dredge test holes in a number of locations, and if treasure were found, then expand the hole. But if the silver or gold were there, it eluded them. Seven months passed before their first treasure coin was recovered, but then what a beauty it was! It was a fully-dated 1732 Pillar Dollar, and in great condition. One had recently been auctioned off for $2,500. Not only was it a valuable coin, but it also gave them positive proof that their site was the *Populo*. Only the 1733 fleet was carrying 1732 Pillar Dollars. With no other 1733 shipwrecks known to be close by, they were now sure they had the *Populo*. This recovery produced a new round of enthusiasm and treasure fever. Moving a ton of ballast stone in one day suddenly became a labor of love.

Diving Season 1967

The weather, and Bob McKay's flying schedule, kept the trips to *Populo* limited as the weeks and months wore on. Lee Harding had developed his underwater metal detector, and it turned up some new "hot spots" that began to produce even more unusual artifacts. It also added to the growing pile of cannon balls in Carl Frederick's back yard. There were also weeks on end when nothing at all of interest was found, yet just as patience was wearing thin another great artifact would be uncovered. There were silver pieces-of-eight, scissors, a pair of bronze navigational dividers, and more cannon balls. They tried to visualize just how their ship had wrecked, to determine which end was the bow and which end was the stern. The sterncastle would have been carrying all the treasure, but was that on the north end where the deep silt and mud lay, or was it at the south end where the sandy bottom disappeared into the eel grass? They tried using the dredge on the mud and silt on the north end, only to cover the entire site with a thick cloud of murky water and shutting down the operation until the water cleared. The excavation on this end went slowly, and in the end only more cannon balls and grape shot were recovered. Test holes in the sand at the south end turned up more wooden bottom timbers. The wreck was larger than they first thought. But still no treasure.

It was when they began digging a long trench against the side of the reef where the ballast rested that most of their important artifacts were uncovered. At first it was a number of wooden block-and-pulleys, then several pottery bowls, an ivory tuning pin from a musical instrument, brass buckles, a granite milling stone, a vanilla bean jar, and more silver pieces-of-eight. Even more of the blue and white K'ang Hsi porcelain shards, broken pieces of the fragile cups and saucers carried as cargo, were carefully stowed in a water-filled bucket. Carl Ward began fitting together pieces that seemed to match, and after gluing about twenty pieces carefully together he had almost an entire cup. It lacked a single triangular piece to complete. Carl kept his eye open for the missing piece, but it was like looking for a needle in a haystack. The treasure fever was again pushing them on a daily basis, and they decided to move more ballast so they could dig a trench along the hull. Mendel Peterson, of the Smithsonian Institute, had suggested they might find some great artifacts there. With more of the keel exposed they still found nothing of the treasure they sought. Hurricane "Beulah" churned its way across the Lesser Antilles and into Bahamian waters, cutting the diving season short as bad weather persisted.

Diving Season 1968

Their last year on the site found the group on alternate days working first one end of the wreck site, then the other. They still hadn't figured out which was the stern and which was the bow, but artifacts seemed to be everywhere they looked. But if treasure were there, they hadn't found it as yet. In spite of their not buoying the site, several boatloads of divers had located them while they were still working on the bottom, and now it was merely a matter of time before the site would be open season for salvagers. There now seemed to be an urgency to complete the salvage before this happened, and quite a bit of the ballast had not yet been explored. Lee Harding had put together a hookah rig, or breathing compressor, so that SCUBA tanks were now history. The divers could stay on the bottom all day long without coming to the surface to change tanks. Time on the bottom was now limited to only daylight or the weather. A marker was placed on a nearby reef to enable them to more quickly locate the site, and soon the ballast was producing more pottery shards, cannon balls, musket balls, and even an almost intact communion bowl. One day Carl Ward popped to the surface shouting, giving everyone a scare that he was being attacked by a shark. As it turned out, he had finally located the last piece of triangular K'ang Hsi to complete the cup he had been working on for over a year.

The end of their dream came in September. Other salvagers had located the site, and one day as they were passing through Black Caesar's Creek on the way to the *Populo* they noticed a cabin cruiser towing a large object slung under several 55-gallon drums. They recognized one of the local salvagers, and stopped to chat with him across the few feet of water separating their boats as they moved in opposite directions. The object turned out to be one of their cannons. When they reached the site they were astounded at finding all their cannon missing and large areas of the hull exposed, where airlifts had probed deep beneath the sand. As they sat in their boat over the *Populo* it was truly a moment of sadness. They had the wreck site to themselves for nearly two years and had recovered some remarkable artifacts. Never the treasure they had imagined, because the piles of gold and silver were never there to begin with. The *Populo* carried no registered treasure. But what the

Populo did do was provide each of the divers with an experience he would never forget. The companionship that had survived months of frustration and hardship. And the memories of a successful treasure hunt. Although not the pot of gold at the end of the rainbow, it was treasure nonetheless.

They located and salvaged* El Populo*: (L. to R.)
Carl Frederick, Bob McKay, Lee Harding and Carl Ward.

The famed "Pillar Dollar" was virtually unknown in its 1732 and 1733 varieties until the discovery of the 1733 Spanish treasure fleet along the Florida Keys in the 1960s.
PHOTO COURTESY: Ponterio & Associates.

*Dutch "stone-throwing" bronze cannon—with Amsterdam
foundry mark—recovered from* **El Populo.**
PHOTO: Ernie Richards

PHOTO: Denis B. Trelewicz

Ballast mound of **El Populo** *in July 1995.*
PHOTO: Denis B. Trelewicz

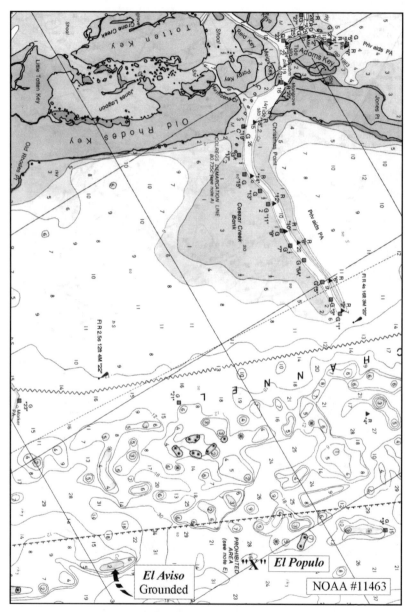

LOCATION CHART: *El Populo.*
(*El Aviso* **grounded where shown, was re-floated.**)

CHAPTER 9: *EL AVISO*
Nuestra Señora de los Dolores
"The Advice Boat"

After the hurricane passed up the channel between the Florida Keys and Cuba, and although the shift in wind direction played havoc with *El Populo*, her sister ship *el aviso* had better luck. Both vessels had been sailing near the head of the fleet of Don Rodrigo de Torres, and at the height of the hurricane the two ships were driven between the reefs at the "Cabeza de los Martires," or head of the Florida Keys. They were within sight of each other when the weather finally settled down, the *aviso* afloat, the *Populo* sunk up to her poop deck. Although afloat, and still seaworthy, the *aviso*'s main mast was gone, as were her top masts and spars. Somewhere along the way she lost her rudder as well. She still had her long boat, and with it Captain Don Pedro Arrambide and his crew made contact with the captain and crew of the *Populo*. Together they rowed the three miles to shore (today's Elliott Key) in an attempt to learn where they were.

By 1733 the Indians were friendly to the Spanish, possibly through fear, but they still hated the English. They were on the shores of Elliott Key when Captain Huboni of the *El Africa* spotted them, sent his own long boat ashore, and eventually rescued the entire crews of both vessels. Some of the *aviso* supplies were transferred to *El Africa* before the ship continued on her voyage. The crew of the *aviso* reached Cádiz, Spain on September 24, 1733, fortunate indeed to have survived the hurricane, but Arrambide was distraught having to leave his ship behind. His crew had been able to rig a jury mast, and with a piece of the main mast they had fashioned, to some extent, a makeshift rudder. But attempting to sail her back to Spain in the condition she was in would have been difficult and dangerous. She carried no treasure, and what little cargo which had been carried on board was transferred to *El Africa*. Surely Arrambide watched from *El Africa*'s sterncastle long after his *aviso* disappeared over the horizon.

"July 31. We learned from the Balandra that dispatched for water to Cayo Biscayno how an Aviso is anchored which sailed with us from Vera Cruz. It is dismasted of the main mast and spars and top masts, and without rudder. They didn't find anyone

aboard, but they found a jury mast made. Likewise a piece of the main mast had been fashioned into the rudder, as though someone had fixed it to try and sail out of there. Some of the ship's supplies were still on board, and from aloft they spotted another ship aground."
(*Indiferente* 57- Diary of the *El Infante*)

"*El Aviso...En Cayo Viscaino quedo a nado.*" [In Key Biscayne stayed afloat.]
(AGI *Contratación* 5102 -2)

The advice boat was a *patache* type vessel, small and in the 100 to 300 ton range, used primarily as a dispatch vessel to carry messages between vessels of the *flota*. Based on the limited information we have on *el aviso* it was the Advice Boat of the Council, joining the *flota* in Vera Cruz for the return trip back to Spain. It had no European trade goods as far as we know, and as a result would not have had much in the way of cargo to be carried back to Spain. It may have carried some passengers with personal possessions, but nothing in the way of registered treasure.

When the vessel was located afloat at the head of the *Martires*, Rodrigo de Torres ordered it towed back to his *real* on Matecumbe Grande (Islamorada) where it was properly repaired and used to carry water to the various *reales* of the survivors. Eventually it made its way back to Havana, but no records exist of it finishing its voyage back to Spain.

To many treasure salvagers who had looked for *el aviso* in the hopes it had sunk in close approximation to the *Populo*, research could have saved them many hours of scouting the reefs off Black Caesar's Creek. But, then again, there are so many shipwrecks in the area they probably found enough ballast piles to keep them busy.

CHAPTER 10: *EL INFANTE*
Nuestra Señora de Balvaneda

Here is a shipwreck site that every avid diver, whether a resident of Florida or a visitor from out of state...or out of the country...will recognize as being one of the greatest thrill dives of the Florida Keys. The *Infante* has had more visiting divers than any other ballast pile along the outer reefs, and more stories have been yarned ashore about this 1733 galleon than any of the other fourteen sites marking the last great Spanish treasure fleet disaster. The story of *El Infante* deserves to be told.

El Infante was one of the four primary war galleons that were consigned by King Philip V of Spain to carry treasure back to Spain from the New World. It was heavily armed and, as a secondary duty, it was a guard galleon to protect the merchant *naos* that completed the fleet of General Don Rodrigo de Torres in 1733. *El Infante* was built in Genoa in 1724 as a *refuerzo*, or merchant supply vessel. The king of Spain purchased the ship as one of his fleet of treasure ships to make the journey to the New World. As a result, before leaving the shipyard, the Genoese shipwrights reinforced her hull with sacrificial sheathing of pine nailed over the outer hull planks. In the West Indies the teredo worms rapidly attack the wood of a ship below the waterline, often rendering the vessel useless within a year or so. It was not unusual that many galleons traveling the treasure route had to remain in the West Indies because damage by the teredo worms was so great they had no chance of surviving an ocean voyage back to Spain. It would have been easier to replace the pine sheathing than the heavier hull planks.

The *Infante* was designed to carry sixty iron cannon, so it was considered heavily armed. In the mid 1650s the English cannon makers were finally able to cast an iron cannon that could be fired repeatedly without the fear of blowing up due to overheating. Prior to this only bronze cannon could be fired without that fear. Very quickly, the Spanish were able to copy the design (some say they kidnapped one of the English cannon makers), and because iron cannon were about one-third the cost of bronze cannon it meant the end of the bronze cannon era. Thereafter all cannons were forged of iron, including the sixty that found their way aboard the *El Infante*.

There are no records available regarding the size of *Infante*, but with an estimated 400-ton cargo capacity the estimated length is 120 feet, with a width of 38 feet. Christened with the name *Nuestra Señora de Balvaneda*, the nickname *El Infante* was adopted early in her sea career and remained with her until she came to grief on Little Conch Reef. It is not known how many trips to the West Indies the *Infante* made prior to 1733, but as General Rodrigo de Torres y Morales gathered his *Nueva España* (New Spain) *Flota* in the harbor of Cádiz in July 1732, *El Infante* was one of the four main galleons. With a consignment of quicksilver on board, as well as general merchandise to be traded, Don Domingo de Lanz was her captain as *Infante* sailed westward from Cádiz on August 2 with de Torres' *flota*.

It was late September when the fleet anchored in the open roadstead behind the fort on San Juan de Ulúa Island. Vera Cruz did not have a protected harbor, and over the years a great many Spanish galleons were sunk in this area due to the unpredictable storms and hurricanes that frequent the Mexican coastline. But Vera Cruz offered the shortest route from the Mexican mint to the coast of Mexico, so storms and hurricanes were the risk the Spaniards were willing to take. Cortez established the port of Vera Cruz in 1519, and it became the primary terminus for the *requas* of mules (a *requa* is a team of 50 mules) that literally mule-hauled the silver bars and coins, as well as gold, over the Mexican mountains from Mexico City to the coast to be loaded on board the galleons. The 1733 *flota* was going to be one of the fortunate ones to be blessed with good weather during its winter stay.

The word was soon spread that the treasure fleet had arrived in Vera Cruz, and the sleepy (almost uninhabited) town began to come alive. Merchants, the operators of the mines, and the local vendors soon filled up the few hotel rooms available. The fair began in earnest when the jingle of bells announced the arrival of the mule trains as they wended their way from the foothills into the town square. The boxes of silver coins and silver bars were unloaded and stacked in the center of town. After a few days of rest, the mules were again loaded with merchandise, and the consignment of quicksilver, and made ready for the return trip to Mexico City. By 1732 the refinement of the silver ore had become fairly efficient (by 1732 standards). German mining engineers had developed the use of quicksilver, the extract of mercury from the ore, cinnabar, which when combined with the silver ore, water, and other chemical additives formed a paste. Over a period of six to eight weeks the silver in the ore gradually adhered to the mercury and sank to the bottom of the mixture. The water was then drained off, and the amalgam of mercury and silver heated to a point that the mercury evaporated, leaving very pure silver. Mercury was necessary in the production of silver, so it became an important part of the control that the Spanish authorities had over the mining of precious metals in the New World. They had the monopoly on mercury production, and the profits from the trade became an important source of the royal revenue. Smart business!

The general cargo that *Infante* had carried from Europe to trade included wines, paper, clothing, armament, glass and other building products from Spain. The local products that found their way into the *Infante* cargo holds were brasilwood, cochineal, Guadalajara ware, Chinese porcelain, leather hides, anil, vanilla, and citrus. For the king's account, there was a total of 186 boxes of silver coins, and at 3,000 pesos to the box that equaled 558,000 pesos. On the 25th of May, 1733, Rodrigo de Torres gave the signal to hoist anchors and, with a westerly wind to carry them, the *flota* sailed for Havana, arriving four weeks later on June 25.

What followed was a whirlwind of activity. Havana had become the primary focus of the king's authority in New Spain. The precious metals from all of Mexico and South America passed through Havana Harbor on their way back to Spain. Over the years El Morro, the fortress guarding the harbor entrance, had gained the respect of the French, English, Dutch, as well as the pirates that roamed the Spanish Main in search of a straggler merchant *nao*. The inhabitants felt safe behind the cannoneers and soldiers that stood ready to drive off any invaders. As a result Spanish culture thrived here, a semblance of the opulence that the mountain of silver and streams of gold had provided to the Spanish autocracy in Europe. When the treasure fleets arrived it signaled the beginning of parties, balls, and a never-ending flow of spirits. There was the additional cargo of sugar, tobacco, and other "fruits of the land" to be loaded on board. Fresh water and provisions were stowed below, and any final repairs or outfitting to the ships were made before the long voyage back to Spain.

It was time to go. In the early hours of July 13, 1733, *El Infante* weighed anchor and followed the *capitana* and *almiranta* past El Morro and luffed her sails awaiting the remainder of the fleet to clear port.

The following is from the diary of the *El Infante*. (*Indiferente* 57 - Diary of the *Infante*, 1733):

"July 13—With all the fleet under sail we left the harbor of San Christobal de Havana at 10:00 A.M. with fair winds from the SE and clear horizons. After leaving El Morro and outside in the open sea, the wind came upon us from the ENE. We stowed the launch and boat and set course to the north. At 3:00 P.M. we changed course to the SE until sundown when we set our course to the N, now finding ourselves north of Jaracas about one and one half leagues.

· "July 14—We continued our course to the north and at 10:00 A.M. we saw the land to the west of the Vacas Keys (Key West), and at noon we were about 3 leagues from them. We then changed course to the SE until 3:00 P.M. when we tacked to the north. At 6:00 P.M. we were off the west point of the Vacas [Marathon], N 1/4 NE, and at this hour we changed course to the ESE and reefed the main topsail. [Began to get a bit breezy.] At 7:00 P.M. the wind changed to the NNE and by 10:00 P.M. it had gone to the north. The top mainsails were taken in with all the reefs, and at midnight we reefed the remainder, leaving only two mains with our course to the east.

"July 15 - At daybreak we brought down the top gallant sails and at 6:00 A.M. we furled the mainsail and the mizzen sail with its reef bands, taking in the sheets and likewise the main sheets. Because the storm was now intensifying and the visibility lowering we reversed course with our bow now to the west. Both sea and wind were rising. Anticipating our arrival to the port of Havana [they were trying to return because of the storm] we put our bow to the SSW. Running in this fashion before the sea we hoped to ease the strain on the ship, but the rudder would not respond and to keep from capsizing we eased up on the fore sail sheet and immediately the wind blew it to pieces, emptying the ship of any sails. At 9:30 A.M. such wind and sea came upon us that we found ourselves unable to work the ship and still maintain the ship upright, and the ship fell away into the sea, unable to right itself. This obliged us to cut away the main mast halyards, after which the mast fell away to the seas.

"We stood this way working the ship with the wind still strengthening and with the water over the Alcázar deck and with the main hatch under water. In this conflict we desired to cut away the fallen top mast, and to achieve carrying away the top mast of the mizzen and fore top mast. Upon doing so, at once the ship righted itself for which we were all heartened. Then we cut away the rigging of the masts and half hour later the foremast fell away, but it fell in such a way that it clung to the side of the ship, it being the only one remaining to relieve our torture and provide salvation. We were unable to cut the stay of the mast.

"It soon became necessary that we cut the bowsprit, which required a lot of work. Having done this by 3:00 P.M. it fell away and we were free of all masts, making us not unlike a buoy, secure in the knowledge that the task before us now was to stay afloat with our pumps and keep out the water which incessantly came in due to the repeated blows of the sea. At 5:00 P.M. the corridor and the privies were filling with water, finding us with more work than we could handle and more when the rudder coat opened up. We stopped this with clothes, mattresses, and odd pieces.

"The ship was now opening up between decks, further filling the hold with water and we worked feverishly at the pumps trying to bail the water out when at 6:00 P.M. the wind changed to the south with as much, if not more, violence than before, the blows of the seas always continuing to add to our torment and we continuously worked at the pumps to keep the ship afloat.

"At 8:30 P.M. the ship struck bottom and continued doing so for a quarter of an hour with horrendous blows, taking on water fast from stem to stern for what seemed surely to pound us to pieces. Thus we suffered through the night.

"July 16—At daybreak the weather was clear and we could see the land and with the light of day we could see the coast of the NE-SW which we recognized as the beginning of the Key Largo at the entrance to the Canal of the Bahamas, about two leagues distant. We also saw a very large ship grounded to the

SW about 1-1/2 leagues and supposed it to be the Capitana. To the NW we saw another ship grounded at about 1/2 league, and we supposed this to be the ship of El Duque [*San Joseph y Las Animas / San José.*] Likewise to the SSW four or five leagues we discovered two grounded vessels which we thought to be Tres Puentes and the one of Herrera. To the west about four leagues we found another close by land which we supposed to be the one of Chaves. [The largest concentration of shipwrecks was around Upper Matecumbe...author.]

"Because the small boat was badly battered by the cruel blows of the seas and winds we had to patch it up with what we could. At 7:00 A.M. we set it in the water and embarked in it an official who could go to land and find the best place for the rest of us to disembark. The launch suffered a similar fate and we patched it up likewise with matting and cloth since we had no carpenter tools [they were all under water in the hold.] With great effort we placed it in the water and embarked in it a sergeant, two chiefs with infantry, and a guardian to defend the people. The officers then ordered a raft built from parts of the ship, since there were no more boats available with which to get the people ashore.

"July 17—In the morning the raft was completed, well made with its quarter casks, and by 9:00 A.M. there were sixty people embarked in it with one official. At 5:30 P.M. we brought aboard our boat and it departed in an hour loaded with nails, caulking, tar, and people to make a launch and a boat on shore. At 10:00 P.M. the ship's launch was hoisted on board.

"July 18—Another raft was made and filled with people and as before the launch towed it ashore. We received notice from the ship of Murgia that it had grounded without taking on water, minus its main mast and some top masts, and that nearby was a balandra which left in convoy with us from Havana bound for St. Augustine loaded with flour. This balandra was afloat but without a mast. Also, we supposed from the said notice that the El Gran Poder de Dios managed to save itself on an anchor but was also dismasted.

"July 19—We continue to send people ashore. Notice was received of the San Pedro being grounded and full of water, and the same fortune befell the navio of Terry.

"July 20—The launch and boat returned about noon with orders from the Commander for the Captain and his officials to go ashore and, if able, leave the ship in the hands of six men of satisfaction. We learned that the San Francisco of Urquijo was grounded along with the Almiranta, and that the fragata going to Florida was in pieces and that only one man escaped from it.

"July 21—We went ashore. We took notice that the San Raphael [*Angustias*], the one of Arizón [*Sueco de Arizón*], and the one of Sanchez de Seville San Fernando were all grounded and flooded.

"July 22—The Captain commanded the crew that were on board to leave the ship, along with the officers, minus the six before mentioned men, and they all headed for this real [camp] where we now all are.

"July 23—The buceo [underwater salvage] of the Capitana commences this day and continues with good results.

"July 25—Notice arrived of the loss of the San Ignacio of Irquijo from which no more were saved than 14, the 12 being sailors and the other two servants of the passengers. All of these ships are cast away in the keys to the west [of this *real*] on Matecumbe El Viejo [Lower Matecumbe], a distance from this real to the last is 12 leagues.

"July 26—The balandra returned from Havana with supplies and were then loaded with people and salvaged silver for the return voyage.

"July 31—We learned from the balandra that was dispatched for water to Cayo Biscayno how an Aviso is anchored which sailed with us from Vera Cruz, it is dismasted of the main mast and without rudder. They didn't find anyone on board but they found a jury mast made. Likewise a piece of the main mast had been fashioned into the rudder, as though someone had fixed it to try and sail out of there. Some of the ship's supplies were still on board and from aloft they spotted another ship grounded [*El Populo*.]

"August 2—The Captain's small boat arrived to this real, which had been sent out as an Advice Boat, and in it were supplies. The Balandra also returned with one launch and one boat, these had gone for water. They encountered the launch of the Aviso on land in a canal. They also found another ship which is El Populo sunk up to its poop deck. They found no one on board and it was determined by the practical navigators to be at the head of the Martyrs. [They had encountered the *aviso* days before near Upper Key Largo.]

"August 4—We received notice that all the silver had been taken off the Almiranta and taken ashore.

"August 7—The ship of Murgia was off-loaded and is now afloat awaiting the trip to Havana. The buceo [underwater salvage] of the Infante started this day and was finished on the 9th, having salvaged 180 boxes of silver coins, lacking just six from concluding the registry."

[They recovered five more.]

[Total recoveries from the *Infante* were: 568,613 pesos, 4 *reales* in *plata acuñada*...coined silver; 1184 *arrobas*, 22 *libras* of cochineal; and 103 *arrobas*, 18 *libras* of anil (indigo).]

Once the silver was salvaged from the *Infante* very little salvage work by the Spanish was attempted. When the grounded vessels were burned to the waterline upon completion of salvage, it is assumed that *Infante* was also burned. Over the years the ballast pile remained intact, with little growth of coral. The ballast stones are a contaminant that resist the growth of coral. The water was only fourteen to sixteen feet deep over the top of the wreck site and as hurricanes crossed the area some of the stones were scattered. Gradually teredo worms ate their way through the timbers, and finally only the timbers under the ballast pile remained. But the pile was a prominent landmark of a once proud Spanish galleon, resting on the seaward edge of Little Conch Reef.

Art McKee, the grandfather of Florida's salvage divers, was the first to look the *Infante* ballast pile over. It was within the lease granted him by the state of Florida, but so was the *capitana*, and from this wreck site he was recovering some great artifacts, including gold and silver coins. As a result he spent very little time on the *Infante*. By 1951 the salvage of sunken treasure was just beginning to take on the halo of a dream come true for those that believed in *Treasure Island*.

Art Sapp, Craig Hamilton, Warren Conway and others began working the site, removing the six remaining cannons (nine-pounders). In 1959 Tim Watkins and his crew, affectionately called "The Bastard Seven" (Jim Hettel, Tim Watkins, Jim Green, Olin Frick, Paul Nixon, Jim Doyle, and Art Sapp) moved out to the site of the *Infante* with their 56-foot salvage boat *Buccaneer*. In a single day they recovered silver wedges, hundreds of silver coins, a few gold rings, rapiers, a flintlock musket, cannon balls, and a number of other artifacts. A photo of the crew on board their salvage boat appeared on the front page of the *Miami Herald*, tagged with the headline "Undersea Swag Sparks Court Battle Threats."

The *Herald* was living up to its controversial nature. The feud was an apparent disagreement between Art McKee and the *Buccaneer* crew over salvage rights on the *Infante*. The disagreement carried over several weeks later on the site of the *capitana*. Suddenly a show of guns brought national attention to the Florida Keys, and the public was made to believe that the sunken treasure being recovered was worth a vast fortune. In fact, the artifacts recovered had little financial value except as a museum exhibit. The end result was an announcement by state officials that the wreck site was outside the three mile limit and beyond state jurisdiction. It became a free for all.

In the years that followed a number of salvagers tried their luck on the *Infante*. It was discovered that the scatter pattern of the site, including the passengers baggage, extended shoreward several hundred yards. World Wide Treasure Research worked the site in 1960. Art Hartman, George Trabor, Harold Still, and Roy Volker recovered five of the 1732 "pillar dollars," a silver shoe buckle, silver knife handle, a bronze religious medallion, twelve uniform buttons, straight pins, a copper *maravedi* coin, and a 2-*real* and 4-*real* "cob" coins. The author, "Frogfoot", as well as Marty Meylach, Don Thomas, Russell Swanson, Dick Hall, Ray Manieri, Pat Patterson, Brad Patten spent many days working under the hull timbers or along the reefs. And no matter how often they worked the site they always seemed to find something interesting. It was a great wreck, the water warm and clear, and five miles from land the sound of traffic and telephones was left behind. D. L. Chaney recovered a 2-*escudo* Mexico gold coin from the sands surrounding the ballast, and Tim Watkins recovered a 2-*escudo* Bogotá dated 1719, as well as a silver wedge and a number of 4- and 8-*real* silver coins. Bobby Klein also spent a great deal of time, both alone and with charters, working around the *Infante* ballast. He recovered over the years several pillar dollars, cob 8-*reales*, and religious medallions. One of the more amusing stories that came out of the *Infante* had to do with Bobby Klein.

In the early 1960s Bobby accepted charters from tourists to "go treasure hunting on a Spanish galleon." His normal fee was $100 per day, and "find treasure or you won't have to pay!" That was a safe bet for the tourist, they would take home "something." Bobby also had an agreement, in case something fabulous came up off the bottom, that the Captain (Bobby) got first choice of the artifacts. A dentist from Chicago was an annual visitor to the Keys and became a customer of Bobby's on a regular basis. This one summer he brought his son along to introduce him to the world of sunken treasure. That particular week Bobby took his guests to the *Infante*. There was a large hole under the turn of the hull that he was recovering some nice artifacts from. That first day they managed to recover several significant artifacts, but one in particular was a conglomerate in which could be seen at least four silver pieces-of-eight.

At the end of the day, as the recoveries were being divided, the dentist remarked, "Let's drop the conglomerate of coins in an acid bath and that should give each of us a couple of nice coins." Bobby (as the story goes) shook his head, "One conglomerate, one artifact, the captain's first choice. Sorry." This agitated the dentist no little bit. So the next morning, as they prepared to head seaward, the dentist asked, "Bobby, if I gave you an extra $100 today, can I have first choice?" Bobby's answer was a resounding "Yes!" They again headed for the *Infante* and anchored over the stern section where the hole had been opened up, extending along the shoreward side for several feet. Soon both Bobby and his charter were busy airlifting under the hull timbers and the sand and coral dust soon reduced visibility to a few feet. Within half an hour the guest came out from under the hull timbers, excitedly waving a large conglomerate that appeared to be a lead tray of some sort. Up in the boat both Bobby and the dentist had an opportunity to see that it was a tray full of the valuable "pillar dollars," encrusted in a cement-like coral, but obviously the only round coins that were on the 1733 fleet.

The rest of the dive was anti-climatic, and when Bobby reached the marina he was the first to pick up the tray full of pillar dollars and head for the acid bath to separate them out. The dentist stopped him. He waved the tray of coins and stated, "Bobby, they all hang together, one artifact and I get first choice. Sorry."

That evening Bobby, the dentist, and his son were having dinner at the Chesapeake House at the north end of Islamorada. The dentist had rented a room at the motel behind the restaurant. It so happened that Ray Manieri and Jack Steffany were heading north from a dive that day and stopped in at the Chesapeake for a last cup of coffee before heading up the road. They spotted Bobby and worked their way over to his table, asking, "How did you do today?" Bobby's face lit up like a candle. "Wait till you see what we've got to show you!" The dentist and his son were grinning broadly as they led Manieri and Steffany back to their room. When the two saw the tray of pillar dollars the response was like electricity in a thunderstorm. Steffany admitted he could sell the coins for as much as $1,000 each, and it appeared as though there were over fifty in the lead tray. They left shortly after, but before Manieri had traveled very far up U.S. Highway #1 towards Miami he was on the phone to me. "You won't believe what I just saw!"—and he went to explain about the tray of pillar dollars. He also said that the guest got "first choice," and Bobby was pretty upset that he wouldn't be sharing in the recovery.

The salvage community was soon aware of the pillar dollar story, and to some it was a chance to circulate the feeling "It couldn't happen to a nicer guy." Bobby Klein was a tough salvor, not many crossed his path on the wrong side of the road. So the story festered.

My wife Margaret and I were traveling through the Keys. I had a company called "Sunken Treasures from Florida" in which I made reproductions of the gold and silver coins being recovered from the old Spanish galleons. The gift and dive shops were my best customers, and Bobby Klein had a nice gift shop and dive center in Upper Key Largo at the Ocean Reef Club. I had always gotten along with Bobby, although we had never dived together, and he was one of my dealers for the treasure coins. As we sat there talking treasure, I mentioned the story about the tray of pillar dollars. "I'd like to hear the story from the horse's mouth." Bobby smiled, then glanced up at a large 24" X 36" photo hanging on the wall. It was a photo of the pillar dollar tray, with coral and sulfide covering the stacks of rounded coins. He laughed, "Bob, you don't even recognize your own pillar dollars!" As it turned out, the dentist and Bobby had taken about sixty of my reproduction 1732 pillar dollars (50 cents apiece), stacked them up in a lead tray about one inch high that Bobby had fashioned out of a piece of lead he had recovered from H.M.S. *Winchester*, then covered them with a concretion of sand, coral dust, and Elmer's Glue. They looked like the real thing. Bobby had to laugh, "You should have seen Manieri and Steffany that night...they were *envious!*" It was a juicy story that evaporated in a whiff of rumor. But that's typical of many treasure stories.

With the passing of the Bennett Bill, "The Abandoned Shipwreck Act of 1987," all salvage of the 1733 Spanish wreck sites came under state jurisdiction. Salvage came to an abrupt halt. It stands that way today on the *Infante*. Look, but don't touch. It's still a great wreck site, with a history that reaches out and touches all that visit this great pile of ballast.

PHOTO: Denis B. Trelewicz

Ballast and timbers on El Infante *in November 1993*.
PHOTO: Denis B. Trelewicz

*Author Bob "Frogfoot" Weller carefully chipping away
at an encrusted object on the site of*
El Infante *of 1733.*

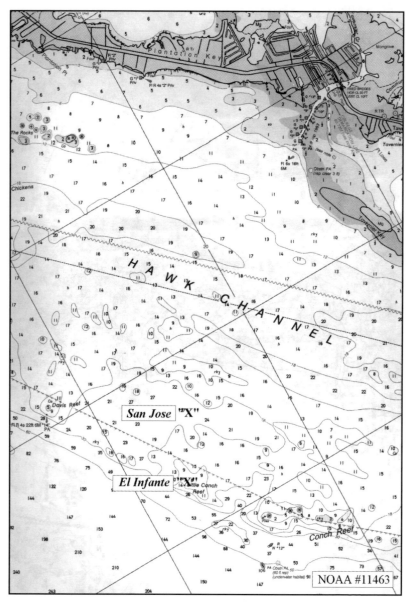

LOCATION CHART: *El Infante, San José.*

CHAPTER 11: *SAN JOSÉ*
San Joseph y Las Animas
Alias: "Del Duque"

Thie launch moved easily around the lee of the island catching a brisk easterly wind, and as the ocean swells sent spray over the gunnels the occupants huddled closer to the center console. The camera cases marked "CBS" were quickly covered with canvas and Captain Gene Geh remarked, "We've got four miles to go, so everyone get comfortable." Behind the launch, at the end of a 50-foot towing hawser, rode a 19-foot fiberglass boat loaded with a strange cargo of sloshing, water-filled containers. It was an unusual entourage that would mark the end of one of the darkest hours in Florida's salvage history.

...the boat sank out from under Tom Gurr! The rough seas finished the job of returning treasure back to the **San José.**

Soon the red buoy that marked the grave of the *San José* bobbed over the top of a wave, and Geh throttled back, letting the launch settle into the wind. The small boat being towed was pulled alongside and bearded treasure salvor Tom Gurr stepped aboard. As CBS cameramen focused on the scene Tom announced, "In protest of the deplorable political situation that currently exists within the Florida Department of Archives, History and Records Management Division, I hereby return to the sea from whence it came, artifacts and treasure recovered from the *San José*! With that he reached into the plastic container he held and began throwing identifiable treasures into the sea. With the cameras rolling he held aloft encrusted flintlock pistols, swords, pewter platters, and threw them overboard. As he worked from one side of the boat to the other the boat suddenly broached between two waves and began taking on water over the side and stern. With the television cameras filming away the unexpected happened...the boat sank out from under Gurr! As he swam over to the launch, the rough seas finished the job of returning treasure back to the *San José*.

The story of the *San José* isn't so much the treasure she was carrying back to the Spain. It became the story of the struggle that erupted between the treasure salvage community and the state of Florida. There was a fence between the two sides, a fence piled high with barbed wire, placed there by distrust. The state of Florida distrusted the salvage divers of not reporting everything that was recovered, and of illegally working shipwreck sites without a state approved lease. Once gold and silver became a major part of the recoveries, and with the media's help, it became a panic situation for the state to control everything that took place within the salvage community. Prior to this, salvage of Spanish shipwrecks had been going on for fifteen years on an amicable basis between the state and salvors. On the part of the treasure salvor, he looked upon the state as an obstacle to overcome. The shipwrecks had been on the bottom for hundreds of years, and no one had paid much attention to them. Suddenly, with the recovery of substantial amounts of gold and silver, "Big Brother" was in their back pocket. Leases were required, and only a very few were granted. Conservation of artifacts was not a concern, and would not be for several years. Artifacts collected by the state were stored in the basement of the old jail building in Tallahassee, where they disintegrated into heaps of rust. Countless reports, fees, and relinquishing the recovered treasure to the state until officials in Tallahassee decided it was time for a division, were a few of the problems that had not been worked out when the *San José* was discovered near the edge of Hawk Channel in thirty feet of water.

Actually, the *Saint Joseph* was constructed in the New England colonies of the New World. English shipbuilders had migrated to the coastal region near Boston where the oak timbers made stout hulls, and the trees grew straight and tall making fine masts. By the early 1700s English-built ships were better sailers than other foreign built vessels. They no longer had the need for high poop decks and rounded hulls, but instead improved cargo carrying capacity with wider beams and sleeker lines above the main deck. Construction of the *Saint Joseph* was completed sometime during the 1727-28 period, and she was listed at 326 tons. Her armament consisted of at least 27 cannon, the number recovered from the site by modern day salvage. A lead water pump dated 1728 was also recovered from the site, attesting to the probable construction time period. By 1730 the Spanish were attempting to rebuild the treasure fleet system, and the *Saint Joseph* was purchased by Don Joseph del Duque and promptly renamed *San Joseph y Las Animas*. Even the English dinner service was included in the purchase. The nickname *"San José"* was adopted and remained with the vessel until she was lost on the Florida reefs.

In August 1732 the *San José* joined Rodrigo de Torres' *flota* in the Bay of Cádiz. Her Captain was Don Cristobal Fernandez Franco, and she carried a cargo of European trade goods when the convoy anchored behind the fortress of Juan de Ulúa at Vera Cruz. The fleet spent the winter months there, suffering through an epidemic of the "black vomit," but the crew of the *San José* seemed to have weathered this well. The captain and merchants on board were able to trade their merchandise for 30,435 pesos in silver coins, 283 *arrobas* of cochineal, 603 *arrobas* of anil, 6 boxes of ceramic ware (probably K'ang Hsi porcelain from China), 27,000 pods of vanilla, sugar, chocolate, dyewoods, sacks of cocoa, earthen jugs, and some hides. When the fleet reached Havana additional strings of tobacco were brought aboard. Captain Franco may, or may not, have known that the merchants had smuggled on board a considerable amount in goods *sin registrada*, or contraband. This amounted to almost ten times the silver coins registered on the manifest, and would bring embarrassment and high penalties when discovered.

Cargo of the *San José*

Two items in the cargo of the *San José* deserve description. The first is the porcelain that had made the long voyage from Manila in the Philippines. This eighteenth-century porcelain was originally made in Chingtechen, an inner China province of Kiangsi. It was manufactured in crude assembly-line fashion consisting of as many as seventy individual operations. Vessels were placed on a potter's wheel, then finished in an exterior mold for uniformity. Artisans painted on the decorations with a different design for each vessel. The container was then fired, decorations re-applied as an overglaze, then re-fired. When this was completed the wares were carefully packed in boxes of straw surrounded by clay for the 600-mile journey from Chingtechen to Canton or Nanking, where the fragile cargo was placed aboard ships for the voyage to Manila. Here they were bartered for primarily Spanish silver. At the time the Chinese valued silver almost as highly as they did gold, so it was a profitable trade for the Spanish. The porcelain was loaded aboard the Manila galleons for the perilous six months (or more) trip by the northern route to the coast of North America.

Once they arrived along the west coast the galleons proceeded south until they reached Acapulco. The cargo of porcelain was transferred to

PORCELAIN from Chingtechen, recovered from San José.

"Ginger Jar" (L.) is 3-1/4" square by 11" tall.

Decorative "Blue on White" Dinner Plate (below) is 9" in diameter.

the packs of mules for yet another arduous trip over the mountains of Mexico to the east coast *feria* being held in Vera Cruz. After being bartered for by the various merchants of the New Spain Fleet, and stored aboard the various galleons, there still remained the long voyage back to Spain before the housewives could entertain with their "china."

The second item of interest on board *San José* was the silver coins stored in her treasure room. Until 1732 the silver coins being minted in the Mexico mint were of the *macuquina* type, or "cob" coins. Native labor simply poured silver into the shape of flat straps, hammered them out until they were the proper thickness, then marked the bars in approximately one ounce sizes. Then, with a pair of large shears, they cut the straps into planchets, weighed them on a beam balance scale, and trimmed them until each planchet weighed exactly one ounce. Once they had a one-ounce planchet of silver, they placed the blank between two dies and struck the upper die with a hammer. Thus a "piece-of-eight" was made and placed in a box that usually held 3,000 coins when filled.

It never mattered whether a date was visible or not, in fact less than 10% had full dates showing in the millions of cob type coins that were struck during the preceding 196 years up to 1732. Not surprisingly, there were never two coins exactly alike. The value of the silver the coin contained was the value of the coin. It could be cut in half to make two "pieces-of-four," or a piece-of-four could be cut in half to make two "pieces-of-two." This actually established the American expression "Two bits, four bits, six bits, a dollar." There were also smaller dies so that pieces of four, two, one, and even half-*reales* could be struck.

With the vast amount of silver flowing from the Lima, Potosí, and Mexico mints this was the most efficient way of putting the silver into circulation. The Spanish silver piece-of-eight was accepted as satisfactory trading money throughout the world, because the silver content was over 90% pure silver. It was the assayer's responsibility to make sure that it was, or his very life was in jeopardy. There were problems over the years with "clip joints," in which shop keepers would clip corners from the odd shaped silver coins! After coins went through a few clip joints they were no longer pieces-of-eight, but closer to "pieces-of-seven," or even less. After awhile the coins had to be weighed to make sure they contained a full ounce of silver. It became a laborious process. Also, the irregular coins wore holes in the pockets, keeping the street urchins busy picking up dropped coins.

By 1732 the king of Spain decided that the mint at Mexico City should institute a coin more worthy of the realm. He sent newly designed screw presses from Europe, and the design and inscription for the first round silver coin to be minted in the New World. And he did a good job. The coin turned out better than all expectations, in fact if the coin were in production today it would be accepted by all world countries as legal tender. It was a beautiful coin, one that attempted to tell a story.

On the obverse side were two pillars that stood for the "Gates of Hercules," or the tip of Africa on one side of the Mediterranean and the Rock of Gibraltar on the other. On top of each pillar rested a crown, the crown of the king of Spain. Across each pillar was wrapped a banner, one bearing the word "*Plus*," the other "*Ultra*," together meaning "More Beyond" the gates of Hercules. Between the pillars were two round globes, or worlds, that represented the Old World, and the New World. And between the bottom of the pillars, and under the globes, were waves representing the ocean that brought the two worlds together. Resting above the two worlds sat a large crown, again the crown of the king of Spain, which indicated Spain claimed dominion over much of the Old World and the New World. The inscription around the outside of the coin was "*UTRAQUE UNUM*," Latin for "Both Are One," followed by oM (Mexico mint mark), and the date 1732.

On the reverse side was the magnificently styled crowned shield of Spain (the House of Habsburg) with the assayer's initial to the left, "F" for Felipe Rivas Angulo, and to the right the value of the coin "8" *reales*. The legend around the outside was "Hispan. Et Ind. Rex Philip V. D. G." meaning "Spain and the Indies, King Philip V, Dei Gratius ("by the grace of God"). The edge of the coin was milled to prevent clipping, and a tulip design was pressed into the edge of the coin. It was a beautiful coin, a design that would endure for almost 40 years with the nicknames "Pillar Dollar," "Milled Dollar," or "Dos Mundos (Two Worlds) Dollar."

An interim coin was also struck and today is called a "*recortado*" or re-cut coin. Another name used is "Klippe" type because it appeared to be clipped. It was a 1733-34 transitional coin until the screw-press pillar dollar was in full production. This coin had changes in the cross and shield that more closely resembled the "royal" issue of coins, and today is a most sought-after coin because of the limited number that were struck.

And so it was that, as the *San José* treasure was recovered by modern day treasure salvagers, these excellent examples of colonial coins began to surface for the first time. They became the coins most sought after by the salvagers, as well as coin collectors around the world, bringing high prices within the numismatic community.

Sinking of the *San José*

When de Torres gathered his *flota* together outside the harbor at Havana and caught a southeast breeze that would carry them to the Gulf Stream, *San José* was positioned near the center of the thirteen *naos*. As the hurricane bore down upon the fleet and visibility vanished, the *San José* fought the huge waves that carried it towards the Florida reefs. It was close to 10:00 p.m. when the ship first struck bottom, having been fortunate enough to miss the dragons teeth, passing between Davis Reef and Little Conch Reef. She bounced bottom at least once before coming down hard on her stern. Her massive 22-foot lead-sheathed rudder was torn away, as well as part of the stern and five cannon. With a gaping hole in her sterncastle, the *San José* quickly filled her hull with water and sank to the bottom 200 yards further shoreward near the edge of Hawk Channel.

> (*Contratación* 5102 -1733 *Flota*):
> "The Navio of El Duque [*San José*] flooded immediately upon grounding and its officials, passengers, soldiers, and sailors sought shelter on the roundhouse [poop deck.] All were saved on rafts."

> In the diary of the *El Infante*, (*Indiferente General* 57 - Diary of the *El Infante* 1733) it gives the "Notices of the sites where the ships of the Flota grounded, over a distance of 20 leagues from the Cabeza de los Martires to the Cabeza de las Vacas; "San Joseph" - Cayo Tavonas & Bocas de Guerrero." [Tavernier Key.]

As the survivors struggled ashore they made their *real* on Matecumbe Grande (Islamorada) where the survivors of the *El Infante* and the *capitana* had gathered. After giving thanks for their deliverance, the merchants approached the appointed Deputies of the

Commander Don Rodrigo de Torres and admitted, in confidence, that "certain *partidas* (shipments) of pesos in the merchant ships had been entered *sin registrada*, (contraband), and that they would be willing to pay the *derechos dobles* (double taxation) if recovered." They then declared 236,247 pesos of *sin registrada* that had been carried aboard the *San José*.

Because the *San José* sank in relatively deep (30 feet) water, very little of her cargo was salvaged by the Spanish. They did manage to salvage most of the silver coinage aboard, but that was about all. When it came time to burn the sunken ships of the fleet to recover the iron and bronze used in their construction, there was nothing left above water for the Spanish to set fire to. *San José* had settled into the sand, an instant photograph of life aboard a 1733 Spanish *nao*.

Salvage of the *San José* 1968-1974

By 1967 treasure salvage fever had already gotten a grip on south Florida. Mel Fisher had managed to change the name of the coast between Sebastian and Ft. Pierce to the "Treasure Coast" with his fabulous gold coin recoveries on the 1715 *patache "Nieves"* just south of the Ft. Pierce inlet. Many of the 1715 fleet of Spanish treasure galleons had yet to be located. But the 1733 Spanish treasure fleet in the Florida Keys had been worked on for about ten years, and of the sixteen ships that were sunk in the hurricane, or never refloated, only five remained undiscovered. They were the *El Populo*, thought to have sunk near Pacific Reef light, the *San José* that on the Spanish charts was shown as sunk between Little Conch Reef and Davis Reef, the *Angustias* which many believed had been refloated and sailed back to Spain, the *El Floridana* or *Fragata Situada* which apparently sank in deep water, and finally the *San Fernando* located somewhere off Grassy Key. Unknown to the salvage community, the *El Populo* had just been discovered by a group of four Miami divers who would work this wreck site in relative secrecy for the next two years. The newspaper and television media would stir the imagination of young and old alike, and on most weekends the boats of wishful treasure finders could be seen criss-crossing the reefs, eyes glued to the bottom in search of a hump of rounded ballast stones.

The more professional salvagers had taken to the air, where they were afforded a birds-eye view of the reefs. Even then it was difficult to discern the wreck sites because they were covered with eel grass or sand with very little of the wreck showing above the bottom. Towing magnetometers behind a salvage boat could locate metal objects such as cannons and anchors below the sand, and although the cost was high, many of the salvage boats were equipped with them. Another aspect of the treasure hunt was the presence of the state of Florida. By 1967 they were in the thick of things, allowing only ten salvage leases within the three mile limit established many years earlier. Salvage outside the three mile limit was under the jurisdiction of the Federal Government, and they had not become involved in the salvage of treasure as formidably as the state of Florida had. Of the undiscovered wreck sites, only the *Populo* and the *San José* were outside the three mile limit. Every treasure salvager in the business was on the prowl, searching in the areas the two ships were believed to have sunk. In the air, with magnetometers, and in the water dragging a diver behind a boat on the end of a line, searching for tell-tale signs of shipwreck on the bottom, it was like waiting for the other shoe to drop. And it did!

Tom Gurr was a successful engineer with the Florida Flood Control District in Miami. Like a great many energetic people in South Florida, the newspaper and TV accounts of sunken treasure being recovered in the Florida Keys stirred his imagination. The photos of cannons, flintlock pistols, swords, arquebuses, and silver coins were enough to convince him he had to give it a go while he was still young enough. Regardless of his decision, his wife, Greta, backed him all the way. He had several associates that had the same enthusiasm to hunt for treasure, enough of a nudge to make him resign his position with the Flood Control and go a-treasuring. It was near the end of 1966, and their first job was to locate a suitable salvage boat, one that a fairly large crew could enjoy working from, but at the same time not cost them their entire budget.

They found the *Parker* on the Miami River, a 90-foot lugger with a 16-foot beam, big enough to mount all the equipment they had in mind. It was an older boat, built in the late 1800s as a New York pilot boat. After spending some time on the Chesapeake as a "lugger," an old sea captain decided to use her as a retirement home, building a sort of out-house on the stern and heading for the Florida Keys and warm retirement weather. He got as far as Key Largo where he ran aground, ripping the rudder off the stern. The Coast Guard pulled the *Parker* off, and Olin Frick towed it into the Miami River where it was to be repaired.

By this time the old sea captain had better ideas about retirement, selling it to Olin for about what the towing charges were. Tom Gurr looked the boat over and decided it would do the job, paying $1,500 for the opportunity to spend a great deal more in repairs and outfitting her for treasure hunting. First he bought a diesel engine, one that had some promise of getting out to the reefs and back. Tom found a surplus air compressor, a big one that would run several air lifts at a time, and deck mounted it amidships. The group located a high volume breathing air compressor to keep as many as four divers on the bottom, and while installing that aboard they located a few planks suffering old age fatigue. When these were replaced it was early summer 1967, and the *Parker* was "ready to go!"

There was a shake-down cruise of sorts that found them digging holes on the "Pillar Dollar Wreck" site off Key Largo. Here was a wreck that had piled in over a moon-shaped reef, settling onto a sandy bottom twenty feet deep. That happened about 1768, the sand soon covering the entire site where she lay undetected until 1965. Art Sapp and Bobby Savage, operating off the salvage boat *Norma* found her with a

***Tom Gurr's salvage vessel* Parker.**

magnetometer and salvaged her the best they could with four-inch air lifts. A number of pillar dollars dated 1760-64 were recovered, but nothing else of great artifactual value. Tom and his crew found nothing on the site at all, and headed further south, towards Marathon.

The Coffins Patch site had been giving up some great artifacts, and a number of silver coins, but here again the pickings were slim. The *San Ignacio* had scattered for miles towards the beach, and without knowing much about the scatter pattern, it would have taken a great deal of time and patience to have been successful on Coffins Patch. The treasure was still there, but Tom and his crew did not have the time.

The next salvage effort was on a ballast pile located between one-half to one mile seaward of Hen and Chickens Light on a direct line with Alligator Light. The wreck lay at the edge of Hawk Channel in 22 feet of water, where the white sand began to blend in with an expanse of eel grass. Tom had heard it was a virgin ballast pile, but someone had to find it "first," look it over, and probably do a bit of salvage before letting others in on the secret wreck. Tom found the ballast pile covered with 28 cannons, but as is usually the case, it was empty of any interesting artifacts. They did, however, recover a small 2-1/2-foot bronze blunderbuss rail gun, which prompted Tom to nickname the site "The Blunderbuss Wreck." Their wreck turned out to be an armed sloop, the *Wolf,* that had sunk in 1741. Cannons brought up had the "Davis" maker mark and a London proof mark.

The wreck did not promise the treasure Tom needed to keep his operation going. The funds were approaching zero, and so far they had found very little that could entice new investors. After raising the 28 cannon and deck-loading them on the *Parker* he headed back to Marathon. Once there the *Parker* sank alongside the dock. Other members of his crew, the original associates, decided to go back to work for a living. Tom was the only one to stick it out. He raised the *Parker*, rounded up new members for a crew, and headed back out to sea. The new members included Jim King, Rudy Paladino, George Hanses, and Dick Williams. Dick had been involved with the 1733 Spanish treasure fleet when working with Mel Fisher. He encouraged Tom to look for treasure on ships of that fleet. The easiest one to locate was the *El Infante*, sunk on Little Conch Reef. Divers had been recovering coins on the site for years. Tom thought, "Why not?" and away they went.

San José **Located**

A captain's gig, retired from the U. S. Navy years before, was added to the Gurr Navy and outfitted with a 30-inch blower. The blower was a 90-degree aluminum pipe which swung down over the boat's propeller, directing the propwash towards the ocean floor. It dusted the bottom clear of sand or coral powder and exposed artifacts that lay on the hard marl bedrock. By the first week in July the *Parker* was in a four-point anchorage over the ballast pile of *El Infante*. It was an operation of frustration because the pile had been worked consistently by every salvage diver in the Keys, including the author. The treasure, what was left, was scattered over the surrounding acres of coral and sandy bottom.

In the meantime, Tom met up with Mel Fisher and struck a deal. One of the only major wreck sites of the 1733 fleet that had not as yet been located, and was outside the state's three mile territorial limits, was the *San José*. Although everyone had been looking for it, it just didn't seem to be where it was supposed to be. Meylach had suggested to Mel an area between the *Infante* and the *capitana* based on the old salvagers charts. He had located a "suspect" area and passed it along to Fisher. Fisher, in turn, struck a deal with Gurr to lend him his Fay Feild magnetometer for a share, if Tom located the *San José*.

The sweeps of the captain's gig, *Revenooer*, trailing the magnetometer behind at the end of a 100-foot electronic cable, began about July 4, 1967, working back and forth about four miles offshore of Tavernier Island. There wasn't a trace of a shipwreck or ballast pile in the vast expanse of sand and eel grass as the gig made pass after pass over an area that covered a mile in every direction. It was soon July 15, 235 years to the day that the 1733 fleet came over the reefs in a hurricane. About noon time the magnetometer "pegged," a reading indicating a large metallic mass on the bottom. The gig's crew threw an anchor over and with face mask and fins the divers were soon in the water looking for their "galleon."

Nothing, absolutely nothing but rolling sand dunes and eel grass could be seen. It was back in the gig for more passes over the area. Each time they got an anomaly on the mag, they dropped a buoy. They criss-crossed the area, dropping buoys on each "hit," until a concentration of buoys favored a particular ridge of sand and eel grass. Rudy Paladino put a SCUBA tank on, rolled over the side with a spear from a speargun, and began probing the bottom. Before long he got a metallic "click" as he pushed the spear into the sand. Bingo! Ballast stones! Lowering the blower over the boat's prop, they revved up the engine and, as the sand was moved off the ridge, the pile of ballast stones emerged. Thoughts of salvaging *El Infante* suddenly evaporated in the summer heat.

They buoyed the spot, then headed over to the *Parker* anchored about a mile away. With the news of the ballast pile, and a possibility that they had located the *San José*, Tom hauled anchors, and soon the *Parker* was circling the buoys near the edge of Hawk Channel. The water was thirty feet deep and gin clear, but there was nothing in sight except rolling sand dunes and eel grass. Soon Tom had the *Parker* in a four-point anchorage near the bobbing float that marked the initial hit area, and his crew was busy firing up the large air compressor. With 6-inch air lifts probing through the sand, the ballast pile was quickly exposed. It lay less than two feet below the sandy bottom. Just as quickly as the sand was lifted from the top of the ballast pile the first artifacts were exposed, and it was enough to get the adrenaline going in the right direction.

Four rapiers and two flintlock pistols lay atop the first level of rounded river rocks. It was evidence enough that Gurr had a virgin wreck site. Artifacts like these are never left behind by salvagers working a shipwreck. By the end of that first week they had uncovered much of the sand over the ballast pile, and it was a big one. Lying NE to SW, with her stern more to seaward, the ballast covered an area 135 long by 40 feet wide. In the center the ballast rose as much as six feet in places. More importantly, there were cannon everywhere. At first count there were over twenty, lying at awkward angles like matchsticks. Gurr whistled, "This has got to be the *San José*!"

Up in the wheelhouse he took careful bearings on a microwave tower and the ends of several islands. Plotting these on the hydrographic chart, the bearings crossed well offshore near the very edge of Hawk Channel. With a pair of dividers he stepped off the distance, "Well, we're certainly outside Florida state waters. It looks like 4.38 miles to the nearest point of land in any direction. This wreck is in international waters." Gurr had a master's license, and a federal salvage permit. As far as he could determine there was absolutely no reason to file for a lease from the state of Florida. They were a happy crew of treasure salvagers as they went about the business of carefully salvaging what would turn out to be the long lost *San José*.

Coincidentally, Mendel Peterson of the Smithsonian Institute was in Miami at the time. He and George Fischer, a Marine Archeologist with the National Park Service, had traveled down from Washington, D.C. to look over a wreck site closer to shore. When Gurr invited them to take a look at his wreck site, Peterson and Fischer jumped at the opportunity. The more the two men looked the site over, the more they wanted to do a complete archeological dig as the wreck was uncovered. Peterson asked if Tom would stop all activity for a week until he could get his complete team to Florida, and Gurr agreed.

The following week Peterson had his group together, including artist Peter Copeland. As the salvage progressed, the site was photographed, measured, and examined in detail. As each artifact was uncovered, it was located on a master chart and tagged, then placed in fresh water until it could be preserved.

In the meantime, members of Gurr's salvage team had decided to mag the area using the captain's gig *Revenooer*. About 200 yards seaward of the pile they had a large anomaly that turned out to be the ship's lead-lined 22-foot rudder. Lying on top of the rudder was an eight-foot cannon, and alongside were four more. It was now easier to visualize the ship's last agonizing moments, striking the bottom hard enough to tear the rudder, pintles, and part of the sterncastle completely off the after end of the ship. It would dawn on Gurr much later that the path between the rudder and the main ballast pile might hold some priceless artifacts that had tumbled out of the stern as the ship sank to the bottom.

For the next several weeks the groups worked harmoniously together. They shared in the excitement as George Hosford uncovered a complete stack of silver dinner plates and, nearby, a matching set of forks and spoons. It was helpful to learn that the maker's mark, "Buckby and Hamilton, London England 1722," pointed more positively toward the fact that this was the *San José*. Ray Manieri one day surfaced with a gold ring on every finger, some with emeralds that would have set any señorita's heart on fire.

The 22-foot rudder of the San José.

A complete barber's kit, with lice comb, ivory handled razors, and barber's shears came off the bottom, still in a leather carrying case! There were K'ang Hsi Chinese porcelain cups, plates, even a square bottle, all with the typical blue and white flowery design work made famous by Chinese artisans. No one quite knew what to make of the small pottery figurines that were being found. There were small bowls no more than two inches in diameter, along with lids, animal figures, fish, ducks, all fired in a dark brown glazed clay. They were similar to those found earlier on the *Herrera*, figurines that *National Geographic* would later label "Tonalaware," small toys being taken back to Spain to stir the young imaginations about the New World. Even a unique glass figurine of a cat, completely intact, was carefully removed from its hiding place near a ship's rib.

By the end of three months a considerable area had been excavated around the wreck site, and some great artifacts had been uncovered. Peterson was convinced that the site was indeed the *San José*. But now it was time for his group to leave, not willingly, but the summer was disappearing, and they had business to attend to back in Washington. Left to themselves, the crew of the *Parker* went back to work, and other members of the local salvage community were invited to dive the site and help out. I was one of the fortunate ones, bringing along my diving buddies Bernie Smith and Kip Porter.

We lived aboard the *Parker*, working harder than we had ever worked before, and enjoying every moment. A barrel full of sailors' palms came up off the bottom, causing some questions as to the reason they would be on a ship going *back* to Spain. As we moved off the main ballast pile and began working the area between the rudder and the pile, we were in for a treat. As we dug down through three feet of

Peter Copeland sketching the **San José.**

sand we reached a compacted layer of eel grass that had been there 234 years earlier. Spread out across the area was rigging just as it fell from the masts, and looped through the hemp were two- and three-sheave blocks, as well as cargo hooks on the end of one of the lines. The hemp came apart at the touch, but as we uncovered the area it was as if we were witnessing the last death throes of this gallant galleon.

Storm Clouds Over the *San José*

It was a simple request by Jim Hardy, newspaper reporter for the *Miami Herald*. "I heard you found a treasure galleon. I'd like to do a story on it." Gurr had nothing to fear, everything was legal, and he was pretty enthusiastic about what was coming up off the bottom. He was following his dream, and he was willing to share the experience with others. On Monday, September 16, 1968, the headlines read "Spanish Treasure Ship Found," along with color photos of Tom and his crew, and with some great artifacts.

When the newspaper came out with the photos of the *Parker* heaped with artifacts and Gurr holding flintlock pistols in each hand, the state of Florida was aroused. The state archeologist, Carl Clausen, was sent to the Keys to determine exactly where the site was located, and whether the state's interests were being looked after. This site apparently had the potential of being the best recovery of the 1733 fleet, a situation the state archeological staff had to take advantage of. The state had been unaware of the salvage activities because Tom had never filed for a salvage lease, and because the site was beyond the three mile limit, he had no legal responsibility to do so. The stage was set for what was to become a black hour in Florida's salvage history.

Clausen and his group motored out to the site on the Florida Conservation Board boat, and upon drawing alongside asked permission to come aboard. They were refused and words were exchanged. Gurr was told that he was operating illegally, that he needed a salvage lease to work the wreck. Tom advised Clausen that he was in international waters, he had a master's license, and a federal permit to salvage. He further advised Clausen that the state of Florida had no jurisdiction over them or their salvage boat. All during this tirade one of the *Parker*'s crew stood near the pilot house with a loaded carbine. As the argument heated up, and as one of the state men tried to force his way aboard the

Parker, a shot was fired into the water near the state boat. That ended the argument, and the state people retired back to Tavernier Key for a telephone conversation with Tallahassee. They were advised to return to the state capital.

Somewhere along the line someone in the state group suggested that there were automatic weapons on board the *Parker*. The next morning a Coast Guard cutter with six armed civilians pulled alongside *Parker* and indicated they would be boarding. This time there was nothing in the way of an argument, the civilians were brandishing Thompson sub-machine guns. The *Parker* was searched without any explanation being offered, and soon the men left without so much as a "have a good day" or a "thank you very much." Later the explanation released was that the Coast Guard had a report that the *Parker* was carrying guns and ammunition for anti-Castro activities. It was October 1968, and it was downhill for Tom Gurr after that.

Salvage work continued, but Gurr knew he hadn't seen the end of the state archeologists. He was right. As he stepped ashore one week later to do some grocery shopping, he was arrested by members of the Monroe County Sheriff's Department and served papers to appear in court in Key West to face charges of salvaging illegally in Florida waters. It was a time when the thirteen Atlantic seaboard states were arguing with the Federal Government over the rights of the submerged land offshore. This included fishing, oil, undersea mining, and other implications that each state thought well worth fighting over. Suddenly the state of Florida felt it could use the salvage situation to help its cause. The state brought up a point of contention dating back to Florida's constitution of 1865, when the boundary was set at the state's barrier reef. The problem with that was the reef extended into Mexican waters, which would have set off an even greater controversy had the state been successful.

The case was heard by Judge Lopez in Key West, and the decision handed down was in favor of the state of Florida for haphazard reasons. Once the decision was made, the state archeological department moved in quickly, confiscating everything that Gurr's team of salvage divers had recovered thus far. The salvage community was in a state of shock. Free enterprise had taken its worse beating. Before the situation became nasty, the state approached Gurr and offered him a contract to continue on a 50-50 basis, and on a 75-25 basis for any new wrecks he might find. But the artifacts recovered thus far had been salvaged "illegally" and therefore belonged to the state. They asked Gurr to put up a $15,000 bond in order to continue salvaging, money Gurr did not have. Even the 10% required by a bondsman was out of the question. Gurr was broke.

The state made a deal with Tom, holding everything he recovered in lieu of the bond. When he could pay for the bond, and a division time was set, he would receive his share of treasure. Before the year ended the *Parker* was back on site, but by this time Gurr's crew had pretty well dispersed, disenchanted with the entire situation. The *Parker* had sprung some leaks in her seams and had to be tied up to the dock until repairs could be made. She promptly sank, ending a year of frustration.

Dumping The Treasure

Gurr did his best to stay in the marine business and still not think about the *San José*. However, the more he thought about the site, the more he realized the job of salvage was far from finished. There were areas on the site that needed to be looked at, and in a way he was frustrated that he never checked the areas out while he was still on site. That summer of 1969 Kip Wagner came to him with a proposal to make a movie on the *San José*. There was a great deal to photograph, and the movie would be about "Tom Gurr—Treasure Hunter." He agreed, and Bob Marx brought his salvage boat *Grifón* down to the Keys. Harry Cannon, Lou Ullian, and Dan Thompson worked with Marx to complete the movie after dusting the wreck site off from one end to the other. In the process they found a few significant artifacts. After they left the sand drifted in and soon covered much of the timbers and ballast pile. But the *San José* still nagged at Tom. The more he thought of the stern section breaking off with the rudder, the more he realized this area had to contain treasure.

Then in the spring of 1972 his opportunity came unexpectedly. A group with very limited finances approached Tom about taking a second shot at the *San José*. Tom jumped at the opportunity. Together they formed "Undersea Mining" and bought a used salvage boat named the *Capitana*...appropriately. By mid-year Tom had the boat outfitted with blowers on her stern, and they were on site working. Tom had buoyed out an area with a sixty-foot diameter around the rudder, and set about moving the sand. Again they reached the packed eel grass several feet below the sandy surface, and there appeared more rigging, blocks, and cargo hooks. The bottom this material lay on was a hard-packed coquina and sand, a bottom that appeared to be very old. Then it happened.

One day Tom was uncovering a section of hemp rope when suddenly it disappeared *downward*! He thought at the time that was odd, because the bottom was hard as a rock. He couldn't break through it with a crowbar. He decided to move the *Capitana* over to the spot and use the blower. After an hour of deflecting the prop thrust directly at the bottom, he went down to check out if he had made a hole in the hard coquina. The prop thrust had done its job, breaking through a hard pan that was almost 18 inches thick. But when Tom looked into the hole the prop thrust had made, he was astonished! Here lay the glitter of gold. Gold rings, gold jewelry, a gold bell, stacks of silver plates, religious medallions, gold brooches, gold chain, it was a bonanza!

What Tom had discovered was in all probability part of the passengers' baggage, and there were a number of wealthy passengers on board the *San José* when she sank. In the days that followed he expanded the hole and discovered a great many new artifacts, including an intact Chinese porcelain jar, and over 300 screw-press pillar dollars.

Just when the salvage of treasure looked too good to be true, the financial budget reached the bottom of the bucket. It was then that Gurr decided to approach the state of Florida in an attempt to get his share of the treasure he had recovered four years earlier. The state had promised him 75% of the recoveries, and there were significant artifacts that Tom could offer for sale and go back to work. The state of Florida had other ideas. Much of Tom's treasure had been cleaned and placed on display at various locations around the state. Clausen had traded some of it for artifacts recovered by the state of Texas at the Padre Island site of three Spanish treasure wrecks. It was obvious that the state had absorbed the entire Gurr recoveries into their own inventory.

At the time ex-senator Williams was the acting director of the Dept. of Records and Management, the office handling treasure salvage. For three months Gurr attempted to negotiate with Williams without success, Williams stated that a division could not be made until all artifacts had been processed by the preservation laboratory. Until that time the state owned 100% of the artifacts. At the time Gurr entered into a contract with the state, no preservation laboratory existed. When it finally was instituted and in business, Williams said that other salvors' artifacts were ahead of Gurr's, and that he would have to wait his turn. Soon all negotiations broke down, with Williams refusing to answer phone calls. They had reached an impasse. The 1973 diving season faded away on that dismal note, and even Christmas didn't bolster Tom's spirits.

After the holidays, when Gurr had time to think over what he was about to do, he called his friend Jed Duval. Jed was with CBS Television in their Washington, D.C. office, and when Tom explained his problems with the state and what he intended to do, Jed agreed to cover the story. It was January 4 when the CBS crew filmed Tom throwing identifiable objects back in the ocean. He stated very clearly, "The state did not pay me to recover this treasure, so I am not breaking any laws in throwing it back in the ocean." It put the state officials in a frenzy, and they were quick to react. No sooner did Tom arrive back home on Merritt Island when agents with the Florida Department of Law Enforcement arrested him. He was charged with Grand Larceny and his bond set at $7,500. His trial was set for hearing in Key West, but upon flying down there he found that the state had fouled up. It was a wasted trip. The next action taken by the state was to dive in the canal behind the house Tom had rented during the salvaging of the *San José*. They did recover some artifacts, but nothing in the way of precious metals.

As the pressure on Gurr mounted, some of his friends within the salvage community stepped forward. Henry Taylor and Joseph Keyerleber decided to set up a legal defense fund for Tom. They called it the "Saltwatergate" Fund. The salvage community was united in the belief that Tom was being wronged by the state. They donated artifacts and coins to the fund to be sold. Gurr and his wife Greta also contributed some coins from their personal collection.

By February 28 they had amassed almost $60,000 worth of coins and artifacts, enough to give Tom a decent legal representation. They met a "buyer" by the name of Earl Yearicks of Ft. Pierce who indicated an interest in purchasing the coins. A contract was entered into in which Mr. Yearicks gave a down payment of $5,000 towards the purchase of seven coins valued at $9,975. Both sides agreed to complete the sale on April 5. The meeting was delayed for a week, and in the late afternoon of April 12, 1974, a meeting was held in room #157 at the Holiday Inn in Ft. Pierce. Tom Gurr was present, as was Henry Taylor and Joe Keyerleber. The agreement at this meeting was that Yearicks could select from about $35,000 in coins and artifacts, approximately $10,000 worth in exchange for $5,000 in cash. Between 5:30 and 6:00 p.m. Henry had laid out on the bed two gold objects, five pewter objects, and 36 silver coins in plastics coin packets. Joe Keyerleber had stepped outside for a minute to photograph the two gold objects, when at exactly 6:00 p.m. Florida Dept. of Law Enforcement (F.D.L.E.) agents Roger Fritze, C.S. Rerell, Jr., and Patrick Stempien knocked on the door.

Tom Gurr thought it was Keyerleber wanting back into the room, so as he turned the door knob the agents burst into the room forcing Gurr backwards against the wall. They flashed their identification badges and frisked everyone in the room for weapons. Then Mr. Fritze looked at the bed and exclaimed "My, my, what have we here!" He followed this with "This is the scene of a crime. These coins and artifacts are from the *San José* and are the property of the state of Florida." Mr. Keyerleber was then brought into the room and everyone read his rights. Each was then asked to sign a waiver to have legal counsel and to answer their questions. Everyone refused to sign. Joe Keyerleber requested permission to photograph the proceedings, but was vehemently denied. When asked if they had a search warrant, the law officers said no, that they didn't need one.

Mr. Yearicks phoned his lawyer who promptly arrived while the law enforcement officials were still there. Yearicks called the local sheriff's office, and when the sheriff asked to speak to Mr. Rerell, the F.D.L.E. agent refused. Not long after that the state law enforcement people left with everything that Taylor and Keyerleber had brought to the motel room. A receipt was signed for what was taken. Unknown to Gurr and his party, the room at the Holiday Inn had been bugged, and a taped recording made of what had taken place. They had been "set up," and it later became evident that Mr. Yearicks was part of the state's set up. The tapes were to be used in the investigation, but somehow they disappeared.

The State of Florida Law Enforcement officers had confiscated about half of the coins and artifacts that had been donated to the Saltwatergate fund. The balance were to be auctioned off by Bowers and Ruddy Galleries in Los Angeles, California. When the state officials found out about the upcoming auction they asked the United States Attorney's office in Los Angeles to seize the coins, assuming they were from the *San José* recoveries. The U.S. Attorney's office did seize 35 coins from Bowers and Ruddy, with intent to turn these over to the state of Florida, Dept. of Archives. The legal council for Tom Gurr began to earn his fee.

In a letter addressed to Robert Bonner, Assistant United States Attorney, Chief, Criminal Complaints, in Los Angeles, Tom's lawyer Harland Braun said:

"This letter is in response to your letter of April 1, 1974, with regard to your proposed action of turning the above coins over to the State of Florida. That action would be without legal justification and in derogation of the rights of Captain Gurr, Bowers & Ruddy, and Henry Taylor.

"Your agents seized these coins pursuant to a Grand Jury subpoena from the person in rightful possession of these coins, to wit, Bowers & Ruddy Galleries. Since you have decided not to use those coins in any prosecution, the appropriate action would be to return them to the person from whom they were seized. Your extra judicial and *ex parte* action in turning those coins over to a third party, to wit, the State of Florida, without appropriate judicial proceedings exposes the United States to substantial liability. Your action is, in essence, a deprivation of property without due process of law.

"The proposed action does not take into consideration the following factors:

1. —34 of these Spanish coins are not even involved in the Florida prosecution.

2. —Many of the coins do not even belong to Captain Gurr.

3. —Bowers & Ruddy were not only in rightful possession of the coins but have a lien on them of over $7,000.

4. —The State of Florida has shown no probable cause or legal justification for the seizure of any coins.

5. —The State of Florida has not used lawful process to try to subpoena the coins.

"The United States Government is at this point merely a stakeholder which, in the absence of any judicial determination, must return the coins to the person last in rightful possession. There is no particular reason for your office to favor and prefer the State of Florida over Captain Gurr or Henry Taylor. Therefore, this letter is a demand that you turn over the 35 Spanish coins to Bowers & Ruddy Galleries rather than to the State of Florida."

The end result was that the coins were not turned over to the State of Florida.

On May 20 Tom's attorney, Harland Braun, in Los Angeles filed a lawsuit naming the United States and the state of Florida as defendants on behalf of Henry Taylor and Tom Gurr. In a letter to Tom, Mr. Braun said:

"Up to this point, the only action the State of Florida has seemed to take against you is to arrest and harass you in a Nazilike manner. Now they have a chance to put up or shut up on the question of the San Jose. Hopefully, this ridiculous charade of the State of Florida carrying on unjustified intemperate vendetta against you will end next month when the State of Florida must produce its evidence in the two criminal matters pending against you and determine whether or not it will submit to a neutral adjudication by the Federal Court here.

"It is unbelievable that the kinds of acts taken against you occur in the United States of America. The conduct of the Florida officials is the type of conduct that I heretofore believed indigenous to Hitler's Germany or the Union of Soviet Socialist Republic."

There was an immediate attempt by the Florida State Attorney to have Gurr sign a waiver to the California coins, which Tom refused to do. Then the state began to take more drastic action to resolve the dispute. Robert Williams, director of the Division of Archives, History and Records Management, and in charge of salvage leases in state waters, wrote a letter to Richard MacAllaster of Peninsular Exploration, a company for which Henry Taylor was a diver of record. It advised MacAllaster that Taylor did not have approval to work on any boat performing activities of treasure salvage. Taylor had been "blackballed" by the state of Florida. The next move by state officials was to threaten to arrest Tom's wife Greta as an accessory to grand theft. Gurr felt he had always been in the right, but by this time he was flat broke. He could not carry on a legal defense against Florida with unlimited resources. Most of all, he did not want to have his wife prosecuted. In a surprise move, through his attorney in Key West, David Paul Horan, Tom negotiated with the State Attorney.

On Friday, June 20, Florida State Attorney Edward Worton dropped the grand larceny charges against Tom, indicating the charge did not warrant the expense of a trial. The following Monday Tom pleaded guilty in front of Circuit Court Judge Wallace Sample in Ft. Pierce to grand larceny and was given a two-year probation sentence. At the sentencing, State Attorney Robert Stone agreed not to prosecute Gurr any further on the treasure issue.

In many ways Tom Gurr was a case of the little guy always losing. But more importantly it was a case of guts and determination that when the little guy felt he was right, he fought a tough battle as long as it did not affect the ones close to him. A final letter from his lawyer in California said it all:

"I am somewhat at a loss to understand how you plead guilty to a crime of theft in Florida when, in fact, as far as I know the items you are charged with stealing are not the property of another. In addition, at least under California law, a *bona fide* claim of right over personal property allegedly stolen is a complete and absolute defense. You surely had such a defense and the fact that it is a *bona fide* defense beyond doubt by the fact that it has taken the United States Supreme Court to resolve this outstanding issue.

"Throughout my association with you, I have never been able to understand one thing. You located and salvaged the *San José*. If the State of Florida wished to take the coins from you under the power of eminent domain, I think that would be perfectly within its right. But for a State to arbitrarily determine that it should take the product of a citizen's skill and enterprise without compensation seems to me to be a variance with what I have normally considered to be the traditions of our country. If the reward that you receive for your enterprise and energy is a criminal conviction, then this country has surely come a long way to abandoning its original ideals of free enterprise and private initiative."

On March 17, 1975, the United States Supreme Court ruled invalid the thirteen state claims to submerged land beyond the three mile limit. The *San José* was determined to be 400 yards beyond the three mile limit. Tom Gurr had won his case.

The *San José* has never been worked completely, and for many years Doctor Ron Molinari had the salvage lease. His recoveries were meager, and he worked alone. The sand would alternately cover and uncover the site, giving the local treasure community a case of treasure fever. They had good reason. In the late 1970s Jack "Blackjack" Haskins was looking over the area to the south of the *San José* rudder with an underwater metal detector. One of the "hits" he fanned up was a five-foot-long flintlock musket, under three feet of sand. Close by the musket two more fainter hits turned out be 8-*escudos*, "Gold Doubloons"! It was late in the day so he took good ranges on the location, noting that it was close by an abandoned lobster pot, and decided to come back the next day. That next day turned out to be a bonanza.

Henry Taylor, Chuck Mitchell, Tom Gurr, George Hosford, and Jim King.

D. L. Chaney, an airline pilot, had a 36-foot salvage boat, *Wasp*, that he and Jack took out to the site. It had a duster on the stern, and although they were not able to anchor right over the lobster pot, they were close. In the first hole they dusted were remnants of rope and a silver coin. D. L. exclaimed, "There are more hits down there!" Haskins went down and began uncovering beautiful gold coins commonly referred to as "royals." These were 8-*escudos* dated 1733 and in mint condition. There were a number of gold coins recovered, twenty eight total, including five of the royal portrait gold coins, each worth in excess of $15,000. A total of five silver coins were also recovered, and a silver reliquary and a pistol with an unusual figure of a face engraved on the brass butt plate. This was in all probability a "bounce" spot of the *San José* as it struck bottom before finally sinking there at the edge of Hawk Channel.

The passengers' baggage holds the key to future treasure finds on the *San José*, scattered shoreward as much as four miles. The *San José* told a story of frustration and political greed, but it remains as a symbol of the indomitable spirit of private enterprise in the face of "Big Brother."

May its flame burn brightly for many years to come!

"Surface boil" over the San José, *as air lifts remove the sandy overburden from the wreck site.*

Diver surfaces from* San José *with a Spanish boarding cutlass.

(Above) Raising a **San José** *cannon aboard the* **Parker.**
(Below) Salvor Tom Gurr with a sackful of **San José** *coins.*

*(Above) Broken shards of K'ang Hsi porcelain from José.
(Below) Artifacts recovered by Gurr's crew on the Parker.*

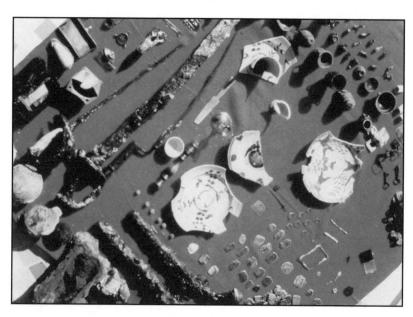

(Above) Twirling figurine of glass, San José *recovery.*
(Below) Glass bottles recovered from the San José.

*(Above) Pottery jars and Tonalaware recovered by
the crew of the* **Parker.**
(Below) Gold rings recovered from the **San José.**

(Above) Lead pump dated 1728 recovered from the San José.
(Below) Underwater view of San José *ballast and timbers.*

(Above) Underwater photo: **San José** *cannons on ship's ribs.*
(Below) Diver working under the **San José** *22-foot rudder.*

(Above) Over 20 cannons were located on the **San José** *site.*
(Below) Two divers working with 6-inch airlifts on the **José.**

PHOTO: Jack "Blackjack" Haskins

Gold "Cobs" recovered by Jack Haskins and D. L. Chaney from the San José "Glory Hole." Mexican and Bogotá escudos *are represented. The second coin CCW from the top is boldly dated 1730!*

PHOTO: Jack "Blackjack" Haskins

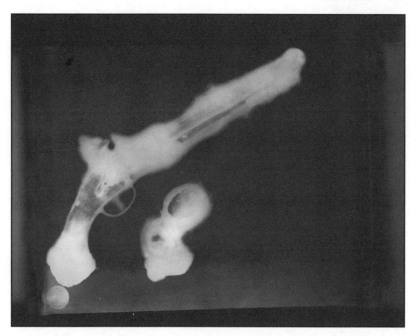

*This X-Ray plate shows the Spanish flintlock pistol
recovered by Jack Haskins concealed within a concretion.
See Color Photo Section for the preserved contents
of this conglomerate.*

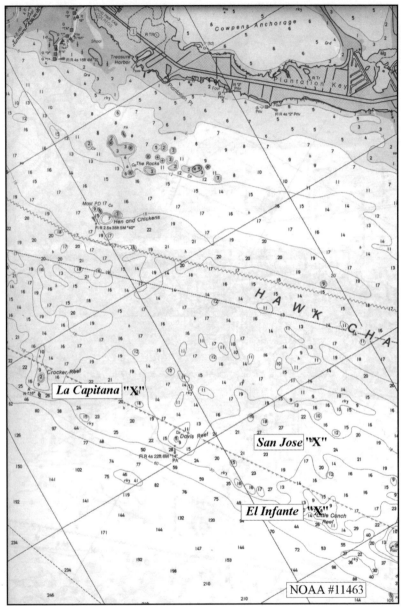

LOCATION CHART: *La Capitana.*
(*San José, El Infante* shown for reference.)

CHAPTER 12: *LA CAPITANA*
El Rubí Segundo
Alias: *"El Rubí"*

Every treasure story has a sunken galleon full of gold and silver coins, and usually that galleon is a "Capitana" or an "Almiranta" of the fleet. Now there's a good reason for this, as anyone in the treasure salvage community can tell you. In every fleet, or *flota*, there was a ship designated as the "Captain" and a ship designated the "Admiral." The official names for the ships were something else, but for that particular voyage these two ships were referred to as...the *capitana* and the *almiranta*. The Squadron Commander, usually a general in charge of the fighting soldiers on board (because the Spanish ships carrying treasure usually had a fight on their hands getting back to Old Spain), rode in the *capitana*. The Admiral of the Fleet, in charge of navigation and the responsibility of getting the *flota* through the reefs and shoals of the Spanish Sea, rode in the *almiranta* and was second in command. These were galleons belonging to the king of Spain, and as such were entrusted to men of honor and courage (usually) who were given the newest ships, and most heavily armed, to sail on. They were designated to carry "The Treasure," usually divided equally between the two vessels, because if any of the *flota* had a best chance of getting back to Spain it would be the *capitana* and the *almiranta*. There would be other treasure, and if the annual output of the mines of the New World produced a considerable amount of gold and silver, then a third major war galleon, normally a "Vice Admiral" or *gobierno*, was designated.

And so it was with the Spanish treasure fleet of 1733 under General Rodrigo de Torres y Morales. The ship he rode in, the *capitana*, was the *El Rubí Segundo*, and it was loaded with treasure. It was a fairly new galleon carrying sixty iron cannon and a large contingent of soldiers on board. At the *feria* in Vera Cruz the registered treasure logged aboard on her manifest was: 1,940 boxes of silver coins totaling 5,080,285 pesos; 104 *castellanos* in worked gold; 3,200 pesos in gold coins; 6,099 *marcos* in worked silver; 4,913 *arrobas* of cochineal; 97 *arrobas* of wild cochineal; 9,230 *arrobas* of anil; 36,000 (arrobas?) vanilla; and 10 boxes of chocolate. Whatever space was left on board was in all probability filled with strings and bales of tobacco when the *Rubí* reached Havana.

The *Rubí* was the first to lead the way out of Havana Harbor, normally because she would be the most heavily armed and a deterrent to enemy vessels standing by the harbor entrance ready to capture a lesser armed *nao*. Rodrigo de Torres watched the remainder of his *flota* form up in a circular convoy, and then led them off on a northerly tack to reach the Gulf Stream that would carry them through the Bahama Canal. The hurricane struck them the following night, scattering his entire fleet and eventually sinking or grounding 20 of the 21 vessels in his command. Only *El Africa*, one of his four heavily armed galleons, survived the hurricane and was able to continue the voyage to Spain.

(*Contratación* 5147 -1733 *Flota*). In a letter written by Alonso de Herrera Barragan, Emissary to the King, and addressed to the President of the Consulate of Cádiz:

"At 10:30 of the night of this day (July 15, 1733) we all grounded in the expressed Cayos, at a distance of 28 leagues on length, with this Capitana off the one called Cayo Largo 2 1/2 leagues [8 miles] from shore. [As usual, the Spanish were long in distance.] I make assurances to Your Lordship that it is fortunate that we grounded this ship, for if the contrary had occurred we all would have drowned since the hull was so full of water, so much so that we were unable to pump it out and it was steadily increasing. We now found ourselves without a main mast or mizzen, having blown the fore sail and the top fore mast entire with its sail. The storm lasted 30 hours. At sunrise on the 16th, the storm having abated somewhat, we set about with the task of salvaging the people from this Capitana with our launch or boat. Although we were badly battered from the blows we had suffered within this ship we didn't lose more than two men from this ship, they having been flung into the sea from the *gallineres* [upper rigging?] The same was executed by the other ships except the San Ignacio, its Captain Don Christobal Urquijo, which had made different pieces on the reef and from which only 10 or 11 men were liberated. The Captain and some merchants from this ship were drowned.

"The salvage operation began on the 4th day after grounding and to this day all of the silver which has been sent [to Havana] has been from the Capitana, Almiranta, and the Infante. Everything that could be was salvaged, not withstanding the fact that efforts are being made to see if more can be encountered. Some of the cochineal and indigo has been saved, although it was badly treated [wet.]

"In these expressed ships we are remitting the silver to La Havana for accounting and relation by disposition of Our Commander with agreement of the Deputies of this Commerce, conforming to that which was salvaged from the named ships. Upon completing all this, the silver was placed in the Castillo de Force where it is free from danger of seizure by pirates or wreckers that occur in these seas, and who are now largely knowledgeable of this loss."

(Letter dated 19 August 1733 from Juan Tomas de la Herrera and Diego Angulo to the President and Official Judges of the *Casa de Contratación*):

"This prompt aid [from Havana] and the 40 divers which were sent in these rescue ships was the major alleviation of those who were shipwrecked. The first thing that was done was to commence the buceo [underwater salvage] which was executed with all effort, salvaging all the treasure from the Capitana, Almiranta, and Refuerzo [El Infante.]"

(Letter dated 25 September 1733 from Alonso Herrera Barragan addressed to Don Francisco de Varras y Valdes, President, *Consulado de Cádiz*):

"In this manner, transported without separation was the amount of 3,917 boxes of silver and between them some bars of silver. 1,923 came from the Capitana, 1,809 from the Almiranta, and 185 from the El Infante, along with 153 loose bars, 48 boxes of fabricated silver from the Capitana, 25 from the Almiranta, 4 from the Infante, and 1 from the navio San Ignacio."

In the *Razón Y Cuenta* (see appendix), the recovery from the *capitana* is listed as:

5,270,167 pesos, 4 reales in silver coins, gold coins and silver bars

729,970 pesos, 5 reales in silver bars

4,145 arrobas, 23 libras of cochineal

995 arrobas, 4 libras of anil

A final count of boxes of silver recovered from the *capitana* leaves 17 boxes unaccounted for. At 3,000 pesos per box that leaves 51,000 pieces-of-eight on bottom when the Spanish salvage was completed. Also, the *capitana* was carrying 592 slabs of Cuban copper, of which 550 were recovered. These slabs weighed approximately 30 to 40 pounds each. With the number of soldiers on board *El Rubí*, the flintlock pistols, muskets, and boarding cutlasses would be considerable, and few of these were salvaged by the Spanish.

It was, indeed, a sunken galleon full of treasure as the 1733 *Flota de Plata* passed into archival history.

Our modern day salvage began in 1938 when a charter boat captain by the name of Reggie Roberts spotted the huge ballast mound four miles offshore from Plantation Key. (*Galleon Hunt* - "Frogfoot" Weller) He eventually led Art McKee to the site, and Art became the "grandfather" of treasure hunters here in Florida as he stocked his treasure museum on Plantation Key with gold and silver coins, and artifacts recovered from *El Rubí*. He introduced many armchair enthusiasts to sunken treasure by actually taking them to the bottom wearing a Miller-Dunn deep sea helmet and letting them crawl over the ballast mound as he searched for treasure. In 1957 the first "Treasure Wars" over sunken galleons in the Florida Keys began when McKee, and Tim Watkins on the *Buccaneer*, locked horns as Tim and his crew raided the *capitana*. The state of Florida backed away from the conflict when it was determined that the wreck site lay outside the three mile limit and came under federal jurisdiction. Without state protection, McKee lost interest in the *capitana*, and the site lay open for the salvagers of the 1960s to try their luck.

I first dived on *El Rubí* in 1962, and I have to admit that it was the most impressive sunken galleon I had ever seen. That was partly due to the wooden ribs that McKee had managed to raise some eight feet above the sandy bottom so that tourists could better visualize what the galleon looked like many years ago before storms flattened the wreck site. The ballast mound was huge, over 100 feet long, 40 feet across, and rising five feet above the bottom. Art had been limited in his salvage work to moving ballast stones, as well as a little sand dredging around the pile, in his search for artifacts and coins. And he found quite a few.

My first salvage effort was in company with Craig Hamilton. We were airlifting the sand along the south side, working under the hull timbers by several feet. The wreck was facing seaward, so her stern was the end of the ballast towards shore. She had rolled on her starboard side, so that most everything of value was recovered on the south side of the ballast. I know of very little that was ever recovered to the north. That first day we had exposed about four feet of the hull timbers and were at a point that we had some concern about the weight of the ballast maybe causing a cave-in. I was working the seaward end, and Craig was working the shoreward end. During the morning we had recovered a small bag full of lead musket balls, a silver buckle, and a silver chain with a round reliquary at the end about 2-1/2 inches in diameter. It had glass on both sides, with what appeared to be a painting inside.

I was working about 25 feet from Craig when I uncovered a flintlock pistol. "Now is my chance to shoot someone underwater," I must have been thinking as I swam towards Craig, pointing it in his direction. About that time I saw him scoop up something that had fallen from the coral which had adhered to the bottom of the wooden hull. He saw me coming, held up the artifact and smiled. It was a *pistolé* (gold two-*escudo* coin) dated 1728. These were old Spanish coins about the size of a nickel, probably pocket change for a passenger on board. It was a great artifact, one that was later sold to a famous coin dealer from Spain. Forgotten for the moment was the flintlock pistol I was waving around over my head. The day continued like that, as we found a number of nice artifacts including a few silver coins, silver buttons, and several cannon balls. Several years later I had a desire to go back to the *capitana* and work further under the hull timbers, but by that time the ballast pile had begun to sink deeper in the sand, and the entire mound would have had to be moved...or a cave-in would have kept this book from being written!

A number of the other salvagers have tried their luck on the "Capitana," and as far as I know each has recovered his share of goodies. Bobby Klein spent many days airlifting the pile. One day that I remember, Bobby had just taken a lunch break when I anchored nearby. He sat there smoking a cigarette waiting for something, and I held my hands out—palms up, asking "what gives?" He pointed over the side where his 20-foot airlift pipe lay alongside the crater he had been working in before the lunch break. It was then I saw the 14-foot shark that had settled in the bottom of his hole, waiting for his own lunch to appear, I guess. But his lunch remained in the boat, smoking a cigarette. Finally the shark became tired of waiting and swam off towards deeper water, and Bobby went back to work.

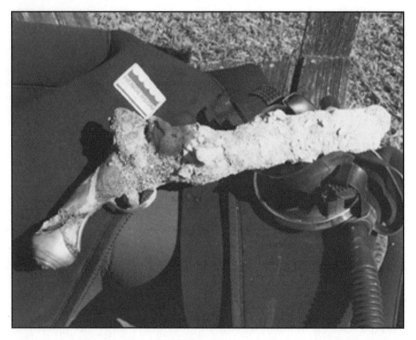

Flintlock Pistol recovered by Jack Haskins from the
***San José.* Grotesque Mask on butt plate (facing page.)**
PHOTOS: John Berrier.

Marty Meylach worked the area to the south and a bit seaward, recovering a handsome gold plated buckle among many other artifacts. D. L. Chaney recovered an ivory compass and sundial one day in the ballast pile, and Jack "Blackjack" Haskins recovered silver coins, a boarding ax, and two flintlock pistols from the sand that stretches towards shore. But there is little doubt in anyone's mind that the greatest artifact to be recovered to date from the entire 1733 Spanish treasure fleet is the 3-1/4 inch by 2-1/4 inch gold religious medallion recovered by Jack Haskins against a reef several hundred yards towards shore from the *capitana* ballast mound. It was originally set with nine quartz crystals, however, one of them is missing. It was hand carved from a casting of 22-karat gold, and probably belonged to a Catholic Bishop traveling back to Spain after serving tenure in the New World. It has been conservatively appraised at $250,000.

PHOTO: John Berrier

In more recent times the state of Florida has allowed divers to place a salvage lease on the *capitana*, and Don Washington, as well as Joe Kimbell, have been actively working the site. But *El Rubí* lies in deep sand, sand that is slowly swallowing all that remains of the once huge ballast mound. Today more than six feet of sand covers the top of the mound, and as quickly as the overburden is moved away by dusters mounted on the stern of the salvage boats, the sand drifts back in overnight. Artifacts, once plentiful, are being lost forever as they sink deeper into the ocean bottom. The one bright spot is the possibility that baggage and cargo which was washed over the side still lies to shoreward. As mentioned before, it will never *all* be found. Searching the "Capitana" site remains a beacon for those with the patience it takes to hunt for sunken treasure along **Galleon Alley**.

Diver Joe Shepherd brings up a trunnion strap...the black item accreted to it is the 1732 "pillar dollar" shown below!

<< Obverse of the 1732 "pillar dollar" found by Joe Shepherd.

Reverse of the 1732 "pillar dollar" found by Joe Shepherd. >>

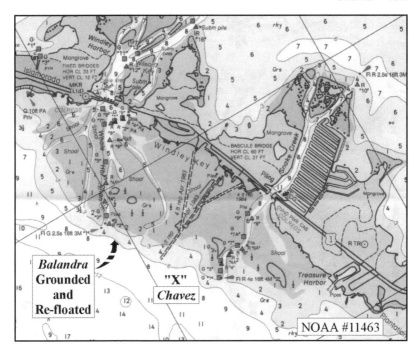

NOAA #11463

CHAPTER 13: *CHAVEZ*
Nuestra Señora del Carmen, San Antonio de Padua
y Las Animas

When the *Chavez* was discovered in 1960, there was very little in the way of artifacts to be recovered from the site by modern day salvagers. There are fairly good reasons for this, and possibly there is a lesson to be learned for future salvagers. It was clear from the research documentation that the *Chavez* carried no treasure to begin with, and apparently little in the way of silver specie was received in trade at the Vera Cruz *feria*. A more basic reason there was little to recover lies in the fact that the *Chavez* was a smaller merchant vessel and was driven through the outer reefs onto the shallow sand banks near shore by some fairly huge waves, where she grounded in seven to eight feet of water. When the hurricane passed, the ship was high and dry in water shallow enough that it seemed the survivors could almost wade to shore less than 1,000 yards away. *Chavez* was clearly visible to the other major vessels grounded or sunk in the same area, with several giving bearings and distance to her from their own locations.

The cargo and supplies on board were taken off and made use of at the *real* of de Torres on Matecumbe Grande (Upper Matecumbe). Because of the shallow depth, everything of value was easily removed. For a time there was hope that she could be refloated, the hull seemed undamaged and her masts, although badly worn by the hurricane, were repairable. But it wasn't to be. Because of the shallow depth, the vessel could not be refloated. With only seven feet of water in her hold, the stores and cargo remained dry and were saved. When the salvage was completed she was set afire and burned to the water line. What remained was only her bottom timbers and small pile of round river rock ballast.

It seems that many of the Spanish ships of the period were built in the shipyards of Genoa, Italy. *Chavez* was built by Genoese shipbuilders as a merchant *nao* of 230-3/8 tons, and although no formal records can be found regarding her armament, it is believed that she carried at least six cannon. When Rodrigo de Torres announced the forming of the *Nueva España Flota* in 1732, Don Antonio de Chavez registered his vessel to make the voyage to Vera Cruz. There were no problems in the crossing; with brisk breezes and the equatorial current to boost the *flota* along, they arrived after a six-week voyage. There is little to do during the winter months in the port at Vera Cruz. The small village of Jalapa, located a few miles inland from Vera Cruz, provided the labor needs of the fleets as well as fresh water and provisions. It would take several weeks for the news to spread that the annual treasure fleet had arrived. Once the word was spread throughout the villages and towns along the Mexican coast, preparations were made to hold the fair, at which time the local merchants could trade local products, including gold and silver, for the Old World goods.

Not all coinage minted in the New World traveled back to Spain. About a third of it was shipped to the Orient aboard the Manila galleons. Some of it remained in circulation in the New World through local merchants, as well as Spanish officials as they bolstered the defenses of Vera Cruz, Cartagena, and Portobelo. Roadways and bridges, as well as buildings of trade and commerce, also had to be built. In the early years of settlement the Spanish brought cattle to Mexico for the purpose of breeding and a source of beef. By 1733 the cattle were so numerous that the price of beef had dropped below a profitable level. In the Vera Cruz area only the few local inhabitants, an occasional merchant *nao*, and the annual New Spain Fleet visit had a need for fresh beef. As a result the hides of the cattle became a principal product to be shipped back to Spain. Often the cattle were slaughtered and the only thing of value was the hide, the remains being left for vultures. Other than hides, the tiny cochineal bug that was the resident of many cactus plants, became one of the most sought after products from the New World. It provided the red dye that so brightly colored clothing. Anil, another product from various plants native to the Indies, provided the deep blue dye for cloth. And by 1733 the fruit groves of the settlers began to produce an abundance of oranges, grapefruit, bananas, and coconuts.

In 1960 the hunt by modern day salvagers to locate the entire 1733 treasure fleet was in full swing. Craig Hamilton had managed to locate a chart by the Spanish salvagers from the British Museum of History in London. It was a chart on which, to the best of their ability, the Spaniards placed the *naufragios sumergidos* close to islands that they could identify with. Of course, the Florida Keys did not have the same names as today, nor did they appear the same as they do on our navigational charts. An aerial survey earlier had turned up several ballast piles offshore Windley Key and the lower tip of Tavernier, but the "piles" were never checked out. With the "best guess," it appeared that *Chavez* had bilged her bottom near the shore of Windley Key. With Whale Harbor Channel to the south, and Snake Creek 1-1/2 miles to the north, the area where the ballast should be would be easy enough to cover. That's where frustration in the salvaging business plays its role. It never seems to be where it's supposed to be!

The ocean was flat calm, the sun bright and shining, and underwater visibility out of this world. Craig Hamilton and his wife teamed up with Dr. Robert Welberry and his wife for a weekend of "looking for the 'Chavez'." Each had a boat, and each knew what to look for. The job seemed simple enough, run parallel passes between Whale Harbor Channel and Snake Creek, spacing the passes about fifty feet apart. "We're bound to find the ballast pile. Piece of cake!" And so it went, beginning about 8:00 o'clock in the morning with a cooler full of sandwiches and soft drinks, the two boats passed and re-passed each other, both salvagers straining over the side to see what had to be a fairly decent pile of round river rocks. There was a break sometime around noon when the women convinced them with an offer they couldn't refuse: "Let's go swimming and cool off!" Then it was back to watching the sand and eel grass slide by the bottom of the boat.

Every once in awhile one of the boats would stop while Craig or Robert checked out an unusual hump in the bottom, or other modern wreckage, causing a blink in the otherwise dull routine. Then it was 4:00 p.m. and the boats had come together, the men discussing whether to call it a day and try again tomorrow, the women displaying their degrees of sunburn towards a frustrating cause. As the two boats drifted with the current less than 1,000 yards offshore, one of the wives glanced over the side and suddenly exclaimed, "Hey guys, there's a pile of ballast stones right under the boat!" They had found the *Chavez*.

The ballast pile showing above the sandy bottom was smaller than they had anticipated, no more than fifteen feet by five feet; sand and eel grass had drifted in to cover most of the timbers. They guessed the pile to be about fifty feet long by 25 feet wide, and it lay in eight feet of water. Their best bearing was taken on the seaward edge of Tavernier Island to the north, lining up with the edge of sand just beyond the last channel marker at the seaward end of Snake Creek. There were no cannons or anchors visible as the divers scanned the area.

Although Craig was aware that the chances of finding treasure on the *Chavez* were slim, he decided to devote a few days to airlifting the sand around the pile. Over the next few weeks he, as well as Bobby Klein, spent several days exploring the ballast and surrounding sand with an airlift. As they expected, the Spanish had salvaged the *Chavez* "clean as a hounds tooth!" There were a few artifacts found, including an intact wine bottle, an ivory handled razor, a gray glazed pottery bowl, a nine-inch pewter plate, a double-sheaved block, a triangular padlock, and a pair of small scissors.

The wreck site was close enough to shore that when the winds kept divers off the outer reefs, the *Chavez* was a good spot to take dive charters. So Hugh Brown and Bobby Klein used the site as a sort of alternate dive. One day Bobby dragged a seven-foot cannon to the site from another wreck nearby (I believe the *Herrera*), so that his dive charters could see something interesting. I happened to drop by the site a week or so later, not knowing it was Bobby's cannon. I thought it had been uncovered by a recent storm. When I secured a rope to the cascabel, I had in mind dragging it close to shore and then floating it to the dock with four 55-gallon drums. By the time I had moved it 200 yards I gave up because the water was shallow, and I didn't want to block the Snake Creek Channel with a cannon. I intended coming back that weekend and completing the job. Before that could happen, I heard through the grapevine that Bobby Klein was pretty upset that someone had managed to drag his cannon halfway to Snake Creek. The track of a cannon being dragged along the bottom is an easy one to follow. I called and apologized, offering to drag it back. He didn't laugh when he said, "I've already done that!" The cannon remained there for a few years, and somehow again "turned up missing." It never made it back to the site of *Chavez*. It's probably resting on a concrete pad somewhere along Galleon Alley, saluting the cars as they pass by.

The *Chavez* is a likely candidate for a state park similar to the *San Pedro* site. It is close enough to shore that visitors can swim to it, or paddle to it on an inner tube or on a surf board. With the thought in mind that there is no hidden treasure, it is easier to visit with a "hands off" attitude.

PHOTO: Denis B. Trelewicz

The Chavez' ballast mound (as of 30 August 1994)
scattering off into the distance.
PHOTO: Denis B. Trelewicz.

(Above) Pottery bowl from the Chavez.
PHOTO: Ernie Richards
(Below) Ivory-handled knife from the Chavez.
PHOTO: Ernie Richards

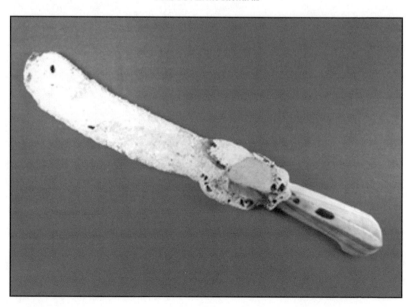

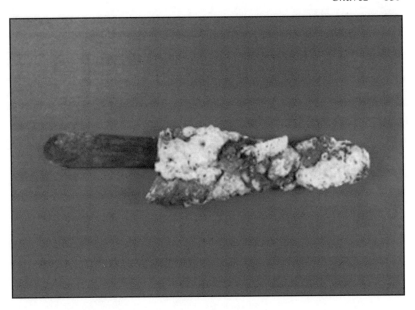

(Above) Encrusted wooden razor handle from the **Chavez.**
PHOTO: Ernie Richards

(Below) Another, cleaned razor handle from the **Chavez.**
PHOTO: Ernie Richards

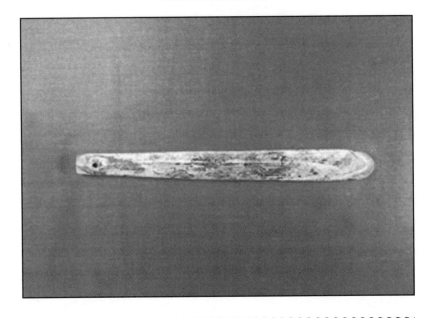

(Above) Single-sheave block recovered from the Chavez.
PHOTO: Ernie Richards

(Below) Encrusted axe-head recovered from the Chavez.
PHOTO: Ernie Richards

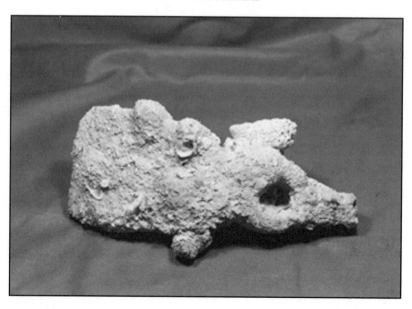

CHAPTER 14: *HERRERA*
Nuestra Señora de Belén y San Antonio de Padua
Alias: *Belén*

It was like so many summer days in the Florida Keys. There wasn't a ripple on the water surface that stretched out of sight to where the horizon met white clouds, which seemed to have no place to go. It just felt right. This was a day for diving, and I was on my way for a first-time visit to the *Herrera*. I lined up with one and a half spans of the Whale Harbor bridge supports showing and, with a purring 35-HP Johnson outboard pushing *Frogfoot*, I pointed the bow towards Hawk Channel. It was a 2-1/2 mile trip that took less than ten minutes, with Harry "Big Splash" Wiseman commenting on how clear the water was and counting big fish darting across a bottom fourteen feet below us. It was an easy wreck to find, once Craig Hamilton pointed it out a week earlier as we passed it on the way to the "Capitana."

He was part of a group that had just completed salvage of the pile, calling it the "Figurine Wreck" because of the almost 100 small glazed clay figurines recovered. They were unusual, and the first discovered on the 1733 fleet. Some speculation had it that they were Mexican Indian playthings. Another suggestion was that they were religious offerings of the Mayas. As it turned out, the figurines were made in the small town of Tonala, near Guadalajara, where pottery making had been an established industry since the early 1700s. The clay mines of Tonala were so unique that their products were valued throughout the European market. In fact it was written, "so soft are they as to aroma and taste that often women eat such clay." The clay products were more esteemed than crystal and china.

The thought of recovering one myself was incentive enough to look forward to this dive. The grayish sand smudge on the bottom appeared just ahead of us, and I throttled back and let *Frogfoot* settle into the wind. It was April 8, 1962, a weekend with pleasure boats "mounting up and riding off in all directions" around us. We had to be careful that they didn't cut our air hoses. As we were putting our gear on I noted the wreck lay in a small grayish sand spot, but to the west about 200 feet was the beginning of a broad sandy bottom which probably was the edge of Hawk Channel. Our air compressor seemed to enjoy the day as much as we did, it started on the first pull, and it kept us on the bottom for three hours without missing a beat. My first impression was, "The other salvage group certainly moved a lot of ballast rocks." They had laid open the hull timbers, piling the ballast along each side. There were sections of eel grass that had been cut into, but most of the salvage had been concentrated on the ballast.

Today Harry and I would be content with just fanning the sand or coral dust off the timbers, it was a "get acquainted with the *Herrera*" dive. Both Harry and I commented that the wreck seemed to be "floating" on a bed of leather. There were sections of leather hides everywhere, coming apart at the touch. They were in layers, stacked against the hull. The previous salvage group had uncovered them, determined they couldn't be salvaged, and left them for others to see and appreciate. We did the same.

I got in trouble early. Along the hull, between two rib sections, I found a curious oval bubble of something soft. It must have been all of six inches in diameter, and I picked it up. When I did, it broke, spilling indigo dye all over my arms. I brushed it off as best I could, fanned away the water that had now turned inky blue, and kept going. It wasn't until I was topside at the end of the day that I realized I had blue arms and hands, a color that would stay with me for two weeks!

Harry was making clouds of turbidity on the other side of the timbers, so I swam towards what was probably the stern at the shoreward end of the ballast pile. I found a likely looking spot just off the ballast pile and timbers and began fanning the bottom. The sand was no more than six inches deep, a hard coquina bottom underneath. It seemed fruitless at first, no signs of artifacts, but after about twenty minutes of fanning I came to a depression in the bottom, a hole that had been missed by the other salvagers. The hole was filled with a compacted gray sand and clay, a little difficult to move at first, but with probing it came apart. It paid off. In the hole were several clay figurines, including an intact small bowl no larger than three inches across the top. A small figure that resembled a fish and a small dog-like figurine lay at the bottom of the hole. All were intact. They were neat, and I brought them to the boat with the same care as if they were gold coins. Harry had also finished for the day, with a hope we would be back the next day. It had been a great dive on a site that should have good possibilities. Passengers' baggage must have been scattered shoreward for hundreds of yards because of the depth at which the *Herrera* had sunk. We agreed that this site deserved a return engagement.

The spring of 1962 was the beginning of a sudden rush of activity in locating the wreck sites of the 1733 Spanish treasure fleet. The sites already located, the *capitana*, *El Infante*, the *almiranta*, the *San Pedro*, and the *Chavez* were all producing great artifacts as well as a few gold and silver coins. It was on everyone's mind that the next site would be a bonanza of coins, like the *San Pedro* that had produced almost 9,000 coins in a single week. To find the wreck sites quickly a few of the salvagers were using "fly-overs" with privately owned airplanes, scanning the bottom for sand patches in the middle of a sea of eel grass. Don Gurgiola had a rag-tag Seabee seaplane that he flew out of Plantation Key, spending day after day in the air...weather permitting. One day while flying at 800 to 1,200 feet above Hawk Channel he spotted what looked like a cigar shaped patch of sand in the center of a football field of eel grass, about 2-1/2 miles east of Whale Harbor on Islamorada's north end. Gurgiola recalled, "The color of the ocean bottom was different somehow, a sort of dark gray."

Art Sapp, Don Knox, and Marty Meylach were riding with Don that day, and there was a disagreement on whether or not it could be the *Herrera*. Meylach said "no," and Sapp said "yes." Don thought "maybe," and dropped a buoy on the spot. Within a few days Don and Art Sapp followed up to see what was under the bobbing buoy. At first they weren't sure they had a 1733 site; partially buried in sand, the ballast pile measured almost 80 feet long, 25 feet across, and three feet high. Water was fourteen feet deep and the bottom flat in all directions. "Must have put a hole in her bottom when she hit the outer reef," was Don's first thought. A single cannon lay across the ballast near one end. It was typical of a number of shipwreck sites near Upper Matecumbe, but located in what was probably the "closest" spot on the Spanish salvage charts to be the *Herrera*. They decided to work it a few days and find out if any 1733 material was there. As Don's group began working the site everything checked out, including the cargo that *Herrera* was carrying when she sank. They had located another missing link in the 1733 fleet.

The *Herrera* was built in England and listed at 242-1/2 tons, possibly designed to carry ten or twelve iron cannon. Her owner was Don Luis Herrera, a Cádiz merchant who had already made several trips to the New World. When he joined Rodrigo de Torres "Flota" in 1732, he carried a general cargo of Old World trade goods to Vera Cruz. At the annual *feria* Herrera was able to trade for a number of hides, cochineal, anil (indigo), several boxes of gifts (probably the glazed figurines), sugar, tobacco, and 12,000 pesos in silver coins. When the fleet left the safety of Havana Harbor, the *Herrera* was positioned near the center of the convoy. As the hurricane drove the fleet through the outer reefs she must have been holed by the dragons' teeth, filling her bilge with water and sinking as she reached the western side of Hawk Channel.

(Letter of September 25, 1733 from Alonso Herrera Barragan, the King's Emissary):

"Relation of the places in which are grounded the ships of the Flota under the command of Don Rodrigo de Torres; Herrera —Cayo of old Matecumbe and those before it. They placed the Real [camp] on this cayo for the bad situation of the horse flies on Tavona [Tavernier]."

(*Indiferente* 57 - Diary of the *Infante* 1733):

"July 16- Likewise to the SSW four or five leagues we discovered two grounded vessels which we thought to be Tres Puentes and the one of Herrera."

"Notices of the sites where the ships of the Flota grounded —Herrera: Matecumbe El Grande, its decks flooded."

(*Contratación* 5102 - 1733 *Flota*. Letter Jesus, Maria, and Joseph— Havana 20 August, 1733):

"The navio of El Duque [*San José*] flooded immediately upon grounding and its officials, passengers, soldiers, and sailors sought shelter on the round house [poop deck]. All were saved on rafts. The same happened to the ship of D. Luis de Herrera."

(*Escribano Real* Rodrigo de Torres, 19 August 1733):

"That the 3rd Deputy Don Antonio Joseph de Herrera, accompanied by Don Joseph Diaz de Guitian, shall remain in the Real of the Capitana to receive and inventory the wealth and other things which are carried to it, such as those coming from the Patache, Navio of Duque, Chavez, Tres Puentes, and the one of Herrera."

Because the modern day salvage of *Herrera* uncovered little or no silver coins, it is probable that the four registered boxes of pesos were salvaged by the Spanish. The hides, tobacco, sugar, and boxes of gifts were considered a loss due to submergence in salt water. The usual items of every day use aboard ship were also left behind, considered by the salvage community as great artifacts. The salvage team of Don Gurgiola, Bobby Klein, Craig Hamilton, Bobby Welberry, and Marty Meylach worked the *Herrera* for several days, recovering a pair of bronze dividers, a cross of Caravacas, twelve pewter plates, twelve large pewter platters, five intact olive jars, eighteen "onion" bottles, twenty teardrop padlocks, close to 100 clay figurines, some exotic brasilwood, brass buckles, bar shot, and quite a number of lead musket balls. The iron cannon was floated to Tea Table Key, where it sat for several months near the edge of the water. It was finally re-located to the front of the Chesapeake Restaurant on the north end of Islamorada, where its muzzle points across U.S. Highway #1 to the site of Don Rodrigo de Torres' 1733 campsite!

Leo Barker took his boat *Norma* a-salvaging on the *Herrera* with Art Sapp, Ralph Weeks, and Bobby Savage on board. They recovered many of the iron fittings, cannon balls, clay bowls, and some pewter artifacts. They also recovered quite a number of the small clay figurines. When the *Norma* docked on the Miami River, most of the artifacts were placed in buckets and lowered to the bottom of the river next to the dock. Not long after, the *Norma* sank at the dock. It sat there for years before finally being removed for demolition. The buckets of artifacts remained, and are probably still there today.

Jack "Blackjack" Haskins often visited the site, as I did many times, recovering three large 16-inch pewter platters in the sand surrounding the ballast pile. I recovered pewter plates and an ivory-handled razor, as well as piles of musket balls and several more figurines.

But the greatest artifact to be recovered from the remains of the *Herrera* was the small wicker basket containing five silver rings and seven gold rings. In the top of the basket was a little rosary of silk thread and wooden beads, the entire artifact encrusted in a coral and mud conglomerate. Bobby Klein had recovered it, and he gave his wife a choice of the gold rings. Afterwards it was put on display at the Ocean Reef Resort in upper Key Largo where, during the exhibit, the case was broken into and the basket removed. It has never been recovered.

The clay figurines have received their share of publicity. *National Geographic*, in the December 1977 issue on page 743, devoted a full page photograph to six figurines. They included a three-inch tall warrior with a headdress that produced a shrill whistle when blown. The Society had determined that the figures were "Tonalaware, fanciful amulets made of clay by skilled Indian hands that must have delighted Spanish youngsters." As recently as 1995 a contractor from Lake Mary, Florida recovered a small clay figurine from the edge of the *Herrera* ballast pile, an artifact he had dreamed of owning for many years before finally finding his own. That's what dreams are made of.

The **Herrera** *is probably most famous for her cargo of clay figurines, made in the village of Tonala near Guadalajara, Mexico and known as "Tonalaware." This statuette of a "seated warrior" was featured in* **National Geographic,** *December 1977, page 743.* AUTHOR'S COLLECTION.

TONALAWARE FIGURINES: Apparently made as toys for children, these miniature statues (above) came in the forms of water fowl, a pig, an anteater, a hare, a cat...? Three of these figures also appear in National Geographic. *And these below depict various fish, a seal, dogs, and a toucan with fruit in its beak!* PHOTOS *by "Seascribe"*

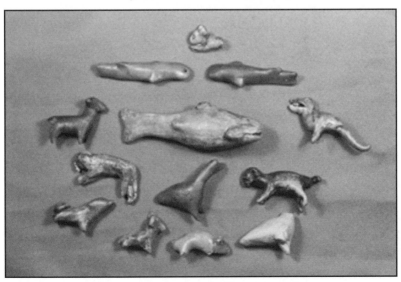

TONALAWARE FIGURINES: *Perhaps made as toys for girls, these miniature utensils (above) came in the forms of bowls (the largest 2-1/2" in diameter), cups, plates, and a pitcher. And those below depict a bowl, a bowl with a cover, a cup, and, perhaps, a pitcher with handles.*
PHOTOS by "Seascribe"

TONALAWARE FIGURINES: (Above): An assortment of utility vessels—cups, bowls, etc.—for the "future housewife." (Below): Larger bowls—one decorated within like a grape-fruit half—and the largest figurine known to have come from the **Herrera,** *the 5-inch-tall "Big Dog" (ref:* **Diving to a Flash of Gold,** *p. 122.) PHOTOS by "Seascribe"*

BRONZE RELIGIOUS MEDALLIONS *recovered from the* **Herrera.** *(Left) St. Joseph with the Christ Child.*

(Below) The Medallion reads "St. Francis, O.P.N. (Ora Pro Nobis—'Pray For Us')."

PHOTOS by "Seascribe"

BRONZE CROSS *from the* **Herrera.** *(Left) This "Cross of Caravacas" is inscribed "Salvator"—Saviour!* AUTHOR'S COLLECTION.

The **Herrera** *anchor.*
PHOTO by Jack "Blackjack" Haskins

(Below) Diver at the extreme end of the **Herrera** *ballast pile is marine historian Chuck Hayes.*
PHOTO: Denis B. Trelewicz

PHOTO: Denis B. Trelewicz

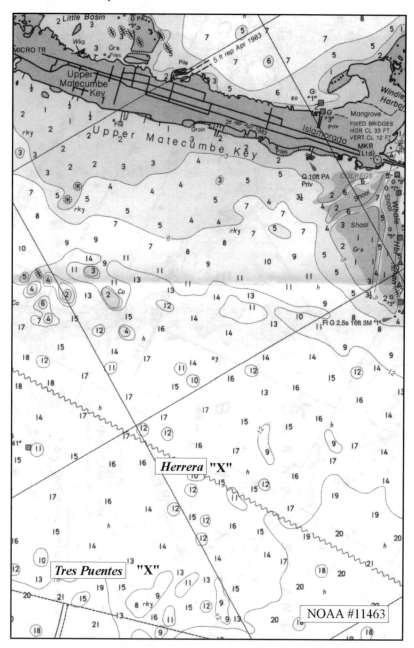

LOCATION CHART: The *Herrera* and the *Tres Puentes*.

GOLD "PORTRAIT DOLLAR" of 1733. *This 8-Escudo coin from the new screw press machinery at Mexico City was recovered from the* **San José** *by* **Jack Haskins** *and* **D. L. Chaney.** PHOTO: *John Berrier.*

*ROSARIES, RINGS, AND RELIQUARIES (above) are
among the fabulous finds from the* **San Ignacio**
by Bobby Jordan.

*THE GOLD SNUFF BOX (below) was also recovered by
Bobby Jordan from the* **San Ignacio.** *PHOTOS: Bobby Jordan*

CHAPTER 15: *TRES PUENTES*
Nuestra Señora de los Dolores y Santa Isabel
Alias: *"El Nuevo Londres"*
Alias: *"Three Decks"*

The modern day salvage of the *Tres Puentes* is really the story of a "Flying Coffin." Back in the late 1950s Don Gurgiola was a fisherman who chartered for bonefishing, as well as other action type fishing trips. He knew the Florida Keys well, he knew how to read the bottom, and he had a side interest in old Spanish galleons. There was another side interest, it involved a Seabee pusher-type four seater airplane that he owned. He loved his fishing business, so he chartered the seaplane to a local pilot who made a decent living running trips up and down the Keys. On days when the weather was good, and Don had a break in his fishing charters, he would take his seaplane up for a "galleon alley run," tracking down the 1733 Spanish treasure fleet. He could spot the outlines of ballast piles, even the dark gray streaks that hid what was left of galleons just below the sand. He was trained to read the bottom, and he was able to locate wreck sites. He was always concerned about his plane, dubbed the "Flying Coffin," not only because it rattled a lot and was subjected to constant mechanical repairs, but you had to know how to fly it or you were a goner. You took off at 90 mph, cruised at 90 mph, and landed at 90 mph. It occasionally had mechanical break-downs, and at sea the service garages are few and far between.

It was the summer of 1962, and it seemed every other month a new 1733 wreck site was being located. His regular companion on the galleon runs was Art Sapp, who sat up front with him and could read the bottom fairly well himself. Art was also a good salvager. On this particular weekend a newcomer, John Knox, as well as Marty Meylach, asked to ride with Don when they learned he was going to look for the *Tres Puentes*. The two hitch-hikers were riding in the back seat as Don taxied his Seabee out to an open stretch behind Plantation Key. As Don gave it throttle he hollered "Hang on!" And the plane began to bounce over the two-foot waves and pick up speed. Soon they were bouncing along at 50 to 60 mph, not enough to lift from the water, but a good speed. But dead ahead of them was a thick stand of mangroves, and they were rushing toward it at a speed that left little margin of error if the plane *didn't* reach 90 mph. Don muttered a comment, "It's not coming off the water!"

as he pushed as hard as he could on the throttle. There was panic in the rear seat, while both Art and Don grinned at each other in the front seats.

As the plane rose smoothly above the mangroves and headed seaward you could hear the chuckles up front, and the cussing back aft, indicating that their passengers probably wished they hadn't asked to tag along. It was about 3:00 p.m., and they were cruising off Islamorada at 900 feet when Meylach suddenly pulled his knees above his seat and shouted, "We've got an oil leak back here!" Sure enough, the oil line to the crankcase had sprung a pin-hole leak, enough to cause Don to head for the choppy surface. He picked a wave and made a downwind landing, one he said he probably couldn't do again if he tried. The wind swung the Seabee into the waves, and a nearby fishing boat captain, who saw them make the emergency landing, soon had them in tow. They dropped anchor near a sandy beach, located tools to make a fast repair, added a quart of outboard motor oil, and within an hour were back in the air.

It was getting late, the sun had already made advances to the west, and shadows were stretching the underwater sand mounds into mountains. Don was the first to see it, a dark patch of sand in the middle of a large sandy area. "That looks like the *Puentes!*" At first Sapp disagreed, "Doesn't even look like a wreck." Meylach also disagreed, "You're wasting your time." Knox was a newcomer and said nothing. Don said he'd make another pass, and turning to Art he said, "Open the door, and drop a buoy as close as you can." He was down close to 200 feet as they passed over the gray smudge on the bottom, and Sapp dropped the buoy as close as he was able. Then they were up and heading for home.

Don suggested they go out the following morning, and Sapp agreed it was worth a look. Meylach still felt it was a waste of time, and he and Knox decided to head back to Miami.

The next morning Don and Art were checking out the buoy, and on the first dive Sapp came up waving a ballast stone. They had found the *Tres Puentes*.

The *Tres Puentes* (Three Decks) was an English-built *nao* of 296 tons owned by Fernandez Del Castillo, and her captain during the fateful 1733 fleet voyage was Antonio de Loaysa. During the *feria* in Vera Cruz the *Tres* brought aboard 20,000 pesos in registered treasure. She did trade for the standard local goods as well: brasilwood, cochineal, indigo, sugar, tobacco, hides, and some citrus products. According to the *"Triaca Producida de un Veneno"* the *Tres* sailed near the center of the *flota* as it made its way northward from Havana Harbor. The *Herrera* sailed close by, and when the hurricane drove the vessels through the outer reefs, both ships must have struck bottom and began taking on water. The *Tres* sank more quickly than *Herrera*, coming to rest on the seaward side of Hawk Channel in nineteen feet of water. The *Herrera* sank 1-1/2 miles closer to shore.

(Letter from Alonso Herrera Barragan—dated 25 September 1733):

"Relation of the Places in which are the grounded ships of the Flota of Don Rodrigo de Torres; Tres Puentes—Cayo of old Matecumbe and those before it. They placed the Real [camp] on this Cayo for the bad situation of the horse flies on Tavona [Tavernier]"

(*Indiferente* 57—Diary of the *Infante* 1733):

"July 16 - "Likewise to the SSW four or five leagues we discovered two grounded vessels which we thought to be Tres Puentes and the one of Herrera."

"Notices of the sites where the ships of the Flota grounded; Tres Puentes—Matecumbe El Grande, totally flooded."

(*Escribano Real* de Don Rodrigo de Torres—dated 19 August 1733):

"That the third deputy Don Antonio Joseph de Herrera, accompanied by Don Joseph Diaz de Guitian, shall remain in the Real of the Capitana to receive and inventory the wealth and other things which are carried to it, such as those coming from the Patache, Navio of Duque, Chavez, and Tres Puentes. A clear account and relation shall be kept."

(*Indiferente General* 2021—1733 *Flota*):

"Below are listed the armed ships which comprise the Flota for the present year (1732) which will make the voyage to New Spain under the command of Chief of Squadron Don Rodrigo de Torres y Morales, including the names of their Lordships and Owners: Nuestra Señora de los Dolores y Santa Isabel [*Tres Puentes*], its owner Don Nicolas del Castillo, its maestre Don Antonio Loaysa."

That first day of salvage for Gurgiola and Sapp really didn't produce much in the way of artifacts. The wreck lay in nineteen feet of water, completely in sand without a cover of eel grass. Over the months to follow they would recover a flintlock pistol, a boarding cutlass, and a few silver coins and pottery. They both had in mind to keep the wreck a secret, possibly for a story that *Saga Magazine* would have an interest in because of the method of locating the sites using an old Seabee pusher aircraft.

Meylach and Knox had already indicated a lack of interest in the site, so they were not called with news that the *Tres* had been located. Unknown to Gurgiola and Sapp, another salvager had been watching the Seabee from U.S. Highway #1 as it dipped over the offshore area opposite the Whale Harbor bridge. The following morning they were spotted as they anchored near their bobbing Clorox bottle and brought up ballast from the *Tres*. The lid was off, no longer was the location of the *Tres Puentes* a secret. It was evident the following day when two salvage boats were found anchored over the ballast pile, airlifts spouting sand and water as the divers uncovered the entire ballast pile. It was a free-for-all, the only one of the 1733 sites that caused a clash of emotions among the salvage community.

Not a great deal was recovered other than the usual artifacts, buckles, buttons, flintlock pistols, pewter plates, honing stones, a grinding wheel, and a few silver coins. The area of sand was airlifted away from the ballast pile as much as 25 yards, up to the eel grass that always spelled hard work for salvagers. It meant cutting through deep roots. That took time and a lot of effort. For the interim, salvage efforts stopped where the eel grass began.

After the initial discovery of the *Tres*, and the converging on the site by several of the salvage groups, Marty Meylach kept busy on other wreck sites. When the first wave of salvagers moved off, Marty visited the *Tres Puentes* and airlifted the area against the eel grass. It turned out to be a bonanza when a group of silver wedges was recovered, along with other artifacts, cemented into a small section of the wreck that had separated from the main hull when the *Tres* sank.

During the Spanish salvage of the *Tres* 13,098 pesos, 5-1/2 *reales* were recovered. This leaves quite a bit of treasure still lying somewhere on the site, probably scattered towards Islamorada because of the depth she sank in. The top decks were flooded, and the waves had to carry much of the cargo—and some personal possessions—away. The site is almost completely covered with sand today, no more than six to eight feet of ballast remains exposed. When I visited the site in 1996 it was by luck that I was able to locate it without a magnetometer. Each of the 1733 sites lying in deep sand are disappearing, and unless private enterprise will consider uncovering them for the public to see and appreciate, they will be lost forever.

What remains of the ballast scatter of the **Tres Puentes**
(as of 22 July 1996.)
PHOTO: Denis B. Trelewicz

Bobby Savage (L.) and Art Sapp
were a couple of the big "movers and shakers" during the
salvage of the **Tres Puentes.**

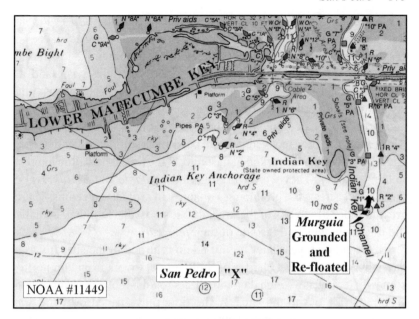

CHAPTER 16: *SAN PEDRO*
No Alias

Each treasure salvor has his favorite wreck site. It isn't necessarily the wreck that produced the biggest, or best, treasure trove. It's a love relation with a particular ballast pile, a site one looks forward to visiting and is comfortable with his surroundings while there. In my case that site is the *San Pedro*. Let me tell you the modern day salvage story of the *San Pedro*, and then my attachment to the site.

The first commercial lease to be issued on the *San Pedro* was state lease # 853 that was issued on June 6, 1952, to Arthur McKee, Jr. The actual lease encompassed the offshore area from the upper tip of Lower Matecumbe to the middle of Key Largo at Rock Harbor. Within this lease were several 1733 wreck sites, and of those, McKee actually did salvage work on the "Capitana." He visited the *El Infante* but did very little work on the site. I am not sure he actually knew the location of any other 1733 sites, and if he did he never salvaged them. The *capitana* lay directly seaward of his museum on Plantation Key. It was an easy four-mile boat ride out to the site, and he recovered quite a bit of 1733 material over the years he worked it.

In 1961 Bobby Klein and Cliff Miller were flying over the Indian

Key area and spotted the rounded ballast pile of the *San Pedro* in fourteen feet of water. It lay in a sand patch surrounded by eel grass, an easy site to locate by lining up the south edge of Indian Key with two small palm trees (the only palm trees) on the U.S. Highway #1 landfill between Indian Key Channel and Shell Key Channel. The ballast pile lay about 1,000 yards seaward of Indian Key. The following week Bobby and Art Sapp located the site by boat and, while fanning the seaward edge of the pile, they recovered a gold bead and a sulfided silver bracelet. Although it was an unworked ballast pile, at the time it held little interest to the salvagers. They were working on the *Infante* and *capitana*, and these wreck sites were producing a quantity of artifacts and coins. There are a number of wrecks in the area, and it's possible that they actually did not know they had the site of the *San Pedro*.

It would be a year later before Klein returned to the site. It was a day when Bobby had a charter of three tourist divers from "up north" somewhere. It was a rough day with three- to four-foot waves providing a bouncy ride out to the site. By the time they arrived over the *San Pedro* one of the divers had become seasick, lying on the bottom of the boat and curled around the console. There was absolutely no visibility, the waves had stirred the bottom up with sand and sediment. Bobby was able to locate the ballast pile by dragging his anchor over the bottom. When they suited up he gave instructions, "Don't leave the ballast pile or you'll get lost!" He asked them to stay close to him as he slid over the side. It would be some time before he saw them again. When he reached bottom the underwater visibility was no more than two or three feet, so he picked a spot at the edge of the ballast pile, sat down, and while waiting for his charter divers to join him, began hand fanning the sandy bottom. Before long he had uncovered several silver *two-reales*, coins about the size of a dime. He had been underwater several minutes, and with no sign of his divers he decided to look for them. Groping around in what looked like green bath water, they finally found each other, and with them in tow he worked his way back to his fanning spot. He showed them what to look for and before long they were fanning out sand potholes too. Before the dive was over they recovered two more of the silver coins, and Bobby found another nine as well.

It was the first coins Klein had recovered from the site, and they were 1733 shipwreck coins. Something stirred in Bobby, because the next day he was back on the site with another diver, Julius Siddon. He had a 4-inch air lift, one of those underwater vacuum sweepers. The water conditions were much improved that day, and they began lifting the sand that covered the area around the seaward end of the ballast. The sand patch stretched some 35 feet out from the ballast rocks, and here the eel grass would make any salvager think of an underwater lawn mower. Near the edge of the grass Bobby and Julius began recovering silver one- and two-*real* coins, small black lumps that had settled into the many pot holes surrounding the pile. Both divers had prior commitments that day, so by 11:30 they were ready to haul anchor. In the boat they counted their recoveries. Even they were surprised to find they had brought up 320 coins in singles, and one lump of coins that later turned out to have over 300 more coins to add to the total.

That evening Klein called Julius and learned he would not be able to dive the next day. Bobby called Craig Hamilton, a Miami fireman and a salvor who had been working shipwrecks for almost ten years. Together they were back on *San Pedro* bright and early the next morning. To the north side of the ballast, the side facing Indian Key, the bottom is a flat, hard marl coquina bottom with numerous small potholes. The sand here is less than a foot deep. As the two divers worked their air lifts over the sea bed they discovered one area of marl bottom that was black, as if someone had spilled a pot of Navy coffee all over it. In the center of the black area was a pothole about two feet in diameter.

As the salvagers cleared the sand away from the hole an encrustation appeared to fill the entire cavity. When they peered closely at the conglomerate, they suddenly realized it was a large lump of silver coins! As it turned out, the entire hole was filled with silver coins, as if a *talega* (sack) of coins had been dropped by the Spanish salvagers. The lump contained 2,000 silver one- and two-*real* coins, a real bonanza. All around the area were other coins, both singles and in lumps. They worked till darkness made them shut down the air lifts and call it a day. When the coins were tallied they had recovered almost 8,000 coins in a single day!

That weekend Craig called me with the good news. He said that he and Bobby were done with the wreck site, and "Would you like to have me show it to you?" I jumped at the chance, and that Saturday I followed Craig's boat out Indian Key Channel, making a broad circle to the southeast as we passed over the natural cuts that the tides have made in the sea of eel grass beyond Indian Key. Soon he lined up the edge of the key with the two palm trees, watched for the sand spot with the gray smudge in the center, and when he found it gave me a "thumbs down." He had other wreck sites to work, so with a wave he left me to take my first look at the *San Pedro*.

I think my first reaction was, "What a neat wreck site!" The ballast pile was about 75 feet long, 35 feet wide near the center, and possibly three feet high at its highest point. There rose near the shoreward end a coral concretion with several large holes. One of them belonged to a rather large jewfish. For awhile the wreck site belonged to the two of us, he swimming motionless around one side, and I trying to ignore him while looking the pile over on the other side. He stayed outside his favorite resting hole the remainder of the day, but every once in awhile I could hear the familiar "thump" as he used his huge tail to let me know of his displeasure. The only area that had been airlifted was the stern section, the part of the wreck site facing seaward, and then no more than fifteen feet into the sand. Very little of the ballast had been disturbed. Along the north side Craig and Bobby had airlifted the sand from the ballast out to the grass some 35 feet away. It was here that I could clearly see the black hole where they had recovered the lump of 2,000 coins.

It was one of those clear, sunshine-filled days, with visibility in the fifty-foot range. I could see every shell, every small crevice in the bottom, the irregular bottom of every pothole. As I looked closer I noticed the small black spots on the surface of the coquina bottom. I took my knife and broke the coquina crust over one of the black spots...and was pleasantly surprised to find a silver coin! As I searched the area of flat bottom I found more black spots, and more coins. The day disappeared so fast I was shocked when I began to lose the sunlight. I had been on the bottom for almost eight hours without even a lunch break. My air compressor had finally run out of gas, shutting down my breathing air, and telling me it was time to wrap it up. I had recovered over fifty silver coins, all one- and two-reales, some of them with dates showing. It had been a pleasant day, one of many to follow.

At the time I was diving with Harry Wiseman, a University of Miami professor and one of my mentors at the University of Delaware. Together we visited the site many times over the next two years, and during that time I never left the site without recovering at least one silver coin. One of my most memorable days was the time I stuck my head into the black hole in which Craig and Bobby had found their bonanza, and looking up I discovered over seventy coins stuck to the ceiling of the hole. And then there was the day that Benn Clouser brought the Boy Scouts out with me while they were on vacation from Newcastle, Delaware. Benn and I were past presidents of the Delaware Underwater Swim Club, and friends for many years. He "claimed" he had instilled in the Scouts what a great treasure diver I had become. That was enough for me to want to make an impression on this young, happy-go-lucky, crew so I led their rented boat out to the site of *San Pedro*. They were all qualified snorkelers, a few of them had rented SCUBA tanks, and it wasn't long before they were "scouting" the pile, disturbing the 400-pound jewfish that had finally gotten used to my visiting his abode, and just having a great time. I had settled on moving a few ballast stone not far from the black hole, and once I reached the coquina bed rock I began fanning out the small holes that squirrel away to nowhere. In one of them I could see coins covering the bottom of the hole, coins that I could just barely touch with my finger tips.

For awhile I was like a kid in a candy store without a nickel, but after retrieving a screwdriver from the boat I began opening up the hole. About the time I was able to pull out the first coin, a two-*real* piece, I had a Scout looking over my shoulder. His eyes were as big as saucers, he knew it was a Spanish silver coin even if it didn't look like much underwater. I handed it to him and he disappeared topside. I was able to bring out a clump of two coins stuck together, and suddenly there was another Scout on my shoulder. Again, I handed the coins to him, and went back to digging. As each coin was recovered, another Scout appeared. The word had gotten out, and you could almost see them lined up, each waiting for his souvenir. There were 22 "pieces-of-two" (2-*real* coins) in that hole, and I had apparently donated the entire cache to the Boy Scouts of Newcastle, Delaware. If it made them happy, it made me even happier. They were bubbling when I finally came up for lunch. I understand they had some great stories to tell when they got back home.

A typical diving log entry of mine during this time:

"September 16, 1963 - Working the San Pedro in company with Bernie Smith and Kip Porter on board Bernie's 18' boat.

Weather calm, visibility 20' underwater. Working the NW side forward, alternating turns on the 2 airlifts. One diver moves ballast stone from his area while the other divers are airlifting. Once the diver clears his area, he uses the airlift to move sand from the pot holes, while the second diver begins clearing his area of ballast stones. This method works well.

"I recovered two silver 1 reals in the ballast pile, and Bernie recovered a whole pottery cup, black, probably Indian-made. A real find, sunk down in one of the pot holes. Later I moved to the sandy flat area north of the stern and recovered fifteen silver 1 and 2 reals. When Bernie and Kip saw the silver coins they moved over to this area as well, and Bernie recovered three 1 reals while Kip recovered 4. Time underwater - 6 hours."

And then there was the Mel Fisher episode, one of the more hilarious times in my years of friendship with the Fisher family. The state of Florida had stepped in when Mel discovered the carpet of gold coins off the Ft. Pierce wreck site of 1715 *patache* "*Nieves.*" They had established a moratorium, not allowing any salvage diving on wreck sites until a system of leases could be worked out. When the smoke cleared, of the 54 applications for leases for salvage rights on various wrecks along the coast of Florida (mine was on the *El Infante*), only ten were granted because the state could only afford to hire ten state investigators, one to watch over each operation. Mel's Armada Research, located in Marathon, was one of the fortunate ones to receive a lease to work the Keys. Within Mel's lease area was...the *San Pedro*.

Mel was using a new device he had come up with to move sand, known as the "mailbox," or "duster" as we know it today. This was a 90-degree pipe about 24 inches in diameter, that swung down over the boat's prop, directing the propwash downward towards the bottom. It did a great job of moving sand, ballast, anything that needed to be moved. Dick Williams headed up Armada Research, and one day he took the salvage boat to the site of *San Pedro* to "have a look." In the years I had worked the site, not I, nor anyone else, had ever really worked through the ballast pile. It just seemed like a typical ballast pile, with usually nothing under the stones except wooden timbers. It took a lot of effort to move tons of river rock just to look at old ship's ribs and bottom planks. We had done a number on the sand surrounding the pile, but the pile to that point was intact. Williams changed all that. When he blew a hole in the center of the ballast pile, guess what...here lay three 8-foot cannons! To this day I do not know how they got *under* the ballast, unless they were used for ballast themselves. The only other explanation is that the *San Pedro* rolled over, spilling the ballast on top of the deck-mounted cannon. He left the cannons there, I guess for another day of salvage.

That weekend Bernie Smith, Kip Porter, and I were out scouting for lobster. With the state of Florida sanctions in place we were not allowed to salvage. We decided to cruise over the *San Pedro* and renew old acquaintances, even though I believed the jewfish had long departed his premises. What we saw was hard to believe. Here, among the ballast stones, lay three big cannon! We swam down for a good look, measured them, rubbed the trunnions and breach end for telltale signs of inscriptions, and then held a conference. We all agreed that we should rescue these three cannons before some swarthy group should come along and steal them from Armada Research!

We made plans that week, gathering 55-gallon drums, rope and some two-by-fours. Bernie and Kip worked for Bernie's brother, Ed Smith, V.P. of Poole & Kent Contractors in Miami.

Rusty Woods, a husky diving colleague who lived on Upper Matecumbe, became our fourth conspirator. Early Saturday morning we were over the *San Pedro* cannons, shifting ropes and rolling water-filled drums into place. Once they were lashed in place, we put an air hose to them and slowly the cannons rose to the surface, one at a time, after spending 232 years under fourteen feet of water. We towed them back to shore and, using an A-frame, hoisted them on the back of a Poole & Kent flatbed truck. We stopped at Rusty Woods' house and lowered one of the cannon onto his front yard. After that we were on our way, singing old sea chanteys and feeling like Blackbeard and his trusty gang of thieves.

Once in South Miami, because it was getting late, we decided to drop the remaining two cannons off at another conspirator's house. We went to bed feeling pretty good. It all changed early the next morning.

I remember it was about 7:00 a.m. Sunday morning when the phone rang. It was Bernie Smith. "We've got to move the cannon! They're on to us." He didn't have time to explain over the phone, he just asked me to me to meet him and Kip where we had dropped off the cannon. It wasn't that far from my home in Perrine, and as the sun decided to chance looking over the horizon, we gathered around the back of the A-frame truck Bernie had parked near the cannon. As it turned out, Rusty Woods' next door neighbor on Upper Matecumbe was a retired colonel in the Florida Highway Patrol. He had seen us backing the truck up to Rusty's front lawn and unloading the cannon. Rusty's father was a doctor, but how friendly he was with his neighbor I'm not sure. In any event, he knocked on Dr. Woods' door that morning, and when Rusty's mother answered the door she was a bit unprepared to answer the colonel's question, "Where did the cannon come from?" She must have known it was a bit illegal to raise a cannon without a lease (shame on us), and to protect her son from the incriminating evidence that was difficult to hide near the front door, she said what came naturally. "Bob Weller, Bernie Smith, and Kip Porter brought that cannon here, and they took the others to Miami. If you want, I'll get their phone numbers for you!"

As we stood there looking at the cannon, we knew we had to hide them some place no one would think of looking. Not far away was a small fresh water lake, near the Jefferson's store that marked the Palmetto Bypass as it intersected U.S. Highway #1. "We'll drop them in the lake, come back for them in a year or so, O.K.?" We agreed, loaded them back on the truck, and with Bernie leading the convoy, we headed for the lake. By the time we backed the truck up to the lake it was just 8:00 o'clock on Sunday morning. We thought we had it made. No one was around as we began to winch the first cannon off the flat bed. Suddenly, out of nowhere, this voice said, "Where did you steal the cannon from?" The voice belonged to a young lad, no more than twelve years old, smiling as if he were part of the plot. You cannot believe the look that came over our faces. Bernie said it all. "I just can't believe this!" In a way this was hilarious, and we would belly laugh about the incident for many years, in fact every time we remember that morning. But we looked at each other, shook our heads, and loaded the cannon back on the truck. I can't remember the explanation we gave that young lad, but I am sure it was complimentary.

Bernie called a friend who owned a dry wall company in Hialeah and explained our predicament. He said we could drop them in his warehouse, "Just lock the door when you leave." We convoyed over to the warehouse, and after building two cannon coffins using plywood and two-by-fours, lining them with plastic, and then filling them with water we finally saw the last of the cannons for that memorable Sunday. But my day wasn't over yet.

About 4:00 p.m. my phone rang. It was Mel Fisher. "Bob, where are my cannon?" By this time I was ready for anything. "Mel, how did you know I got your cannon?" He chuckled, "I've got eyes and ears all over the place." I said, "O.K., I'll tell you where they're at, but I'm not going to put them back in the ocean. If you want them you'll have to get them out of the warehouse." I gave him the address, and he hung up. I called Bernie and Kip and told them of my conversation with Mel. It had been quite a weekend. The next week came and went, and the next, and nothing happened. In fact, the cannons were there months later, and we disposed of them. We each had cannon sitting in our front yards, so it became a matter of financial remuneration. Years later I asked Mel about the cannons, and why he never picked them up. His reply, "Bob, I had cannons laying all over the bottom, so a couple more didn't matter much. I just didn't want you to think you got away with something." It was a great ending to a story we relish of the "good ole days."

The *San Pedro* was built in Holland as a *nao*, a cargo-carrying merchantman. At 287 tons it wasn't considered a large ship in terms of trade with the New World, but certainly seaworthy for the long voyage. Her owner was Gaspar de Larrea Berdugo, and her Captain Gaspar Lopez de Gonzales was in command when the ship joined Rodrigo de Torre's *flota* in Cádiz for the annual *Nueva España* trip to Vera Cruz. During the *feria* when the European goods on board were traded for silver specie, cochineal, anil, vanilla, hides, and brasilwood, another treat awaited the 1733 fleet. The Manila galleon had reached the west coast of Mexico after an arduous trip across the Pacific, depositing ivory, worked-gold jewelry, porcelain cups, bowls, and saucers, spices, and other assorted Oriental trade goods to delight the hearts of the European housewives. Captain Gonzales, and merchants aboard his ship, were able to trade for 16,000 pesos in silver specie, all in smaller coins of the one- and two-*real* denominations, as well as 323 *arrobas* of anil, 124 *arrobas* of cochineal, three boxes of porcelain, and other general cargo. It is quite possible that some tobacco was brought aboard in Havana when the fleet arrived there.

When the *Flota de Plata* left Havana on July 13, 1733, the *San Pedro* was located near the head of the "freight trains of the sea" as the *naos* were herded northward by the war galleons. Don Jose Ignacio de

Toca Velasco, in his "*Triaca Producido de un Veneno*" (Antidote Made From Venom), described the fleet as it sailed up the Bahama Canal, placing the *San Pedro* in close proximity to the *El Infante*. When the hurricane struck, Captain Gonzales was very fortunate to have missed the outer dragon's teeth as his ship was driven into the shallow waters of the Florida Keys. He finally grounded in sand just shoreward of Hawk Channel in 2-1/2 *brazas* (14 feet) of water.

In a letter written by Alonso de Herrera Barrigan, the Kings' Deputy, on September 25, 1733, he described the *San Pedro* as "*sinking near Cayuelo de Matanzas, its decks flooded.*" In the diary of the *El Infante* on July 19 it was recorded: "*Notice was received of the San Pedro being grounded and full of water.*" In a letter written by the *Escribano Real* of Don Rodrigo de Torres, it outlined that Don Antonio Navarro shall work in off-loading the *San Pedro*. He used Indian Key as the *real* to assist survivors and store the cargo saved from *San Pedro*. During the salvage most of the cargo and specie of *San Pedro* was recovered. We have to assume at this point, that in the transfer of boxes and *talegas* of silver coins from the hull of *San Pedro* to a launch, one or more of the boxes or *talegas* fell overboard (the coins recovered by modern day salvagers have been found a short distance away from the ballast pile). With many sharks in the area, the Spanish salvagers were hesitant to jump overboard and retrieve the silver. For that, the salvage community today is forever grateful.

(Above) Silver "cob" 1-real and 2-real coins recovered by the author from the San Pedro.

(Below) Platinum cross with turquoise stones, recovered by Kip Porter from San Pedro.

(Above) Intact olive jar recovered by author from
San Pedro.
(Below) Tea kettle recovered by author from **San Pedro.**

(Left) Pewter medallion with unicorns, recovered by Bernie Smith from **San Pedro.**
(Below) Bernie Smith and Kip Porter using an airlift on the **San Pedro** *ballast.*

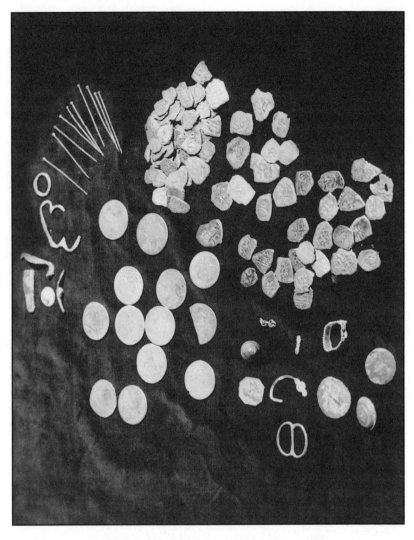

San Pedro *silver coins and other artifacts*
recovered by the author over the years.

CHAPTER 17: *MURGUIA*
Nuestra Señora del Rosario y Santo Domingo
Alias: *"Rosario de Murguia"*

The *Murguia* was a fairly large Spanish-built *nao* at 522-1/2 tons and believed to have mounted twenty cannon. Her owners were the heirs of Don Andrés de Murguia, and she sailed from Cádiz on August 2, 1732, with Don Thomas de Apodaca as her *maestre*. Reaching the safe anchorage off Vera Cruz in October, she remained through the winter, until the *feria* (fair) brought the sleepy village alive in May 1733. Her European trade goods were bartered, and her cargo hold was soon filled with New World products.

(*Indiferente General* 2021—1733 *Flota*):

9 cases of worked silver —5,486 pesos

In 835 arrobas, 21 tomines of dry cochineal at 70 pesos per arroba —50,508 pesos, 6 1/2 reales

In 903 arrobas, 11 tomines dry anil —11,293 pesos, 4 reales

In 3,358 arrobas, 18 tomines of tobacco at 3 reales per arroba —1,259 pesos, 4 reales

291 arrobas, 1-1/2 tomín tobacco at 8 reales per arroba —291 pesos, 1-1/2 reales

28 cases of gifts (usually clay pots or porcelain) at 30 pesos each —840 pesos

3,353 arrobas, 16 tomines white sugar; 2,107 arrobas, 14 tomines rough sugar (raw), all at 8 reales per arroba —5,461 pesos, 2 reales

2,071 arrobas of tobacco powder at 3 reales per arroba —776 pesos, 5 reales

1,410 arrobas, 14 tomines of purgative of julap (a laxative)
—4,231 pesos, 5 reales

60,800 vanilla pods at 20 pesos per 1,000 —1,216 pesos

176 arrobas, 13 tomines of annatto tree (a dye) —1,103 pesos

9 sacks of cacao —170 pesos

When Rodrigo de Torres' *flota* came together outside Havana Harbor and sailed northward to pick up the Gulf Steam's two-knot current, the *Murguia* was stationed somewhere near the forward van of 21 vessels. When the hurricane came upon them on July 15, she lost her main mast and some top masts, and was driven aground to the northeast of today's Indian Key. After the hurricane passed, Captain Apodaca found himself about five leagues south of the *capitana* which was submerged to her gun decks near the edge of the outer reefs. Although battered by the high winds and waves the *Murguia* was afloat and her hull was intact, and by a miracle his people came through without a casualty. Just to seaward was the overturned hull of the *San Pedro*, to the south the *El Lerri* and *Poder de Dios*, and to the north near shore was the *Chavez*.

In a letter written by the King's Deputy Alonso de Herrera Barragan (*Contratación* 5147—1733 *Flota*):

"I don't think we will have to remit more than a little of that which was salvaged from the ship of Murguia, since it is being off loaded at small canal where it grounded, in efforts to sail the ship into deeper water. I think this ship will be able to return to Havana with its cargo."

The survivors set up a *real* on Indian Key, and the off-loading was successful. The salvagers were able to move the *Murguia* into deeper water and reload the cargo on board under the supervision of Don Antonio Navarro. This was completed by August 7, and new masts stepped so that she could be used carry survivors and treasure back to Havana.

The *Murguia* was one of the more fortunate vessels to survive the hurricane, returning to Cádiz in 1734.

(Reference: Diary of *El Infante*, *Contratación* 5102—1733 *Flota*.)

As a salvager I would like to share a few thoughts with you regarding the off-loading of the *Murguia*. The *Murguia* ended up in Indian Key Channel where the water is ten to fourteen feet deep, depending on the tide. The Spanish salvage charts place the *Murguia* a very short distance northeast of the *San Pedro*, "between two islands." The two islands would be Teatable Key and Indian Key. Because the *Murguia's real* was on Indian Key it stands to reason that the ship had found itself in the Indian Key Channel. The wind and waves of the hurricane caught the *Murguia* and drove it shoreward, clearing the outer reefs that line the Gulf Stream, and with high cresting waves carrying the vessel like a surfboard she had a good chance of not striking bottom until reaching the shoreward side of Hawk Channel where the bottom rises abruptly to eight or ten feet of depth. When the hurricane passed, I can visualize the predicament in which Captain Apodaca found himself. His ship was intact, although badly treated by the high winds and waves, and when his anchors finally grabbed bottom it had settled in a narrow channel surrounded by shallow water.

Because of the recent man-made bridges and islands that carry U.S. Highway #1 westward towards Key West, the channels today are more distinct, and probably deeper, than they were in 1733. Today the channel narrows down to seaward and gets pretty shallow for several hundred yards before it begins deepening towards Hawk Channel. I am sure that in order for Apodaca to lighten his ship enough to pass over the shallows he would have to remove a lot of cargo, and probably ballast stones as well. The *Murguia* was drafted at about 14 to 15 feet, and the shallows between the Indian Key Channel and Hawk Channel, even today, are between 8 and 10 feet.

The *Murguia* was a fairly large *nao* at over 520 tons, with at least 120 tons of that in ballast stone at the bottom of her hull. Considering the range of tide, at least five to six feet of draft had to be reduced to get *Murgia* into deeper water.

The cargo was taken off and stored on Indian Key. Some of the cannons may have been lost as the ship came into the shallows. At this point we have to assume that some ballast had to be removed. In 1974 Jack "Blackjack" Haskins, Jimmy Jones, and Henry Taylor, three local salvage divers, decided to scout the bottom of Indian Key Channel. About

200 yards from the point where the channel narrows down to seaward they found a considerable scatter of ballast stones. They were not mounded as in the case of a shipwreck, a possible indication that ballast was thrown overboard until the vessel's draft was low enough to clear the shallows. More ballast stones were discovered closer to Indian Key, where a smaller channel branches off to swing southeastward around the key. It was during this scouting trip that Jones spotted a bronze mortar near the edge of the channel. It had been lost the night of August 7, 1840, when two U.S. Navy medics poled their way across the shallow flats between Teatable and Indian Keys after hearing gunfire on Indian Key. As it turned out, the Seminole Indians were raiding Indian Key, killing sixteen people, including Dr. Henry Perrine. The Navy corpsmen tried firing the mortar, but never having fired one before they over-charged it with powder, and when the gun went off it promptly tumbled off their raft.

Nearer the center of the channel Haskins and crew discovered a three-foot swivel gun, and several hundred yards closer to the bridge, carrying U.S. #1 southward, they located a five-foot iron cannon. Both the swivel gun and iron cannon could possibly be from the *Murguia*. Another indication that a Spanish vessel had been there were the two intact olive jars they discovered in the sand of the channel bottom. They raised the bronze mortar and swivel gun, but the cannon is probably still lying on the bottom near the middle of Indian Key Channel.

In the winter of 1976-1977 John Gardner, Jr., was running charter boats from the Chesapeake House located on the north end of Islamorada. On one of his trips he located several iron cannon about a quarter-mile seaward of Indian Key, again possibly ones from the *Murguia* that may have been jettisoned. The cannon are also still there as far as I know, covered and uncovered by sand, as storms and tides change the bottom landscape off Indian Key.

[See the San Pedro Location Chart on page-175 for the position where the *Murguia* grounded and was re-floated.]

CHAPTER 18: *PODER DE DIOS*
El Gran Poder de Dios y Santa Ana
Alias: *"El Gran Poder de Dios"*

Not a great deal is known about the *Poder*, except that she held on an anchor through the hurricane and, although dismasted, she remained afloat. She did lose most of her cargo, but fortunately her crew was saved along with the 14,000 pesos in silver carried aboard.

El Gran Poder was a small vessel, in fact, at 181-3/4 tons she was the smallest vessel in the treasure fleet that left Cádiz with Rodrigo de Torres in 1732. Upon arriving in Vera Cruz, her Captain, Don Francisco Sanchez de Madrid, was able to trade his European cargo for not only the 14,000 pesos in silver, but also 139 *marcos* of worked silver, 261 *arrobas* of cochineal, 15 *arrobas* of *añil*, 12,000 pods of vanilla, 12 *arrobas* of sugar, as well as tobacco and a few boxes of gifts.

During the voyage up the Bahama Channel the *Poder* was positioned near the center of the *flota*, probably close by *Murgia* and *San Pedro*. After the hurricane passed she found herself on the sand flats that stretch from Hawk Channel shoreward. To the southeast lay the *El Lerri*, flooded up to her decks in eighteen feet of water. To the southwest the *San Francisco* had grounded in nine feet of water, rolling on her side so that her decks were flooded as well. Don Pedro de Iriarte and Don Manuel Gabriel de Céspedes were placed in charge of the off-loading of the *Gran Poder*. It is interesting to note that in the final list of recovered treasure from the *flota*, this entry is made:

"El Gran Poder de Dios debe por gasto de efectos," translated— *El Gran Poder de Dios* owes for cost of effects.(*Contratación* 5147)

In the diary of *Infante* is the first mention that the *Poder* had survived the hurricane and remained afloat:

"July 18—Also, we suppose from the said notice that the El Gran Poder de Dios managed to save itself on an anchor but was dismasted."

In the description of where each vessel was grounded:

"Notices of the sites where the ships of the Flota grounded, over a distance of 20 leagues from the Cabeza de los Martires to the Cabeza de las Vacas...Poder De Dios—Cayo de Viboras, [Long Key] less its cargo."

The Spanish salvagers' map actually locates *Poder* opposite today's Lower Matecumbe, but the important thing is that she remained afloat.

(*Contratación* 5102 - 1733 *Flota*) also mentions:

"The Gran Poder De Dios was saved like the before mentioned."

I assume the salvagers did not make a great deal out of the *Poder* being afloat, as in the case of *Murguia*, because of her size and the fact that she did not carry much in the way of treasure or cargo. She eventually did sail back to Spain, although on her first attempt she had to return to Havana when her seams opened up and she began taking on water.

(*Carta* of 21 ???, 1734, a letter from the King's Emissary Alonso de Herrera Barragan to Don Francisco de Varras y Valdes):

"On the 8th of the month the Fragata Incendio, accompanied by the Gran Poder de Dios, sailed for Cadiz from Havana, along with an Advise Boat from Cartagena. The Aviso and Gran Poder de Dios returned to Havana because they were taking on water. The Incendio continued to Cadiz."

Most of the previous historians who have written about the 1733 Spanish treasure fleet reported that the *El Gran Poder* had disintegrated against the reefs of Lower Matecumbe. Today, considerable translation of the *legajos* from the *Archivo General de Indias* has given us a better picture of the salvage efforts and recoveries. We now know that *Poder* did not leave her ballast pile somewhere off the Florida Keys, awaiting some lucky treasure salvager to locate and bring her back to life with tales of recovery. **[Contemporary Spanish charts indicate that the *Poder* was dismasted seaward of *El Lerri*.]**

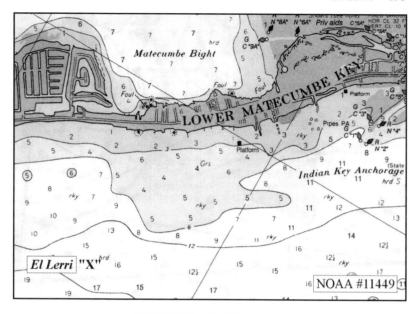

CHAPTER 19: *EL LERRI*
San Phelipe
Aliases: *"San Felipe"*; *"El Terri"*;
"El Tyrri"; *"Therry"*; and *"Navio of Terry"*

There seems to be a story surrounding each of the 1733 shipwrecks, some of them humorous, some of them rewarding, some mysterious. The *El Lerri* story is humorous, and it involves the modern salvage of the site. Years ago, when I was a Honeywell engineer in Greensboro, N.C. I met Ray Manieri. During the development of our friendship I put him through a SCUBA course in the YMCA pool, and then we became members in the "Scuba Slobs," a nefarious club of divers whose shining light in the underwater world was covering a rip-rap dam with a plastic sheath so that the water behind could be pumped out and the leak in the dam repaired. It was in the dead of winter, and we took turns sitting in a tub of water over a fire to thaw out. Those were in the "no-brainer" days.

When I was transferred to Miami, Florida and wrote raving revues of the warm, clear waters of the Keys, it wasn't long before Manieri managed to work his way to Ft. Lauderdale, and we were diving together again. This time it was on old Spanish galleons, the 1733 *Flota de*

Plata. I had formed the "Royal Fifth" group, and Ray was an integral part as divemaster. He fit the job perfectly. He was energetic, he bubbled, and had an Italian smile that put everyone at home in an easy chair. And...he had a nose for gold. Harry Lowe, of Lowe's Marina in Key Largo, one day painted a pair of sunglasses with gold paint and gave them to Ray, saying, "Now *everything* you see will be gold!"

We salvaged the *Sueco de Arizón* and found a pile of silver coins. It was the door that opened for Ray to form "American Power Spraying," with some financial backers that must have been swayed by his Italian smile. One of the sites he worked under a contract with the state of Florida was...the *El Lerri*. I believe Dick Barnes actually located the wreck site, and the *El Lerri* anchor sits against the front wall of what used to be his dive shop at the south end of Plantation Key, at Cobra Marine—mile marker 84. Barnes' group worked the pile to some extent—it was one of the largest of the 1733 fleet—and never really recovered much of interest. As usual, the pile was welded together with the iron fittings that had fallen across the ballast mound, making it a tedious and back-breaking task of taking the pile apart. There was still quite a bit of the mound that had not been gone over when Manieri's group worked on it during the summer of 1967. After two weeks they also gave up, although by that time most of the mound had been thoroughly gone over. They also came up with very little from the pile. The Spanish had salvaged the *El Lerri* as clean as a hound's tooth!

The *El Lerri* site lay about one mile offshore of Lower Matecumbe Key, and its scatter trail to the beach would have carried ashore close to what is today "Port Antigua." In 1967 there stood alongside U.S. Highway #1 a sign by Jerry Eagan, a real estate agent, that stated for the potential home buyers from the North, "Yankee don't go home!" That summer Ray and I were working Delta Shoals off Marathon out of my 16-foot Mohawk boat *Frogfoot*. We were staying with our wives at the Siesta Motel at the south end of the airport, parking my boat on its trailer behind the motel each night.

One morning, as we were putting our gear in the boat and hitching it up to my car, a man and his young twelve-year-old son who were also staying at the motel, approached us with, "Ginger, the owner of the motel, said you guys were treasure divers. I'm down here on vacation with my family, and I was wondering if there might be some place that we could just walk the beach...and maybe find something from an old shipwreck?"

Ray and I looked at each other and nodded, the treasure bug bites young and old alike. Ray offered, "I just finished working a wreck site not too far north of here. Tell you what you might do, drive to Lower Matecumbe Key and look for a real estate sign on the east side of US #1 that says "Yankee don't go home!" If you walk out in the water until it's about up to your knees, then look around, you might find something that washed ashore." The father and his son thanked us for the information, we hitched up *Frogfoot*, and our day began.

**"Scuba Slob" divers sitting in tubs of heated water,
thawing out our "brains!"**

It was a long day, the "Ivory Wreck" on Delta Shoal is scattered but produced some interesting artifacts. We pulled *Frogfoot* behind the Siesta Motel just as it was getting dark. We hadn't even had a chance to unhitch the trailer before the father and his son came rushing out of the motel, grabbed Ray, and began pumping his hand. It caught both of us by surprise. We did begin to understand his excitement as he tried telling us what had happened. "We went where you said, my wife, son and I walked out right where you told us, and sure enough...look what we found!" He then excitedly offered an encrusted Spanish dirk and several encrusted silver coins for us to see. One of them was a 1732 pillar dollar, a rare and valuable coin. "I've got to give you something for a really terrific day!"—and with that he forced a $50 bill into Ray's hand.

After he left, and as we cleaned up the boat, all we could do was shake our heads. Ray spoke up, "And after all the work I put into that wreck site, he walks out on the beach and finds more in a day than all of us did." The next day he and his wife, Gloria, spent the day walking that beach themselves!

El Lerri was one of the largest ships of the 1733 *flota* at 485-4/5 tons. She was English-built, but there is no record of the number of cannon on board. Her owner was the Marqués de Cañada, a name that would pop up again in 1765 as the owner of the "last galleon" of the Spanish treasure fleet, the *Santa Barbara*, which sank off the Bahamas on her way back to Spain. The captain of the *El Lerri* during the voyage of the 1733 *flota* was Don José del Villar y Andrade.

(*Contratación* 2021 - 1733 *Flota*):

"Armed ships which comprise the Flota for the present year 1732 which will make the voyage to New Spain under the command of the chief of Squadron Don Rodrigo de Torres y Morales: "San Phelipe"—of the Marques de Canada, its maestre Don Joseph del Villar y Andrade."

During the Vera Cruz *feria* the *El Lerri* took on a registered manifest of 34,000 silver pesos, 326 *marcos* of worked silver, 675 *arrobas* of cochineal, 57 *arrobas* of wild cochineal, 5,145 *arrobas* of *añil*, 6 boxes of chocolate, 51 barrels of molasses, 245 [Tajilla???] (orange or lemon relish), 21 earthen jars, and 8 boxes of gifts. Because of the ship's size I am sure that a considerable cargo of tobacco (a money crop in Cuba) was loaded on board when the fleet reached Havana. The *El Lerri* was stationed somewhere near the center of the convoy as it made its way towards the mouth of the Bahama Canal. At the point where the high winds and waves drove her onto the Florida Banks there were no major reef structures. When she reached the shallows close to Matecumbe

Nuevo (Lower Matecumbe) her hull opened up and she sank in eighteen feet of water.

(*Contratación* 5102 - 1733 *Flota*):

Letter of Jesus, Maria, and Joseph —Havana 20 August 1733: "All of the people were saved of the ship of Terri."

(*Indiferente* 57 - Diary of the *El Infante* 1733):

"July 19—Notice was received of the San Pedro being grounded and full of water, and the same fortune befell the Navio of Terry."

"Notices of the sites where the ships of the Flota grounded: Terri—Cayo de Viboras, its decks flooded."

(Letter by Alonso de Herrera Barragan, the King's Emissary dated 25 September 1733):

"Relation of the places on which are grounded the ships of the Flota under the command of Don Rodrigo de Torres: #13 Terri —Cayo de Viboras" [Long Key group includes Lower Matecumbe.]

When Ray Manieri's American Power Spraying group salvaged the *El Lerri*, her cannons wound up, for awhile, on Siesta Motel property. Where they are today, along the Galleon Alley, is anyone's guess. Several years later, when Jack "Blackjack" Haskins and Carl Fismer were checking out the shallow area close to shore they recovered several silver forks and spoons. The ballast mound is a large one, about 100 feet long, 40 feet across, and stands in some sections as much as five feet above bottom. The shoreward end of the ballast pile has pretty well been worked over by modern salvagers, but the offshore end has been hardly touched. There are several large brain corals growing on top of the ballast, and eel grass surrounds the area. But the wreck site itself sits in a sandy patch and is easy to locate. The Indiana University archeology group has spent a year or so on the site, doing a series of measurements and suppositions as to what the construction of the *El*

Lerri looked like when she sank so long ago.

There remains an aura of intrigue surrounding the *El Lerri*. Here is a rather large galleon that sank in what must have been considered deep enough water to cover her main deck. This meant that the huge waves very quickly moved her deck-stored cargo shoreward, soon followed by her passengers' baggage. It is quite possible that a small boat from the ship overturned in the surf at the shoreline, with some of the passengers' pocket change, a dirk, and even spoons and forks, being lost in the knee-deep water. But the fact that little was recovered from this large ship attests to the Spanish salvage efforts...or else it is still there in the unworked section lying seaward. There is a deep surrounding layer of sand and clay, covered with eel grass, that may hide the secret of the *El Lerri* treasure. The ship had registered 34,000 pesos in silver coins on board, and yet only 22,292 pesos, 1-1/2 *reales* were recovered. So we are missing 11,708 pesos in registered treasure. I am fairly sure that modern salvagers did not recover it, so there is a chance that it's still on site...somewhere.

PHOTO: Denis B. Trelewicz

The El Lerri *ballast mound, as of 13 May 1994.*
PHOTO: Denis B. Trelewicz

*(Above): Beach opposite Port Antigua, looking south along
U.S. Highway #1*

*(Below): Beach opposite Port Antigua, looking north along
U.S. Highway #1*

The **El Lerri** *anchor saluting travelers along the side of "Galleon Alley" in the Florida Keys.*
PHOTO: Jack "Blackjack" Haskins

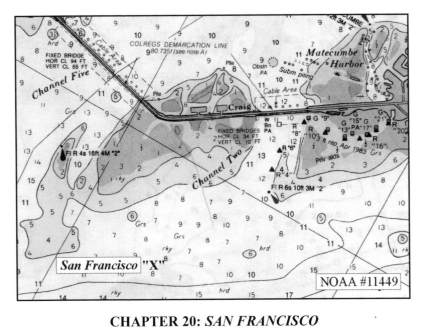

CHAPTER 20: *SAN FRANCISCO*
Nuestra Señora del Rosario, San Francisco Javier y San Antonio de Padua
Alias: *"San Francisco de Asis"*

By 1964 we had narrowed the undiscovered 1733 wreck sites down to *El Populo, San José, Las Angustias, "El Gallo"* (the *almiranta*), *San Fernando*, and the *Fragata Situada*, which we believed sank in deep water. Somewhere along the way the entire salvage community had tagged the large ballast pile that Tim Watkins and his *Buccaneer* crew had discovered near the seaward end of Channel #5 between Long Key and Craig Key as the *San Francisco*. It was in the right location according to the Spanish salvage charts, and most of us expected to find a large number of cannon on the site of the *almiranta*. There were several clues that, if we had the research, would have led us to the conclusion the Channel #5 site *was* the *almiranta*. Dr. Marshall Hall and I made a number of aerial surveys over the Long Key area in an effort to locate the "Admiral" of the fleet. We saw a large number of sharks, but no other ballast pile. Other salvage teams looked the area over on a regular basis, all coming up empty.

In 1965 my group Royal Fifth was salvaging the *Sueco*, located between Duck Key and Crawl Key. Our salvage boat the *Big Fisherman* was docked at Fiesta Key (Greyhound Key in 1966). With a normal run out Channel #5 past the *San Francisco* ballast pile, then southwest to the Duck Key area, it was a 35-minute boat ride, usually made early in the morning with the sun over our shoulders so we could see the reefs better. One morning we got a late start, and as we made our way up to the Channel #5 turn I noticed a group of boats fishing directly under the bridge. I had a choice of creeping through the channel, or having irate fishermen contend with our boat wake. Instead I steered toward the Channel #2 opening , and besides, we hadn't gone that way before.

As we crossed the shallow flats opposite Craig Key I could see a gray smudge in a sand patch ahead, and throttled back to have a look. The sun was just right or I may have missed it. Pat Patterson was with me, Brad Patten and Ray Manieri were resting on deck, and we all agreed it deserved a closer look. Without a current over the sand flats we dropped one of our stern anchors, put on face masks, fins and snorkels, and in minutes we were scouting the pile. The water was only nine feet deep, and the top of the ballast lay no more than five feet under the surface. It wasn't a large pile, about 65 feet long and 30 feet wide, but the metal fittings had welded the pile completely together. It had never been touched as far as we could tell. "Let's leave it for another day and a closer look." And with that decided we climbed back aboard *Big Fisherman*.

By the end of the second week in July we had completed the salvage work on the *Sueco*...and we found a *pile* of silver coins! It was time to take a closer look at our virgin ballast mound.

That first weekend we concentrated on what we thought was the stern section, facing seaward. As we removed the ballast we found large timbers and a few cannon balls, but no indication that it was a 1733 wreck site. In a conversation that evening with Mel Fisher I remarked that we had located a virgin ballast pile off Craig Key. He asked if we intended to work it the next day, and I said that we intended to if the weather held up. "I'll meet you at the dock." And he hung up. The next morning he was at Fiesta Key, and so was "Big Tony" Clausen, the state archeologist. "Show me your new ballast pile!" Tony was very pointed with the remark. It took us about twenty minutes to line up our bearings and drop anchor, and before long we were all picking our way over the ballast.

Mel and Tony decided to move ballast near the center of the pile, while the rest of us continued working near the stern. Tony recovered a silver spoon, and all the rest of us got were cannon balls. As we approached our dock at Fiesta Key that afternoon, Tony came up on the bridge and advised me, "You know that's a 1733 wreck site, don't you?" I replied that I didn't. "Well, Bob, you don't have a lease on it, so I want you to stay off. No more dives on the wreck, O.K.?" I nodded, no sense in upsetting the state of Florida. At the time it didn't seem like much of a loss after all the coins we had recovered on *Sueco*. He then picked up the cannon balls we had recovered and dumped them over the side before we reached the dock. "Without a lease it's illegal to remove anything from the site. I'll tag the spoon with your name, possibly you may get it in your division some day." (I never saw the spoon again.) So ended, for the time being, our exploration of the Craig Key wreck site.

Within a week we had things figured out. The large ballast pile that everyone had mistaken for the *San Francisco*, was really the "Almiranta." The pile we had discovered was the *San Francisco*. Two years later I was invited to attend a seminar on Miami Beach by Frank Allen, a highly regarded advocate of the salvage community. We sat in the front row, and on the stage were a number of state dignitaries, including "Big Tony" Clausen. The seminar, or lecture as it turned out to be, was on the state of Florida suggesting that they make a project, paid for by the people of Florida, of salvaging...the *San Francisco* off Craig Key. "Here is an undisturbed, intact 1733 wreck site. We can learn a great deal about Spanish shipbuilding if we go forward with this project." (She was English built!)

Some point early in the discussion Frank Allen was on his feet and shaking his fist at Clausen. "The state does not belong in the salvage business. You don't have the experience nor the technology. Bob Weller found the wreck and he should be given a lease to salvage it!" Up until that moment I had never considered a request to salvage the *San Francisco*; I was involved in the salvage of the *San José*. But I went along with Frank's contention that the state was ill-equipped to salvage anything. I did have to drag Frank out of the meeting room before he came to blows with Clausen. The 100 or more people in the room were a bit shaken up by the outburst, and so was Clausen. The project never got off the drawing board, and the *San Francisco* slept undisturbed for a few more years.

The *San Francisco* was not a large *nao* by contemporary standards, weighing in at 264-2/3 tons. She was English, built as a merchantman, and purchased by Don Christobal de Urquijo sometime before de Torres' *flota* left Cádiz in August 1732. It is unclear who the captain was, but Urquijo was sailing on his other vessel, *San Ignacio*, when the fleet cleared Havana Harbor July 13, 1733. The hurricane sank both his vessels; Urquijo did not survive.

In the diary of *El Infante* (*Indiferente General* 57 - Diary of *Infante* 1733):

"San Francisco: Cayo de Viboras [Long Key], its decks flooded."

"July 20th—We learned that the San Francisco of Urquijo was grounded along with Almiranta."

In a letter written by the King's Emissary Alonso de Herrera Barragan dated 25 September 1733:

"Relation of the places in which are grounded the ships of the Flota under the command of Don Rodrigo de Torres: San Francisco—Cayo de Vibora [Long Key]"

(*Contratación* 5102 - 1733 *Flota* : Jesus, Maria, and Joseph — Havana 20 August 1733):

"From the San Francisco of Urquijo, only the people were saved."

Although the supplies and cargo on board *San Francisco* could not be saved, salvage divers were able to retrieve 19,934 pesos in silver coins (*Contratación* 5147 *Razón y Cuenta*). Considering that only 20,000 pesos in registered treasure was on her manifest, the divers did exceedingly well. The 273 *arrobas* of cochineal, 282 *arrobas* of *añil*, and other general cargo were lost to seawater.

In the years following discovery of the *San Francisco* site, it was visited by a number divers of the salvage community. Richard MacAllaster located a pothole several hundred yards towards shore and recovered about 400 silver coins. Jack "Blackjack" Haskins recovered 500 silver coins and two gold rings while working with a metal detector, about thirty feet away from the ballast pile under two to three feet of sand. John Berrier, working with Jack, was excavating in the ballast mound, when a spotted moray was disturbed from his hole in the pile. He attacked John, biting him on the cheek and arm before disappearing on the other side of the pile. John persevered, recovering several *"recortados,"* or recut coins after the eel left.

I was on the pile during the 1990 period while writing *Famous Shipwrecks of the Florida Keys*. It was a day that I spent working through a bit of ballast near the center edge of the site. On board my salvage boat *Pandion* was Betty Smith, a registered nurse and daughter of a diving buddy, Bernie Smith. Don Kree, another diver, had a bit of food poisoning, and was flaked out on the bow of the boat. I had just recovered two six-pound cannon balls and had surfaced behind the boat. I put them on the diving platform, then headed back for the bottom. My wife Margaret, and Betty, heard me put something on the platform and walked back towards the stern to see what it was. The added weight in the stern of the boat did the trick.

The cannon balls promptly rolled off and dropped "like a cannon shot...literally." I was about five feet under the boat, heading for the bottom, when one of them hit me on the head. I can tell you it was a real "thud!" I knew what had happened, and picking up the two cannon balls as they hit bottom, I swam back to the surface and handed them to the two girls as they leaned over shouting something. I paddled back for the bottom. I had been on the bottom only a matter of minutes, when I noticed the green swirl around my head. Blood looks green underwater!

In the meantime, the two girls had been trying to shout to me that I was bleeding badly from a cut on my head. When I disappeared back towards the bottom, they feared for the worse. They thought I had passed out. They ran to the bow and woke up Don. "Bob's bleeding badly, and I think he passed out on the bottom!" Don, still half asleep, said, "I'll get him up; I'll shut off the air compressor!" About that time I was sitting up on the dive platform, trying to stop a bleeding head and not being very successful. Nurse Betty took over, and everything worked out just fine. It was the first time, and hopefully the last, that I was ever hit with a cannon ball.

The *San Francisco* has still never been completely salvaged. The ballast pile is still relatively untouched, and the surrounding area should contain potholes with silver coins. If I don't answer the phone, I'm probably out diving the *San Francisco*.

An excellent example of a ballast mound of 1733 wreckage is the **San Francisco** *site, shown at a distance (above) and close up (below.)* PHOTOS: Denis B. Trelewicz

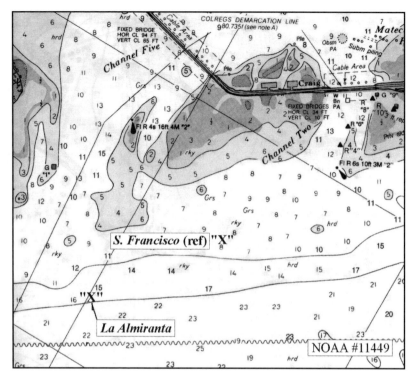

CHAPTER 21: *LA ALMIRANTA*
El Gallo Indiano
Alias: "Cock of the West Indies"

Two galleons carried the bulk of the king's treasure in the ill-fated 1733 *Flota de Plata* of Don Rodrigo de Torres y Morales, the *capitana* (*El Rubí*) and the *almiranta* (*El Gallo Indiano*). Of the total registered treasure carried by the entire 1733 *flota*, amounting to 12,286,253 pesos in silver coins alone, the *almiranta* carried in her hold 5,654,979 pesos. At 3,000 pesos to the box, that translates into 1,884 boxes of pieces-of-eight! As it turns out, there were actually 1,809 boxes of coins, and the remaining 225,000 pesos was contained in *talegas*, or sailcloth money bags.

(Letter dated 25 September 1733 from: Alonso Herrera Barragan, Emissary of the King):

"In this manner, transported without separation was the amount of 3,917+ boxes of silver and between them some bars of silver. 1,923 boxes came from the Capitana, 1,809 from the Almiranta, and 185 from the Infante."

(*Indiferente* 57 -Diary of *El Infante* 1733):

"August 4th—We received notice that all of the silver had been taken off the Almiranta and taken to shore."

The *almiranta* of the 1733 silver fleet was a 60-cannon warship that belonged to King Philip V of Spain. Normally the two primary war galleons, the *capitana* and the *almiranta*, belonged to the king and were designated as the primary vessels to first transport cinnabar, the red mercuric-sulfide used to refine silver ore, to the New World, and on the return voyage carry the bulk of treasure back to Old Spain. The one strong hold that the king held over the miners in the New World was the royal monopoly on the production of mercury. Not only did the king profit from the sale of the mercury, but it was his method of monitoring output of silver from the mines to prevent fraud. To carry the mercury overseas was nearly as important a task as bringing the silver home, so for this reason only the king's galleons were used. Often they were newer ships, or ships with lead-lined hulls to make sure that teredo worms never cut short the voyage. As Rodrigo de Torres put together his 1733 fleet, the king designated the *El Gallo Indiano* as the *almiranta*. In a *flota* such as this, General Rodrigo de Torres would ride in the *capitana*, and the Admiral of the Fleet would ride in the *almiranta*.

This was a fighting armada, and General de Torres was in charge of the entire convoy, so that he could direct the battle in the event of an approach of enemies. The galleons had a large contingent of soldiers, and their charge was the safe conduct of the fleet through enemy waters. The *capitana* rode at the head of the convoy, where the general could direct any battle that might present itself. The admiral, riding on the *almiranta*, was responsible for the safe navigation through the Spanish Sea and back to Old Spain. In many ways, as a result of this arrangement, the soldiers looked down upon the sailors as "hired hands," tending lines, scrubbing and holy-stoning decks, and working the sails and rigging at all hours of the day and night. They, in turn, had little to do except amuse themselves with deck games or fishing for sharks or other surface fish. However, when the hurricane struck, and everyone's life depended upon the manner and efficiency with which the sailors handled the sails and anchors, the soldiers' attitudes must have changed considerably.

There would be no *sin registrada* goods, or contraband, aboard the *capitana* and *almiranta*. Because they were the king's galleons, merchants had no share of cargo nor space aboard them. It was highly unlikely that an appointed official, such as General Rodrigo de Torres, nor the Admiral of the Fleet, would tempt fate by carrying unregistered silver and gold aboard their vessel. Therefore, when the records state that "all the treasure was removed from the Almiranta," modern-day salvors have to accept the fact that little or no treasure would be found in her ballast pile.

Upon leaving Havana Harbor the *Gallo Indiano* took up her position at the rear of the convoy. Her job would be to provide safe navigation for the armada, but also to keep any merchant *nao* stragglers from drifting outside the protection provided by the four major galleons, *El Rubí, El Africa, El Infante*, and *El Gallo Indiano*. In the poem *"Triaca Producida de un Veneno,"* written in prose by a survivor on board the *Angustias*, Don Jose Ignacio de Toca Velasco, he described the fleet of Don Rodrigo de Torres as it proceeded up the Bahama Channel:

"Strong in combat, soft in health, at the head a Rubí,
a rose of prominence. It had the beautiful vanity of
a bird...with feather, which lifted Spain, from Gallo
[proud rooster] its curly tail."

Because *El Gallo* was the rear guard of the fleet, it caught the brunt of the high hurricane winds. Its size probably kept the galleon from disintegrating, a fate that befell the *Ignacio* and the "Florida Fragata" sailing close by. It passed through the outer dragon's teeth close to Tennessee Reef, probably bouncing bottom before reaching Hawk Channel. Filling with water, she sank at the shoreward edge of the Channel in fourteen feet of depth. Just inshore, and no more than a mile away, the *San Francisco* lay submerged with her hold flooded.

(*Contratación* 5102 - 1733 *Flota*):

"The Almiranta grounded at a great distance from the Capitana, saving all its officers, passengers, soldiers, and sailors less a child of Ariscum of young age, one soldier, and two sailors."

"That the 2nd Deputy, Don Pedro de Cordova, shall assist in the Real of the Almiranta [Long Key], along with Don Alonso Balcarcel and Don Francisco de la Razabal for the expressed ends."

(Letter dated 19 August 1733 - *Escribano Real* de Don Rodrigo de Torres):

"The treasurers of the Capitana, Almiranta, and Patache are all busy salvaging and sending the goods to Havana. So far 1,100 boxes have been taken from the Capitana, 1,525 from the Almiranta, and 180 from the Patache [*El Infante.*]"

(Letter dated September 25, 1733 from the King's Emissary Alonso Herrera Barragan):

"25 boxes of worked silver recovered from the Almiranta, and placed in the Royal Castle of Strength. The Capitana contained 592 slabs of copper belonging to His Majesty, from which amount the divers salvaged 550, lacking 42. The Almiranta had 517, from which 438 were salvaged, lacking 79."

(AGI *Contratación* 5147 dated August 13, 1733 Havana):

"The disputant of the fleet Don Pedro de Cordova tells us about how they saved all the ships of the fleet [??], that immediately upon arrival had divers go down into the Almiranta, and that with success were able to recover 19,839 trunks [??] of silver, stamped, and 26 bars of Labrada and different bales of grain with very little damage. The rest is under water, was regretfully not recovered as of yet because of the location in the cargo bins. It is recognized that some of the bales of grain broke open and were lost also. All was not recovered because of the expense of the divers and the transportation to Havana was not worth the effort to those interested. Meanwhile seeing impossible to benefit from the mentioned and the main cargo recovered and in transit to Havana, to the Governor, where taking to storage 670 cannons in brief, will recover the rest and only two or three cannon were considered missing."

As modern day salvagers converged on the sunken galleons along the Florida Keys, one piece of the identification puzzle lay in the fact that *only* the *capitana* and the *almiranta* were carrying copper slabs back to Spain as cargo. The slabs were Cuban copper, and they would have been used for copper *maravedi* coins or ship's fittings. The copper was no longer needed for the making of bronze cannons. The English had perfected iron cannons in the mid 1600s that would allow firing many salvos without fear of the cannons overheating and blowing up. Iron cannon were less expensive to cast, and copper was at a premium.

In 1960 Tim Watkins, and his crew on the *Buccaneer*, located the *almiranta* at the seaward end of Channel #5 between Craig Key and Long Key. It was an extremely large ballast pile, but based on the salvagers' map of the positions of sunken 1733 vessels, the location of this pile of ballast more closely matched the position of the *San Francisco*. For the next six years the mound would be mistakenly called the *"Frisco,"* and hours were spent surveying the bottom to the south of Long Key in search for the *almiranta*. I spent a great deal of time in the air with Dr. Marshall Hall studying the mounds of sand and eel grass within the three square miles that we felt the *almiranta* had to be. At the time, if we had the copper slab information, it would have saved us looking in the wrong location. When Watkins and his crew salvaged the Channel #5 ballast pile, I can remember a photograph of Tim Watkins standing alongside a five-foot-high pile of copper slabs he and his crew had salvaged from that location. It would have convinced us that this large ballast mound was, indeed, the *almiranta*. I would have shifted my survey to the north where eventually I found the *San Francisco* in 1965.

Where the *El Gallo Indiano* lies at the edge of Hawk Channel, the water rushes past at each change in tide. Some days it is clear, other days not so clear. Watkins dismantled most of the mound and found a copper pot with the lid still intact, two double-headed claw hammers, several boarding axes with different logos stamped into their heads, two bronze mortars—one plain and the other with five Neptune heads around the rim, each with pestles—the top of a copper powder keg or storage box, several pewter plates, and many cannon balls. Over the years following Watkins' discovery, we all visited the site for nothing more than becoming acquainted with the new wreck site. Without metal detectors we would not realize until later that personal baggage had to have been swept seaward, as well as shoreward, by the strong current that swirls through the channel between Long Key and Craig Key. There was a large mound of coral that stood in the center of the ballast mound. It was too big to break up, too large to move, and we used it more as a reference point than anything else.

One day Art Hartman came to the site on his 85-foot salvage vessel *Dare*. In the channel the sand is not very deep, and with a strong current running, the *Dare* could not hold anchor. Art sent his engineer over the side with orders to "wrap the anchor line around something solid." The engineer spotted the large coral encrusted mound and wrapped the anchor chain around her several times. The *Dare* stayed in place most of the day, even though the current was running fairly strong. About 4:00 p.m., Art decided he would leave and asked his engineer to "go down and unwrap the anchor chain." His engineer spent several minutes on the bottom but finally surfaced with the anchor, both being dragged seaward as the tide caught the *Dare*. Once on board the engineer went up to the pilot house and said, "Art, I think you should know that when I unwrapped the anchor chain, the *Dare* had pulled that whole coral conglomerate over on her side. And you know, the bottom was covered with artifacts!" Hartman was tempted to turn the *Dare* around and go back for a look himself but said, "Another day." He never returned to the *El Gallo* ballast pile again.

In 1990 I last checked out the mound, found the overturned coral conglomerate, and sure enough you could see a number of large cannon balls encased in the coral bottom. They are still there as far as I know. The *almiranta* has never really been salvaged the way we would salvage a site today. The surrounding sands should be detected and, I am sure, will turn up much of the ship's dinnerware such as silver and pewter platters, knives, forks, spoons, and some of the Chinese porcelain that is still missing. And although most of the silver is accounted for, the *El Gallo* was carrying 196 *castellanos* in worked gold, and 3,200 pesos in gold coins. Only 838 pesos of *oro acuñado* (gold coins) were listed on the recovered cargo from the *almiranta*. It might still be there, covered by drifting sand and time. Follow your dream!

PHOTO: Denis B. Trelewicz

PHOTOS: Denis B. Trelewicz

These photos of the **Almiranta***'s ballast mound—another beautiful example—exhibit the expanse of such a pile, this view giving an indication of its length as the pile disappears at the extent of visibility.*

In the view below we get the feeling of the width of a major 1733 ballast mound, and...

PHOTO: Denis B. Trelewicz

PHOTO: Denis B. Trelewicz

*...the view above offers some perspective of the height of the **Almiranta**'s ballast mound. Below is a close-in view of the large, rounded river rocks which comprise the ballast pile of a typical Spanish galleon...and a welcome home for these banded butterfly fish.*

PHOTOS: Denis B. Trelewicz

PHOTO: Denis B. Trelewicz

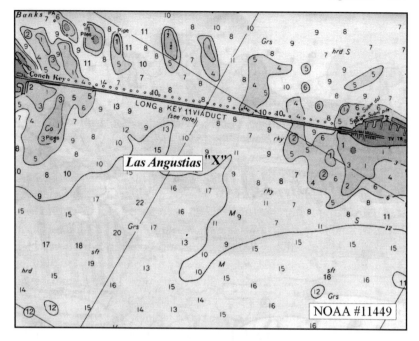

NOAA #11449

CHAPTER 22: *ANGUSTIAS*
Nuestra Señora De Las Angustias Y San Raphael
Alias: *"Sanchez Madrid"*
Alias: *"Charanguero Grande"* or **"Grand Coastal Trader"**

The story of *Angustias* really begins with the modern day salvage of the site. As I look back to 1972, the project began with a phone call. While working with Craig Hamilton on the 1733 fleet I had received a copy of a poem written in prose by José Ignacio de Toca Velasco and published in 1734. The title was, *"Triaca Producida de un Veneno,"* and it was part of the book, *Naufragios de la Flota Española*, published by Joachin Sanchez in Spain. As it turned out, the author was one of the survivors on board *Angustias*, and in his poem he described the *flota* of Rodriguez de Torres leaving Havana Harbor, the hurricane striking the fleet as it moved up the Bahama Canal, and a vivid description of the sinking of his ship. I had my secretary at Honeywell translate the poem. She was well qualified, having graduated from the University of Havana with a degree in History. The poem, when translated, was full of flowery prose and descriptions of ships by their nicknames, which was difficult to sort out. I filed it with the rest of my documents gathered on the 1733 fleet. The year before, I had moved to Riviera Beach, about sixty miles up the road from my former job with Honeywell in Miami. One afternoon I received a phone call. "This is Richard MacAllaster. We've never met, but I'm a salvage diver here in the Keys. Someone said that you had a copy of the "Treacle" translated. Is that right?" I answered that I did have it filed someplace. "Would you mind if I brought a friend up with me and had a look at it?" I said the invite was open, "just give me a chance to dig it out."

The next evening I had a knock on the door, and met Richard MacAllaster and Jack "Blackjack" Haskins for the first time. Haskins was a diver/translator, having been on several trips to the *Archivo de Indias* in Seville chasing down documents on shipwrecks. Mac was head of the Florida Keys division of the Department of Transportation which maintained the numerous bridges that leaped from key to key on their way to Key West. They both sat down with the "Treacle" and began reading, while I was busy in another room. I suddenly heard Jack Haskins say, "That's it!" I came back in the room as Jack looked up, "Bob, do you know what you've got here?" I shook my head. "You've got the *Angustias*!" That was the first indication of the reason for their visit. Jack apologized and explained, "You've been involved in salvaging the 1733 fleet, so I think you can understand all the confusion about ships' names and locations. Everyone thought the *Angustias* had been refloated because a vessel by the name "*Charanguero Grande*" passed over the bar at Cádiz in 1734. No one has ever looked for it down in the Keys. Let me read something for you." With that, he read a single passage:

"On those of a stoney reef she stumbled impelled, and almost hit a reef, and in her death throes our tormented ship was caught by that great iron ring, which in chain of strong flint was seriously shaken, until her side was dented with rage, and such fury that the valiant keel broke."

"Bob, when a galleon breaks her keel, she's not going anywhere. The *Angustias* is still there where she sank. If I can make one more trip to Spain, I think I can find her."

They thanked me for letting them see the *Treacle*, and I offered to send them a copy. What followed next was a plane trip by Haskins to

Seville, for a final search in the *legajos* to nail down the more exact location of where *Angustias* sank.

Nuestra Señora de las Angustias was built in England and was a typical *nao* at 328-1/2 tons cargo capacity. When she joined Rodrigo de Torres' fleet in Cádiz, her captain was Francisco Sanchez de Madrid, and her owner José Sanchez de Madrid (possibly the captain's father.) In Vera Cruz the *Angustias* was able to trade her Old World merchandise for a general cargo of indigo, cochineal, anil, and 27,000 pesos in silver coins. An additional 605 *marcos* of worked silver, and some of the Manila galleon K'ang Hsi came aboard. (Marx: Shipwrecks of the Western Hemisphere.) When the armada departed Havana, *Angustias* was stationed near the rear of the fleet and close to the *almiranta* and *Sueco*. She finally sank less than three miles from the grounded *Sueco*, and without any loss of life. Because the ship did sink in fairly shallow water, the Spanish were able to salvage her silver and cargo. Haskins had guessed this before he ever started the salvage operation.

Within two weeks he was back from Spain, sporting a big grin and the assurance that he could find *Angustias*. It was up to Mac to get the state lease for an exploration contract. A meeting with ex-Senator Robert Williams, the new director of the Division of Archives, History, and Records Management produced an exploration contract which allowed the team to look for the wreck site.

Haskins was no stranger to salvage work. He had been a corporate pilot who was involved in flying clients to Florida. Somewhere along the way he decided that hunting for sunken Spanish treasure was a better way to make a living, a decision he often has second thoughts about. (But he does enjoy it a lot more.) He made a decision to fly to the source of the Spanish documents on shipwrecks, the *Archivo de Indias* in Seville, Spain. Once there he discovered that all the *legajos* were written in an old Spanish script that was hard to decipher, "even assuming that you knew what you were looking for to begin with." Without anyone to help him with the English translation, he had the documents of the 1733 fleet microfilmed and headed back to the States. Eastman Kodak made xerographic copies of the documents, blown up to their original size, making it easier to translate. With a Spanish dictionary in hand he spent hours tediously translating, until soon he was able to read the documents like a newspaper. After four more trips to Seville he wound up with a file of 12,000 microfilms on various wrecks. When Richard MacAllaster asked if he had a "secret" wreck in his file that the two of them might look at, Jack responded, "How about the *Angustias*?" That's when they called me.

With the exploration lease signed, it was time to go magging. Haskins had a 36-foot Mathews that he used for the magnetometer survey. Jack and another diver, Jimmy Jones, left the Toll Gate Inn dockage on the *Trident* and headed south towards Long Key. The survey got off to a bad start that first day. As they rounded Teatable Key the boat's transmission filled with water, throwing oil and water all over the engine compartment. The boat slowed to a chugging halt, and Jack threw an anchor over the side. It took them about an hour to fix what was wrong and get the engine turning over again. They almost called it off; with a suspect engine it would have been understandable. The site was about fifteen miles away, a long way to paddle a 36-foot ex-charter boat. They decided to give it a try, and within an hour they were approaching the Long Key channel.

The Florida Keys separate the Atlantic Ocean from the Gulf of Mexico. Between each key a natural channel has been formed over the years, providing a free flow of water between the two bodies of water. On incoming—or outgoing—tides the water moves rapidly through these channels, sometimes at a rate of four to six knots. This was what the two divers found as they guided the *Trident* into Long Key Channel. Jack had pinpointed the most "potential" spot for the *Angustias* ballast pile: about a mile seaward of U.S. #1 passing over the Long Key viaduct on its way westward towards Duck Key, three miles away.

They marked the area with four buoys roughly half a mile apart, forming a square. They didn't know it then, but one of the buoys had been dropped within fifty yards of *Angustias*!

After streaming the magnetometer behind the boat on the end of the 100 feet of electronic cable, they began their first sweep near the shadow of the bridge. They began picking up "hits" on the "mag," but dismissed them as probable debris from building the bridge. Without knowing it, they had chosen to ignore the scatter pattern of their target. On the fourth pass, with Jimmy Jones standing on the bow of the *Trident* and surveying the bottom, Jack saw the magnetometer recorder do a sharp spike, indicating a large anomaly. He hollered for Jimmy to "throw a buoy on the hit." In the meantime Jimmy had spotted two big anchors, three cannons, and a ballast pile as they passed under the boat. "Which one of the hits do you want to mark, the anchors, cannon, or the ballast?" They had found the *Angustias* in less than five hours from leaving the dock at the Toll Gate Inn.

I received a call from Mac. "We found the *Angustias*. Because you helped us find it, how would you like to help us salvage her?" I jumped at the chance, but with the promise that I could write the story. To salvage the site Mac had established a salvage company under the name Peninsular Exploration and Salvage Corporation. Under the exploration lease, the state of Florida allowed the group to dig two test holes and an exploratory trench to determine if they did indeed have the *Angustias*. Anchors sometimes help to identify vessels, and there were four good size anchors lying near the seaward end of the ballast pile. They were Spanish, and about the right vintage, but the group needed more proof than that. Two cannon lay off to one side, and a third just seaward a few yards away. Again, they were Spanish and the right vintage, but not proof enough to spend many hours and days salvaging a site that may not be what they were looking for. There were many cannon wrecks in the Keys, few of them were treasure wrecks. They were looking for *Angustias*. It would take time and money to receive a salvage lease from the state of Florida. They wanted to make sure of what they had before they started that process.

The first test hole near the seaward end of the ballast pile produced very little to indicate they had a 1733 wreck site. The second test hole near the shoreward end of the pile uncovered a number of rosary beads and a few pottery shards. They carefully picked the spot to start the test trench across the ballast pile, their last hope to make a decision on. Halfway across the trench they had their answer. A gold two-*escudo* coin, about the size of a nickel, tumbled out of the edge of the trench. Although undated, it was unmistakably a 1724-27 gold coin from the Mexico City mint, and in excellent condition. They had their proof; all they needed now was the state to issue a salvage contract for them to get started.

The contract was issued in December 1972, and during the winter months the weather in the Keys would not cooperate. The wind blew, it rained, the water turned cold and murky, it was quite miserable. There was plenty of opportunity to plan the project. They needed a larger salvage boat, and they found the R.V. *Geo-Search*, a 60-foot research vessel owned by Don George, that had been used to work the sites of the

1553 Spanish galleons which sank off Padre Island, Texas. By the spring of 1973 the group was ready to start, and I made the trip south to Marathon. I can remember the current running pretty strong as we anchored up over the site. A 200-foot rope, with two rubber inner tubes tied to the end, was made fast to the stern. Mac gathered us around him and explained the need for the inner tube. "This current has to be dealt with every time you leave the bottom on a dive. Crawl over the bottom until you get near the dive platform, then jump for it. If you miss the platform, then grab the line or the inner tubes and haul yourself back to the boat." As an afterthought: "If you miss the inner tubes, let the current carry you out the channel, swim the mile to Long Key, walk over the bridge and jump off. The current will carry you back where you can take another shot at it." No one ever missed the inner tubes.

The ballast pile was 90 feet long and 35 feet wide, with an average of four feet in height, representing about 100 tons of smooth river rock that had to be moved by hand. Like the *Sueco*, much of the ballast rock was welded together by iron fittings and had to be sledge-hammered apart. On some stages of the incoming and outgoing tide the water became very murky, as well as laying the airlifts almost flat over. It was an uncomfortable feeling knowing that large sharks feed in the various channels. I can attest that on several occasions I saw what appeared to be a gray freight train passing by our work site. I kept telling myself there was indeed an underwater railroad in the channel somewhere. As we got started, a large barracuda began a silent vigil over our heads. In spite of the current he seemed to remain motionless. Magic, or imagination I guess, but as each diver headed for the boarding platform he followed him...right to the ladder. It helped the diver get out of the water a little faster.

I was working near the seaward end of the pile during that first weekend, and I heard this "rubbing" sound, like a boat rubbing up against a tire hanging from the side of a dock. I looked up, and side to side, but couldn't determine where the sound was coming from. Another diver, Jimmy Janda, saw me looking and swam over. When he pointed towards the anchors, I saw the reason for the unusual underwater noise. A large 400-pound jewfish was rubbing his back on the inside of one of the large anchor rings that stood upright from the bottom. The anchor was twelve feet long, and the anchor ring at the end was 3-1/2 feet in diameter. Later that day I swam over to take a look (after the fish had disappeared) and found the inside of the ring rubbed bare. He had been using this rubbing post for years apparently.

That first weekend produced a whole K'ang Hsi porcelain bowl, valuable and extremely rare to find intact, particularly under the ballast. In the weeks to follow we recovered a silver dinner bell, a jade Buddha, and quantities of silver-dipped rosary beads. One day we began uncovering pewter crosses about two inches high. And then it was an exuberant diver coming up the boarding ladder with a grin on his face...and a pewter jewelry box tucked under each arm. You can imagine the excitement that caused. In moments he had all of us crowding around the engine hatch cover as the lids were gingerly pried open. Inside...a string of rosary beads. It was a let-down, but still, the beads were historically significant. We felt like kids looking at a Christmas tree with out any presents underneath. Within the hour up came a silver locket with a glass front, encasing what may have been a painting. Jimmy Jones was working on a "pretty big cannon ball on one side of the ballast pile." When he couldn't dislodge it, he swam over the pile and motioned Mac to give him a hand. Mac took one look, then waved Jimmy over to the other side of the pile that he was working on. He had uncovered another seven-foot cannon, and what Jimmy had been trying to dislodge...was the cannon's cascabel!

Near the seaward end of the pile we began recovering some silver pieces-of-eight. Finally, we thought, we're getting into the treasure! But it soon petered out. George found a silver buckle and a pewter spoon with an ivory handle. The most excitement of the whole salvage project was about to happen. As the ballast was being removed near the seaward end, a box was uncovered! It measured 20 x 16 x 14 inches, and it was too heavy for a diver to pick up by himself. Silver coins were shipped in boxes, 3,000 pieces-of-eight to the box, and when we pried this one off the bottom it weighed in at 236.6 pounds. That was about the right weight. The state inspector, Larry Murphy, took charge of the coral concreted box and whisked it off to Tallahassee. I never found out what was in the box, but my guess is it did not contain silver coins, or we would have heard about it.

We were sitting on the deck rail about noon one day, having lunch, and a Greyhound bus had stopped in the middle of the bridge on U.S. #1. Suddenly we could hear the loudspeaker over the water less than a half mile away: "That's a treasure salvage boat anchored on your left, bringing up gold doubloons and silver pieces-of-eight from the remains of an old Spanish shipwreck." Even if the pronouncement wasn't true, we had hopes. It was a time when the salvage of sunken treasure was big news. It brought many tourists and would-be treasure hunters to Florida in hopes of finding their own El Dorado. It felt good to be part of the action.

As the ballast pile narrowed down we uncovered a three legged stone *metate*, the kind of breadboard that was used to roll out and mash corn, or flour, on board ship. The salvage had been a great experience, and I guess none of us wanted to wind it down. We found ourselves dawdling on the bottom, being more meticulous in fanning out each hole and crevice. We had time to watch the fish on the site, and by this time they had certainly gotten use to us. One diver made the mistake of opening a few scallops for a five-pound sheepshead that had been following him around. A scallop slipped down the ballast pile a few feet away, and the diver didn't see it. The fish began darting back and forth from the diver to the scallop. Finally the fish actually picked the scallop up in his mouth, swam over, and dropped it alongside the diver. After the scallop was opened and devoured, the fish was off looking for more scallops. Another diver had hair that was long enough to stream out in the current. One day a black angel fish must have thought it was something edible and, sneaking up behind the diver, the fish grabbed at the hair and made a run for it. That was as unnerving as the small damsel fish, all teeth, that would swim out of nowhere and nip at your knees or elbows. The big green moray eel gave us fits as well. He lived in the ballast pile, everywhere in the ballast pile, and we never knew under which ballast stone he would pop out. As we narrowed the pile down, he became more aggressive. The day he followed Mac up to the dive platform was his judgment day. Mac was back in the water in a few minutes with a spear gun, and the eel no longer presented a problem.

By the end of May we finished the pile. It had been a great wreck site, but it didn't have the treasure we had hoped for. It did provide us with a number of great artifacts, and the experience of working a virgin 1733 shipwreck. The last job was raising the cannon. While we were winching them aboard the *Geo-Search*, "Blackjack" Haskins was making a last tour of the bottom, searching out any holes that were missed. About thirty feet shoreward of the now flattened pile of ballast, he spotted a shallow sand hole no more than a couple of feet in diameter. Fanning the sand out of the hole he was greeted by the flash of gold! Cemented to the bottom of the hole was a perfectly round dated 1732 gold four-*escudo* coin. It was the most valuable artifact recovered from the site, and it later sold at auction in California for $17,500. What a way to end the salvage!

The wreck site is now abandoned to the fish characters who miss all of us, I am sure. We miss them as well, but we treasure the hours and days we spent on the *Angustias*. The friendship among the divers exists even today, the greatest treasure of any salvage project.

PHOTO: Denis B. Trelewicz

"Las angustias" means "the anguishes" (religious), but one can forget his grief in such an absorbing dive spot as the ballast mound of Las Angustias.
PHOTO: Denis B. Trelewicz

(Above) "Iron Mike," the 5-foot barracuda, keeps vigil over
Angustias.
(Below) A 6-foot green moray eel keeps divers alert.
PHOTOS: Mike Cassaday

(Above) Gold 4-Escudos dated 1732, recovered by Jack "Blackjack" Haskins on the Angustias. PHOTO: Haskins (Below) 3-foot anchor ring of Angustias frames a black angel fish. PHOTO: Jimmy Janda

(Left) One of the **Angustias** *cannons being raised by Jimmy Jones.*

(Below) Bob Weller (author) and Jack "Blackjack" Haskins take a break on the **Geo-Search** *during salvage of the* **Angustias.**

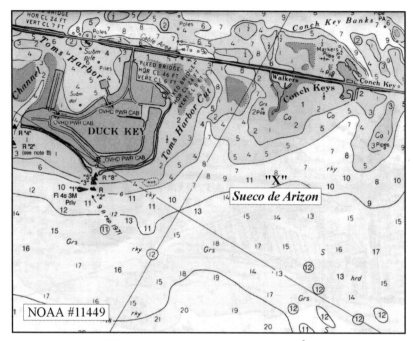

CHAPTER 23: *SUECO de ARIZÓN*
Nuestra Señora del Rosario, San Antonio y San Vincente Ferrer
Alias: *Sueco*

I have a personal interest in telling the story of the *Sueco*. Without a doubt it was my first big treasure recovery and, of course, it would be one of my favorites. As I look back to those emotional days in 1965 I remember the people involved much more than I do the treasure we recovered. If anyone were to ask, I would have to confess that those early years of salvaging the 1733 galleons were made most memorable by the salvage divers who worked the Florida Keys. None of us was highly professional. We put together the equipment we thought would do the best job, and there never seemed to be a need to find a financial backer because, for the most part, what we were doing was a hobby supported by a full-time job in the city. When I first began salvaging on the 1733 Spanish fleet in 1960 I bought a 16-foot Mohawk, a plywood boat with a 35-horsepower Johnson motor on the back. Cost was $850, a bargain at the time. It took me wherever I wanted to go, weather permitting, and I could trailer it to any point in the Keys I had a mind to.

The nearest point of land to the wreck I was working was where I would back it up to the water and slide it in. The one problem I had was that I suddenly had a number of friends, and getting them into a 16-foot boat, along with all their equipment, was like shoe-horning sardines into a can. By 1965 I was ready to step up to a bigger boat, and better equipment.

At the time I lived in Green Hills, a sub-division in South Miami. One day the real estate agent who sold me the house was following up on a standing water complaint we had about our patio. While there he noticed the sunken treasure artifacts I had in the spare bedroom, and as it turned out he had two friends that together invested in "hare-brained" projects that kept them out of their wives hair during the summers. He asked if I needed financial support for my favorite wreck project. I have to admit the first thing that came to mind was a bigger boat and newer equipment. Before long a group of people was gathered around my dining room table. My neighbor across the street, Pat Patterson, and I had quickly put together a prospectus aimed at working under the timbers of the *El Infante*. Craig Hamilton and I had recovered some great artifacts under the turn of the hull of the 1733 *capitana*, and I felt there might be some great things under the *Infante*. Together we called into the group two of our closest buddies, Ray Manieri and Brad Patten, and formed "Royal Fifth," named after the king of Spain's 20% tax on all precious metals shipped home from the New World. Across the table from us were the three business partners, Al Greenberg, the real estate agent, Norman Somberg, a lawyer, and Manuel Serkin, a businessman who owned the Army-Navy surplus stores in Miami.

I didn't know it then, but Somberg had come to the meeting to "shoot me down" on this treasure hunting project. The group had invested in a wild salvage scheme three years before, and the people they had invested in went south somewhere with the money. After a formal introduction and handshakes around the table, I looked at the three men across the table, and my first words were, "Why do you want to throw your money away on a treasure hunting project?" This caught the three of them by surprise, particularly Somberg. He said later, "It took the wind out of my sails! I had no choice but to listen, and the more I listened the more I wanted to get started." Al Greenberg spoke up, "We want to be a part of the diving operation. We want to get in your way, bring our families, take photos, and some day we can tell our grandchildren that we dug for treasure on an old Spanish galleon." Before the evening was over they became eager partners in the hunt.

They formed a corporation and called it ALMANO, after their first names. They asked me how much I thought I needed to work the *Infante* for a year, and Patterson and I had worked out a $6,000 budget. We got it. Within a week or so we found a fairly used (I use this term lightly) charter boat owned by a young man who had been running diving trips. She was called the *Big Fisherman*, 36 feet long, wide of beam, and with two (suspect) gasoline engines. The following week Patterson and I cast off from Dinner Key Marina in Miami and headed south, down Biscayne Bay in a fog. It was early morning, and we hoped the fog would burn off by the time we reached the Featherbed Bank, a narrow opening in the channel. It didn't, and suddenly we found ourselves grounded in a couple of feet of water. It took both of us getting out of the boat and pushing *Big Fisherman* off the bank before we could get back on track. The rest of the trip was uneventful as we passed through Caesar's Creek and finally out into open water. What a great feeling. Our first big boat, and up on the flying bridge you could see every reef and bed of eel grass for several hundred feet in all directions. We took turns steering, weaving around the coral heads that seemed to lie just below the surface. It seemed like we owned the whole ocean.

We had made the mistake of inviting our respective families to meet us at the Mandalay Boat Basin in Upper Key Largo. As we approached the channel leading in past the breakwater we could see our welcoming committee waving from the dock. We had a little old tin horn on board, and Pat began tooting on that while I maneuvered into the channel. About that time one of *Big Fisherman*'s engines decided to take a rest. We were already in the narrow channel with the wind threatening to ground us again, so I kept her on course with one engine the best I could. As I made the turn into the basin I discovered that with one engine, and the wind in the wrong direction, I was in trouble. I saw the dockmaster, the woman that owned the marina, pointing at the slip she wanted me to back into. That was a laugh. I tried backing her down four or five times, getting it pointed in the right direction, only to have the current or a gust of wind push it in the direction of the row of fancy-looking boats already tied up at the dock. Our welcoming committee seemed to evaporate when it was obvious I hadn't handled a bigger boat before. Finally, the little old lady that owned the marine threw Pat a line and hauled us backwards into the slip by herself. That was a most inauspicious way to start our first commercial venture. I often wondered whatever happened to that little tin horn, particularly after one of the welcome committee suggested a permanent place for it.

During the next three weekends we furiously outfitted the boat with tank racks, four air-lift systems working off some 40-cfm air-conditioning compressors I had purchased from Eastern Air Lines maintenance. We also bought a 7-1/2 horsepower Hale fire pump, rigged two-inch fire hose to it, plus a 6-inch suction dredge that Brad Patten would soon remember. We tried to build racks for everything, masks, fins, gloves, towels, spare gasoline cans and anything else that might have gotten in the way. We found ourselves running down the dock just to get a can of oil. The enthusiasm was building fast. It suddenly seemed as though the treasure would disappear if we didn't get out on the wreck site soon.

I can remember that first Sunday we felt we had to take a break. The investors, their wives, and their kids were visiting, and we decided to take *Big Fisherman* out on a trial run. With both engines running, I took her out behind Rodriguez Island, about a half-mile offshore, throttled back and dropped an anchor. I then let the boat drift into shallow water where the bottom was white sand. I remember sitting up on the flying bridge and watching everyone jumping off the stern, splashing around, just having a great time. I thought to myself, "It can't get any better than this."

A week later we were on our way to the *Infante*. It was just turning springtime, and the waters were flat calm, crystal clear, and we knew we were going to find treasure. In spite of all the luck I had previously on the *El Infante*, we were to find out what patience and perseverance have to do with treasure salvaging. We worked under the hull timbers... Nothing! We worked through the ballast pile and were rewarded with a sulfided four-*real* coin and a single gold link of a chain. We picked our way through the reef to the north of the ballast mound and found a few bronze spikes, remnants of H.M.S. *Fly*, which sank in front of Little Conch Reef. After a month of frustration we held a meeting at my house. The general consensus was that what we were looking for was not under the hull timbers of the *Infante*. We wanted to give our investors something for their money, but where to look was the big question. We decided to give a luau party for the investors and show them the appreciation we all felt for their giving us the chance to at least look for treasure. I made up book-ends, using teak and some preserved cannon balls I had recovered the year before from the *Infante*. A brass plate had each investors name and the "Infante 1733" on it. We polished some bronze spikes for each of them, as well as a ballast stones, each with a brass nameplate. I had silver replica tie tacks made from a full-dated 1731 one-*real* coin Pat Patterson had from the *San Pedro*. Finally, a friend of mine, Bob Page in New York City, sent me seven medallions depicting the Manila Galleons, and I put these on chains for each of our wives.

We held the party out on our patio, with a long luau table you had to sit cross-legged at, and the Hawaiian drinks certainly didn't hurt the camaraderie we felt around that table. When it came time for speeches I stood up and made some kind of comment about how grateful we all were for having this chance to follow our dream, and began to apologize for not finding any treasure as yet. Al Greenberg cut me off, "Bob, don't apologize. We're having a ball helping you out on the 'Infante.' The cake we already got. If we find treasure...that's the frosting on the cake. Just keep doing what you know best, the treasure will come." It was a great evening.

During the following week I decided to give Mel Fisher a call. I had met Mel not long after he moved to Florida in 1963, and by 1964 he was already famous with his gold recoveries on the 1715 fleet. He had said, "Bob, if you ever want to dive with me, just let me know." He had a group, Armada Research, in the Florida Keys, and they were finding a number of wreck sites with Fay Feild's magnetometer. I said I wanted to talk, and Mel answered, "Come on up to Vero Beach." The following evening I sprang for dinner at the Driftwood Inn on the ocean in Vero Beach. Fay Feild had joined us, and I explained that I had a good salvage group that knew what it was doing, a good boat, and the equipment to salvage anything they threw our way. After dinner Mel said, "Dick Williams is in charge of our group in Marathon. They've got about 28 wrecks that I know of, so I'll call and tell him to put you on one of them for a 50-50 split. O.K.?" I left Vero Beach that night feeling pretty good.

That week Dick Williams met with us at Christensen's Motel in Marathon. Bobby Jordan was his chief diver, and of course Bobby and I knew each other from a passing wave to each other as we worked various wreck sites over the previous six years. Dick was on an ego trip—with every right—based on the box of gold and silver coins he flashed as his share from the 1715 fleet recoveries. He referred to us as "weekenders," and I bristled. "If you give us a wreck site, and there's anything at all on it, we'll find it!" We followed his station wagon to Crawl Key, and there on the hood of his car he spread out a chart of the area. Pointing to a spot about 700 feet offshore, and then to the same spot on the chart, he said, "We've got a wreck buoyed out there with three red Clorox bottles. Water's about seven feet deep, and the ballast pile is about 80 feet long. We've worked part of it and found a piece-of-four. I'll show you exactly where it came up, but I don't think there's much else on her. We think it's the *Sueco de Arizón*, one of the 1733 Spanish plate fleet merchant *naos*. It's all yours! When you finish digging her, I'll give you another to work on." We came out of that meeting like a football team out of a huddle. The action was about to begin.

The *Sueco* had the usual proper Spanish name, *Nuestra Señora del Rosario, San Antonio y San Vincente Ferrer*," and it was an all day job for the quartermaster just to log in the ship's name. As a result the name *Sueco de Arizón*, (Swede of Arizón) was adopted after the ship's captain Juan José de Arizón, and its owner Jacinto de Arizón. We have to assume from this that the vessel was constructed in Sweden, but no official records indicating this have been located. The *Sueco* was part of the original *Flota de Plata* of de Torres that left Cádiz with Old World trade goods, arriving in Vera Cruz late in 1732. During the months that the fleet lay at anchor in Vera Cruz an epidemic of "black vomit" swept through the small town. Tragedy struck Captain Arizón who had members of his family aboard *Sueco*. Two of his children died as the disease spread (possibly cholera), and there seemed to be no cure at the time. During the *feria*, merchants on board *Sueco* were able to barter successfully for a variety of New World goods, as well as 24,000 pesos in silver coins. The Manila galleons had recently brought K'ang Hsi porcelain to Acapulco, and this arrived in Vera Cruz while the *flota* lay at anchor. Some of the porcelain, in boxes packed with straw and clay, found a place aboard the *Sueco*, as well as leather hides, dyestuff (cochineal and indigo), and when Arizón reached Havana there remained room in his hold for strings and sacks of tobacco.

Sueco's place in the fleet that left Havana Harbor that fateful morning July 13, 1733, was towards the rear, close to the heavily-armed *almiranta*, *El Gallo*, the last vessel in the convoy. When the hurricane passed between Cuba and the Florida Keys the strongest winds were on the north side.

Those vessels in the rear of the convoy were hit the hardest, particularly the *San Ignacio* sailing close to the *Sueco*. The *Ignacio* literally disintegrated as it was driven through the reefs at Coffins Patch, five nautical miles west of where the *Sueco* was driven ashore. *Sueco* was not a large vessel, although no official records of her tonnage have been located, which probably accounts for the fact that she was carried into fairly shallow water by the hurricane. After the hurricane passed, the *Sueco de Arizón* lay in close to the *Cayo de Vacas del este*. The depth of water around her was only nine feet, and her hull was intact, although she had lost her rudder and masts. There was no hope of refloating her. Fortunately no lives were lost, and the major part of her supplies and cargo were saved. (Letter dated 19 August 1733: *Escribano Real* of Don Rodrigo de Torres.)

We could see the three Clorox bottles bobbing on the surface about 1,000 feet due east of Walker's Island. Duck Key was to the west about the same distance, possibly a bit more. In 1966 Canaveral International had offices in the Indies House on Duck Key and was responsible for selling waterway lots on the island. At $4,000 a lot, the building boom hadn't hit the Lower Keys as yet. The president of Canaveral Int'l. offered us free dockage, if they could use our salvage project as a publicity approach, and we agreed. We ran our boat *Big Fisherman* down to Duck Key during the week, running a few circles around the Clorox bottles before we docked.

Anticipation in treasure salvage is half the fun. By the weekend we were on the site before the sun was up, swimming the ballast pile and running a tape over the length and breadth of this fairly intact site. It measured 60 feet in length and 20 feet across the middle. It rose about 3-1/2 feet at its highest point. What surprised us most was the fact that the entire pile seemed welded together. There were iron fittings over quite a bit of the pile, and what wasn't covered with iron, was welded together with a white coral concretion. It was obvious to us that no other salvage effort had been made previously on this wreck site.

We joked later that Dick Williams crew felt it was too much work to break the pile apart for salvaging. The coin they had recovered was off to one side of the main pile. We dug five random holes that first day, sledge-hammering the stones apart to reach the bottom. By the end of the day we were exhausted, but we did manage to recover several pieces of Chinese K'ang Hsi porcelain shards, and a few brown olive jar shards.

It was typical 1733 wrecksite material and, as far as we were concerned, it was an untouched wreck site. You could cut the enthusiasm with a knife.

The next day we drove a stake into the bottom at the eastern-most point of the ballast pile, then ran a line 80 feet to the north-northwest, where the pile disappeared into the eel grass.

With the line knotted at five-foot intervals we began our assault on the ballast stones, drawing the width and depth of the pile as we went. Before noon we found our first coin, a silver four *reales*, about seven feet from the eastern stake. Just north of the stake, a section of a blue wine jug with gold etching was uncovered. Quite a bit of brown pottery was in the area, and before the day was over we had three four-pound cannon balls. It was the following weekend that we fired up the sand dredge for the first time. It was a six-inch pipe with a 90-degree elbow at the end. The two-inch fire hose was attached to a venturi at the elbow end, so that water pumped from our Hale fire pump shot a stream of water up the pipe, creating a vacuum effect. We had welded handles on each side of the pipe for easier handling, but we forgot to add a cut-off valve. Brad Patten, the lightest diver in the group, offered to be the first to use it, so when everything was ready...I fired up the pump. The next thing I saw was Brad coming out of the water at the end of what looked like a bucking bronco. He disappeared in a burst of bubbles before I could get the pump shut down. I think I commented at the time, "I wonder where the hell Brad is going now!" When it was all over I had to admit that Brad rode the dredge like his life depended on it. We quickly installed a cut-off valve to control the force of water, and after that the dredge worked like a charm.

This was weekend work only. We all had jobs, but you can imagine the speculation and phone calls every day, and the eagerness to get back on site. By the fourth weekend we still hadn't found much in the way of artifacts. Every once in awhile another cannon ball could be heard bumping down the dredge pipe, but for the most part the wreck was fairly clean of artifacts. It did have a lot of broken olive jar shards, very typical of a Spanish wreck site. Then it was Sunday, July 1, a day we would always remember.

We arrived on location by 8:00 a.m., and by lunch break we had a chance to swim around the site. The ballast pile had been narrowed down to an area five feet by fifteen feet that we had yet to uncover. Pat

Patterson was on the binnacle list, he had broken a couple of ribs the week before when a big wave dropped him down on the ballast chest first. He had it taped up and was content to sit on the stern and tend our hoses. Brad had been working hard all morning and decided to take a break as well. Manieri and I were on the bottom, he was working the north side of the pile and I was on the south side. I had located a large piece of a K'ang Hsi porcelain cup welded to the bottom. At first I thought I had an intact artifact, but after several minutes of careful excavation it turned out to be just half a cup. Still a pretty good artifact. It was about 4:00 p.m., probably time to start heading for home. I swam over the pile to where Ray was working, tapped him on the shoulder and waved the porcelain in front of him. I gave him the signal that I was heading for the surface and he followed me up.

When we broke the surface he had a real gleam in his eye. "Bob, I've got five pieces-of-eight!" He pulled the coins out of the yellow rain jacket he had been wearing to keep warm on the bottom, handed them to me and said, "Tell the guys not to shut the pump off. It looks like there's more down there!" It was that time of the day when the divers on the boat felt we should be wrapping it up. Their signal was simple, they shut the compressor down. No air, no diving. I swam back to the stern of the *Big Fisherman* and leaned over the transom. "Don't shut off the compressor...we hit it!" Brad and Pat were sitting on the deck with their backs up against the cabin. Neither of them moved. I opened my hand, and the five coins dropped out on the deck. The response was a flash of energy I hadn't seen in some time. Both of them were on their feet to look at the coins, and I headed back for the bottom.

By the time I got there Ray already had a small pile of coins sitting next to him, and as he removed ballast stone you could see the edges of coins everywhere. I looked around and Brad was beside us, the only problem was he forgot his fins and face mask. I gathered up the loose coins and headed back to the boat for a bucket of some kind. Brad asked to use the hookah rig, and within minutes he was helping Ray dig into the ballast pile. I began carrying the mounting pile of coins to the boat a bucket full at a time. After three buckets full we began to lose our daylight. I looked at my watch and was surprised that it was 7:00 o'clock. Time flies when your having fun! Another concern was that I had drained gas from our main tank to keep the air compressor going, and we were low to begin with. Now I was sure a long-legged fly could walk around the bottom of our gas tank without drowning. We had to wrap it up. I swam over and got Ray and Brad up to the surface. They agreed, but wanted to cover over the area with ballast rocks in case someone should check the pile out. The edges of coins could still be seen everywhere under the remaining stones.

I had mentioned to our wives that if we ever "hit it" we would return to the dock with our dive flag upside down. Patterson now turned the flag upside down as we headed into the Duck Key channel. All of us were on the flying bridge, and as we rounded the last channel we could see our wives standing on the dock. I made a fist and held it up in the air, but no one caught on. As soon as we came alongside we jumped down on the dock, and I grabbed my wife, lifted her up, swung her around, and so no else on the dock could hear, whispered, "We hit it!" Down in the cabin she saw the three buckets filled with coins and she squealed. Pat Patterson had made a beeline for the phone at the end of the dock to call his wife, Joanne, with the news. Ray and his wife Gloria, were there as well, and I ran down to suggest we get hold of our investors and break the news over a champagne party at my house. It was a wild moment, standing there at the phone booth, when I looked up and saw the *Big Fisherman* drifting away from the dock. We had forgotten to tie her up!

It was a wild celebration that evening. The coins were counted a hundred times, spread out on the counter top by my pool. We then put them in envelopes and marked the number of coins in each, sealed the flaps, and initialed over the seals. The conglomerates containing coins were wired with tags and placed in a fresh bucket of water. I can remember a bar shot with 28 silver pieces-of-eight stuck to it. What an artifact! What a week that followed! The Fourth of July was that Thursday, a holiday for everyone. Each day everyone was on the phone, making plans and trying to guess how many coins were still out there on the bottom. Among the three buckets of coins we had recovered eight pillar dollars dated 1732, and these were extremely valuable coins. Plans were made to rent six rooms at Christensen's Motel, and bring the wives and kids with us as we finished the recovery. Ray Manieri brought his older son along that day as well. Wednesday evening we were all up late, kicking ideas around. We decided to tie off yellow ski rope around the area within ten feet of the pile and check the bottom over within that area very carefully so that nothing was missed.

When the sun finally came up we were already anchored on the site. And we actually did drive stakes into the bottom in a ten-foot square around the small pile of remaining ballast. With good intentions, we spaced ourselves around the outside of the yellow rope, and began a very slow and careful search of the bottom. That lasted...perhaps 30 seconds, and we dived into the ballast pile, pulling the rocks apart to get at the remaining coins. I can remember uncovering two pillar dollars stuck together, flat to the bottom. When I carefully pried them loose they turned over, and the date 1732 was like a shining star. We filled more buckets with coins, and the young sons of the investors would dive down, grasp a bucket, and swim it to the surface, where a lot of helping hands brought the bucket into the boat. By noon-time we had finished the remaining pile of ballast, recovered all the coins that were visible, including a total of four more pillar dollars; then we sat on the stern of our boat, satisfied and smiling.

It was the treasure at the moment that fired up our enthusiasm, but years later we still kept that same enthusiasm whenever we got together. We realized then, as we do today, that the friendship that bonded us together would last long after the treasure became nothing more than artifactual history.

PHOTO: Denis B. Trelewicz

The Sueco *ballast mound as of 31 August 1996.*
PHOTO: Denis B. Trelewicz

<< Bob Weller: "Hey, guys, I'm finding pieces-of-eight down there!"

Pat Patterson: "I think I've got a Spanish flintlock pistol!" >>

<< Ray Manieri: "It's pieces-of-eight for me, too!"

Brad Patten: "Help me on with my gear, or get the hell out of the way! It's my turn!!" >>

PIECES-OF-EIGHT, indeed! This large conglomerate (left) gave up many, many of the fabled Spanish silver coins (below)!

PHOTO: Pat Patterson

**The author, Bob "Frogfoot" Weller, on the deck of
the Big Fisherman *with the conglomerate of
Spanish silver coins and some bar-shot.*
PHOTO: Pat Patterson

THE *"SERIOUS"* SIDE OF SALVAGING *for the "Royal Fifth" group...*

"Frogfoot" bringing silver coins up. (He's serious!)

Ray Manieri checking out his gear (above) and Brad Patten performing maintenance on a pump (below.)

While Pat Patterson (above) "has the wheel"— and the duty of getting the boat to the dive site.

THE "ROYAL FIFTH" GROUP, Brad Patten (left front), "Frogfoot" (left rear), Pat Patterson, and Ray Manieri celebrating the recovery of hundreds of pieces-of-eight and twelve rare "pillar dollars" from the **Sueco de Arizón.**

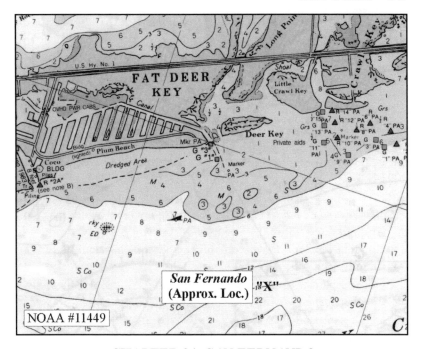

NOAA #11449

San Fernando
(Approx. Loc.) "X"

CHAPTER 24: *SAN FERNANDO*
Nuestra Señora de los Reyes y San Fernando
y San Francisco de Paula
Alias: *"Sanchez de Sevilla"* Alias: *"San Raphael"*

E veryone loves a mystery, and although *Galleon Alley* is not that kind of book, there still remains an enigma to unravel. That mystery is the location of the *San Fernando*! Of the 21 vessels that went through the 1733 hurricane, only one has not as yet been located and salvaged. There has been considerable speculation, even misnaming some recoveries and attributing them to being the *San Fernando*, but the fact remains that the ship has never been located nor salvaged as of this date. It is possible that the ballast pile has been "looked over," but has never been identified as a 1733 wreck site...at least officially, or within the salvage community.

The *Fernando* was built in Genoa, like a great number of Spanish galleons, and was a rather large vessel of 328 tons capacity. (Marx: *Shipwrecks of the Western Hemisphere*.)

Although Marx lists the *Nuestra Señora de los Reyes y San Fernando y San Francisco de Paula* under the command of Captain Jose Cabeza, and her owner as Francisco de Soto y Posada, she was referred to by the other fleet captains as the *Sanchez de Sevilla*, which usually is a reference to the ship's owner or captain. In the Spanish records at the salvage camp her owner was listed as Don Manuel Sanchez Duran. Obviously this is where the "*Sanchez de Sevilla*" nickname came from. There may have been a change in ownership during the fatal 1733 voyage to the New World. In *Indiferente General* 2021—1733, letter dated 4 August 1732—the list of vessels leaving Cádiz on August 2, 1732, with Don Rodrigo de Torres' *flota* includes *Nuestra Señora de los Reyes y San Francisco*, whose owner was Don Francisco de Soto y Posada, and its *maestre* Don Joseph Cabeza. It is possible that the "*San Fernando*" name was somehow omitted in the translations.

On all Spanish salvage charts of the wreck sites, #18 is always listed as *San Fernando*. And more importantly, the *Angustias* #16, *Sueco de Arizón* #17, and the *San Fernando* #18 are all grouped closely together on the salvage chart—within two miles of each other. I have salvaged on the *Angustias* and the *Sueco*, and they are, in fact, two miles apart. Plotting the *San Fernando* two miles to the southwest would place the wreck site in front of the northeast end of Grassy Key. The nearest 1733 wreck site to Grassy Key is the *San Ignacio*, which began its disintegration over four miles to the south and scattered westward. In the area directly seaward of Grassy Key is our mystery area, and a question yet to be answered: "How, and why, did we miss locating the *San Fernando*?"

At the *feria* in Vera Cruz the *San Fernando* is recorded as taking on board 16,000 pesos in silver coins, 226 *marcos* of worked silver, 853 *arrobas* of refined cochineal, 315 *arrobas* of wild cochineal, 1,011 *arrobas* of *añil*, 2,000 *arrobas* of vanilla, and five boxes of chocolate. Upon reaching Havana some tobacco and sugar were probably added to the cargo manifest. As the fleet sailed out of Havana towards the mouth of the Bahama Canal the *Fernando* was positioned near the rear of the convoy, close to the *almiranta*. During the hurricane she was driven through the outer reefs of Coffins Patch, somehow missing the shallow reefs that line Hawk Channel. Based on the fact that all the silver, supplies, and later the cannon, were salvaged usually means that the vessel sank close to shore. **"Flooded up to its poop deck"** usually indicates water no more than twenty feet deep, unless the vessel has rolled on her side. That would put her on the shoreward, shallow side of Hawk Channel.

(*Indiferente* 57 - Diary of *Infante* 1733):

"July 21—We went ashore. We took notice that the San Raphael [*Angustias*], the one of Arizon [*Sueco de Arizón*], and the one of Sanchez de Seville [*Fernando*], were all grounded and flooded."

"Notices of the sites where the ships of the Flota grounded: Sanchez de Sevilla—Cayo de Viboras [Long Key], flooded up to its poop deck."

(*Contratación* 5102 - 1733 *Flota*):

"The ship of Don Manuel Sanchez Duran [*San Fernando*] lost no people, none of the supplies were saved, and only one passenger named Don Mateo Ronquillo, a citizen of Sevilla, perished." [A later letter says they salvaged the supplies and cannon.]

As the salvage work began on the sunken *Flota de Plata*, General Don Rodrigo de Torres y Morales directed efforts to control the removal and storage of silver and cargo from the sunken ships. He was suddenly faced with the fact that more silver was being salvaged than was registered with the *Maestre de Plata*. This became a two-bladed sword. He was going to recover *all* the king's treasure, and as a result not lose favor in the royal court. But, on the other hand, it was suddenly evident to the royal officials that he had allowed a great deal of *sin registrada* (contraband) on board his fleet, contraband from which the king would have been cheated out of his 20% *avería* (tax). This became an embarrassment to him, even more so each day as the silver was salvaged.

(*Escribano Real* Don Rodrigo de Torres, dated August 19, 1733):

"That in the same manner Don Juan Valentin de Villaneuva

and Geronimo de Ariscum [whose two sons were lost when the *almiranta* sank] shall assist in the off-loading of the navios Nuestra Senora de los Reyes y San Fernando, the Rosario of Arizon, and the Angustias of Sanchez Madrid, to these ends likewise shall be made in particular the responsibility for scouting the beaches close to where the ship of Urquijo wrecked and to pick up whatsoever things the sea happens to bring in."

(*Contratación* 5147):

"Razon Y Cuenta. Del prorrateo de la plata, Y effectos, que se salvaron de los Navios de la Flota de Nueva Espana, del cargo del senor Theniente General Don Rodrigo de Torres y Morales, que naufragaron en los cayos de antes de Boca de Canal de Bahama, el 15 de Julio de 1733, en que se manifiesta el gravamen de los interesados en cada Navio a saber." Translated: Account and Information. Of the proportion of the silver, and goods, that were salvaged from the ships of the New Spain Fleet, in the charge of Lieutenant General Don Rodrigo de Torres y Morales, that shipwrecked in the Cayos before the mouth of the Canal of the Bahamas on July 15, 1733, and which is manifested for the tax [in salvaging] each vessel." (see Appendix)

From the *San Fernando* the salvage crews recovered 25,633 pesos, 5-1/2 *reales* in silver and were charged 17 pesos, 6 *reales* per 100 pesos recovered. The problem was that only 16,000 pesos in coins, and 226 *marcos* in worked silver (1,864 pesos) were on the registered manifest, a total of 17,864 pesos. *Sin registrada* accounted for the almost 7,000 pesos *over* the manifest that salvagers brought up!

One more interesting bit of information came from a map found in the *Biblioteca Nacional*—Madrid, *Sección Geográfica y Mapas*: On a map drawn by Miguel Hurdel de Montellon of places where the ships of the 1733 *Flota* were lost. At the bottom of the map, a note:

"La Fragata que iva para la Florida se sumergio al SE del No. 18 como 6 millas." Translated: "The *fragata* going to Florida sank southeast 6 miles from the #18 [*San Fernando*]."

The lone survivor of this vessel came ashore at Crawl Key where Andrade, the First Deputy, had set up a *real* for the survivors of the *Fernando, Sueco,* and *Angustias.*

As a final note on the *San Fernando,* it was a large vessel and, as such, would leave behind a fairly large ballast pile. It did *not* disintegrate when it came ashore, but stayed fairly intact. Only one person was lost, and the supplies, silver, and cannon were salvaged, something that would not have happened unless the ship stayed in one piece. The charge for salvaging was a bit higher than some of the other vessels, which meant that it may have sunk in a little deeper water, or may have rolled on her side, making salvaging a bit more difficult. Andrade made the *real* close to where the ship he was on (*San Fernando*) had come aground, which puts the vessel somewhere in front of Crawl or Grassy Key.

Davey Wolfner did locate some cannon in front of East Turtle Shoal, and they were raised and placed in front of his home and museum on Crawl Key. There is today a trail of ballast over East Turtle Shoal, but whether or not the trail belongs to the *Fernando* is unknown. Coffins Patch is a graveyard of shipwrecks. The *San Ignacio* did begin her

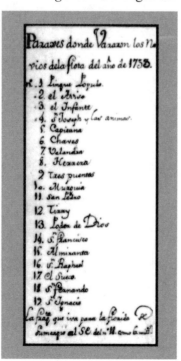

disintegration out by the remains of the old beacon, about two miles seaward of East Turtle Shoals, and her trail leads directly towards the Marathon High School just shoreward of East Sister Rock. The two trails are far enough apart that the recoveries from the *Ignacio* should not be confused with the *Fernando.* Artifacts from the *Fernando* will be located very close to her ballast pile, or just inshore, and the recoveries by the salvage community in Coffins Patch over the years do not fit this pattern.

So we have a mystery, one that hopefully will be solved by someone with the patience to endure the state of Florida requirements for a lease, and then to locate and salvage this last of the Spanish silver fleet of 1733.

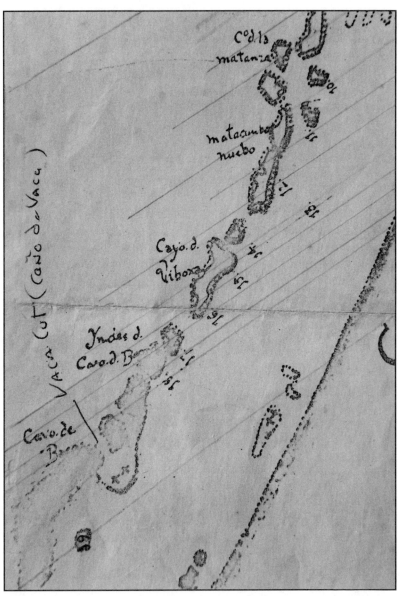

Note on this 1733 Spanish salvage chart the close proximity of the "Sn Fernando" #18, to the "Sueco de Arizon" #17 and the "Angustias" #16. They all lie in close relationship to Grassy Key and Duck Key. [Numbers are inverted on chart.]

CHAPTER 25: *SAN IGNACIO*
Alias: *"San Ygnacio"*
Alias: *"Sumey de San Ygnacio"*

When the hurricane struck the 1733 *Flota de Plata* only one vessel literally disintegrated with great loss of life. That vessel was the *San Ignacio*. The path of the hurricane took it between the Florida Keys and the western province of Cuba, and because the *Ignacio* was sailing near the rear of the fleet, it was caught in the strongest winds. It first struck the Florida reefs four miles off shore, directly seaward of *Cayo de Baca* (eastern end of Marathon and Grassy Key.) Here it grounded on a reef in eleven feet of water, and as the mountainous waves battered the helpless ship, the top decks separated at the gun deck and were sent dancing across the waves nearly seven miles, scattering cargo and cannon as far as the western end of *Cayo de Baca*. Of the 111 crewmen and 51 passengers and officials who were on board, only ten sailors and two servants survived, struggling ashore on what today is called East Sister Rock near the western end of Marathon. The captain of *Ignacio*, Don Christobal Urquijo, was one of those lost.

(*Contratación* 5147 - 1733 *Flota*):

> "The same was executed by the other ships except the San Ignacio, its Captain Don Christoval Urquijo, which had made different pieces on the reef and from which only 10 or 11 men were liberated. The Captain and some of the merchants from this ship were drowned."

After the winds subsided, salvage of de Torres' treasure fleet began, and for most of the ships the salvage was not a difficult task. Many of the ships had grounded in fairly shallow water and the salvage boats had only to come alongside and transfer the treasure.

Where the treasure was in the flooded hull, divers were brought in to dive it up. In the case of *Ignacio*, nothing was visible above water. Where the hull lay four miles offshore, it was probably never located by the Spanish. The top decks had separated and, as the huge waves carried it westward, it spilled treasure across the sandy bottom. The passengers' baggage, as well as that of the officials who were on board, were carried ashore by the waves and current. The treasure recovered at the time was

54,000 pesos of *plata doble*, which in all possibility was eighteen boxes of silver coins (at 3,000 pesos to the box), two boxes of worked silver, and baggage that had washed up on the beach. (*Indiferente General* 2300—1733 *Flota*.) The trail of treasure across the area that is now known as Coffins Patch has become one of the bonanzas of the modern salvager. But the real story of *San Ignacio* is the tale of the people involved, both in 1733 and today. The site has been a subject of lawsuits and controversy involving treasure salvage groups and the state of Florida. It also involves the story of a destitute mother and two daughters, and finally a tale of treasure found. The story continues even as this book is written.

When the *Ignacio* prepared to sail from Cádiz harbor in August 1732, Don Christobal de Urquijo was listed as its owner and *maestre*. Another vessel, the *San Francisco*, also listed its owner and master as Don Christobal de Urquijo. No other captain has been located in the documents for the *San Francisco*, however, on board the *San Ignacio* not only did Don Christobal Urquijo drown, but so did "The Captain Don Diego Raphael Benitez" and "the Maestre Don Mathias Canuto." It is quite possible that Urquijo was sailing on *Ignacio* as overseer of both his vessels. He was also involved in considerable *sin registrada*, possibly in conspiracy with the owner of the *San José*.

The *Ignacio* was English-built and had a cargo capacity of 292-4/5 tons. It is not known what armament she carried, but in all probability there were two decks of cannon, with the larger cannon being carried on the lower deck. The New Spain Fleet reached Vera Cruz six weeks after leaving Cádiz and remained anchored there for the winter. The *feria* was held in May 1733, and it was then that the silver and gold was loaded aboard the various vessels of de Torres' *flota*. As it turned out, more silver was loaded aboard the *Ignacio* than was listed on the official manifest. Only 12,000 pesos (four boxes) in silver coin was listed on the official manifest, and yet 54,000 pesos (eighteen boxes) were recovered. Of the 696 *marcos* of worked silver in six boxes, two boxes were recovered when it washed ashore on Cayo Baca. Also loaded on board at Vera Cruz were 272 *arrobas* (an *arroba* is about 25 pounds) of cochineal, 53 *arrobas* of vanilla, 35 boxes of chocolate (cocoa) and 265 leather hides.

As it turned out, Urquijo was carrying his total wealth back to Spain when his ship was sunk by the hurricane. His wife petitioned King

Philip V, via a letter from a lawyer, to recover some of the treasure.

The names Cayo Baca and Cayo Vaca were used interchangeably by the Spanish and were adopted by the English, as well as the United States (when Florida was admitted to the Union in 1845.) The name "Marathon" is attributed to the aftermath of a 1906 hurricane that disrupted construction of the Keys railroad that Henry Flagler built. One of the railroad workers made a statement, "This is a real marathon!" and the name stuck. (*Yesterday's Florida Keys*; Windhorn & Langley.) When the Spanish drew a map of the salvage area, Cayo Baca included Fat Deer Key, Crawl Key, and Grassy Key. It is quite possible that the Spanish set up a temporary *real* (salvage camp) on Crawl Key in 1733 in an attempt to salvage the passengers' baggage and cargo that lay strewn along the beaches. When the Boy Scout camp was built on Crawl Key, and the area cleared, a quantity of pottery shards, glass, and artifacts was recovered. This would indicate another possibility as well. The *San Fernando* is shown on the maps (several) as being grounded off the eastern end of Cayo Baca, probably at the edge of Hawk Channel, where Crawl Key is today. This would make a salvage camp more realistic at that location.

The wreck site of the *San Ignacio* was the most difficult of all the 1733 sites for the Spanish to salvage. It was the only vessel that disintegrated over the reefs for almost seven miles. The sand quickly covered the scatter pattern of treasure, shipboard gear and personal possessions. The remaining vessels, other than the *fragata* that sank in deep water, were relatively easy to salvage. As a result the salvage divers spent their time on those sites. The *San Ignacio* slipped into archival history, leaving behind a tantalizing trail of treasure.

"Afterward, the knight Commander (Torres) ordered the Florida Balandra repaired and a new mast stepped. In it he sent Joseph de San Vicente with orders to Havana. He then repeated this act with the launch of the Navio of Don Reimundo de Soto in which he embarked an Official of Orders. They encountered a Balandra off Cayo Hueso which had been dispatched from Havana to scout the coasts, and they related information to them. Then said launch returned to the Real transporting the men freed from the ship of Urquijo." (San Ignacio) Dated 19 August 1733.

In 1965 Armada Research, a Mel Fisher salvage company working the shipwrecks in the Florida Keys out of Marathon, located the first signs of cannon, anchors, and ballast piles in the Coffins Patch area. One rather large ballast pile, covered with a twelve-foot cannon and at least fourteen nine-footers, was located several hundred yards from the remains of an old beacon, destroyed years before by storms. Only a vestige of her frame remained above the sandy bottom marking the edge of the deep blue Gulf Stream. Using a proton magnetometer, the Armada Research salvage vessel began marking "hits" around the pile, dropping green buoys to mark each spot. When Dick Williams and Bobby Jordan ran out of green buoys, they dropped red buoys. One morning, as the salvage boat approached the site, Dick Williams exclaimed, "With all the red and green floating balls, this site looks like a Christmas tree. Since that moment this area has been known as "The Christmas Tree Wreck."

Although it appeared to be an interesting site, it was one of 28 sites that Armada Research had located. Some of the others had seemingly more potential, and as a result very little salvage effort was expended on the Christmas Tree site. I visited the location in 1965 while actively salvaging the *Sueco* near Duck Key. I was thoroughly impressed with the huge ballast pile that rose almost six feet above the bottom, and the fairly large nine-foot cannons that lay atop the ballast. I recovered a number of bar-shot and cannon balls that day, some that still find a place on my artifact shelves. But not much of interest was recovered by Fisher's group. By 1971 Fisher moved his *Atocha* operation from Marathon to Key West, and the various sites were literally abandoned. In 1973 another salvager, Art Hartman, obtained a lease on the area under his company name Doubloon Salvage. While magging the area in the immediate vicinity of the old beacon he got a good anomaly. Using a blower over his prop wash he uncovered a 410-pound wooden box and a Spanish rapier. It was what salvagers dream of, the right weight to be a box full of 3,000 silver coins or bars. The state of Florida took possession, and while they pondered its contents, Hartman's investors, including the wife of the CEO of General Motors, waited impatiently to learn how "rich" they were. When the state finally pried into a corner of the box, under the glaring lights of publicity, only iron "sail needles" were discovered. The box of "treasure" may have been a disappointment, but it triggered a serious salvage effort that began to uncover a trail of treasure and artifacts.

Jack Richards, in the early 1960s, had located three cannons and a small galleon anchor about two hundred yards south of the old beacon, which seemed to be the beginning of the trail.

In the late 1960s salvor Jack Steffney, on the *Johnnie C*, began recovering Spanish coins beyond the ballast pile towards Marathon. Over a period of a month 625 coins came up off the bottom, as well as a cutlass and an encrusted musket he recovered under the 13-foot, 6-inch galleon anchor. That seemed to start a stampede of divers to the area. Chuck Mitchell, working with Steffney, discovered an area of artifacts that included pillar dollars dated 1732, pieces-of-eight, an onyx sand-shaker, five pewter plates, and a pair of miniature pewter cannons weighing two pounds each. Ray Manieri, heading up a group, American Power Spraying, was working down the trail of artifacts when they took a lunch break. Only Manieri remained on the bottom. When he finally surfaced and climbed aboard the salvage boat, the other divers were sitting with their backs against the cabin taking a cigarette break. Ray leisurely had his lunch, and when he was finished turned to the group with a smile, "Are you ready to go down and pick up the silver?" They smiled back, a frustrated smile that belied the several weeks of fruitless effort at finding absolutely nothing on the bottom. He pulled off his glove and dumped a dozen sulfided silver pieces-of-eight on the deck. The reaction was instantaneous. Divers scrambled for gear, splashed over the side without fins or face masks, and playfully argued who would use the SCUBA gear to help Manieri recover the coins. The hole Manieri had located produced over 1,000 coins that day. Before they completed the salvage season on Coffins Patch they recovered other artifacts, but the 1,000 coin hole was their best find. The trail of artifacts and coins seemed unending, stretching westward along a bearing of 270 degrees, towards Key Colony Beach.

The Shugar brothers followed a trail of ballast from the old beacon, recovering several "frying pans" and other artifacts as they worked their way towards a reef that rose to within eleven feet of the surface in Coffins Patch. From the hump, the ballast trailed directly towards West Turtle Shoal (a light beacon on the edge of Hawk Channel). On top of West Turtle Shoal were more scatterings of ballast, and then the trail disappeared into Hawk Channel in the direction of the Marathon High School on land several miles distant. Salvor Art Hartman located two cannon in eight to twelve feet of water on the shoreward edge of Hawk Channel in front of the High School. About 200 yards away he also located a ballast pile, recovering four ivory tusks, some African copper-ring coinage, and several slave bracelets. This is close to Boot Key, and very near East Sister Rock where the *Ignacio* survivors came ashore. This wreck site was most probably a "slaver", certainly not the *Ignacio*. There would be no ballast stone on the top decks of *Ignacio*, so all indications are that several "contaminate" wrecks are in this particular area. Artifacts can be intermingled, and care should be used to not confuse these with the 1733 recoveries.

Soon there developed a controversy over the "rights" to work the wreck site. Late in 1989 Stefan Sykora and Richard MacAllaster went before a district court in West Palm Beach to settle salvage rights. They were told by the judge that they could both work the site as long as they kept at least 100 yards between salvage vessels. Both salvors were able to recover a considerable amount of treasure. Mac and Whitey Keevan recovered over 100 pillar dollars dated 1732, hundreds of silver cob coins, a silver bar, and buckets of artifacts. Stefan also recovered many pillar dollars—dated 1732 and 1733—and thousands of silver coins himself. The site was a literal mine of silver.

Then, in the early part of 1990 the "first gold" was recovered. Bobby Jordan was back on the Patch with his large salvage vessel *Castillion*. He had formed American Salvage Co., and together with Paul Moranville, and their wives, they began a systematic search towards Key Colony Beach. In April they hit a bonanza when they recovered a gold jewelry box 2-1/2 x 3-1/2 inches and weighing nearly three ounces. Before they could catch their breath they uncovered eight gold rosaries, two gold rings, a silver ring, a silver bell, silver buckles, and other artifacts. It renewed an even greater interest in other salvors to "try their luck" on the Patch. Soon Geoff Zitver, working out of a small 21-foot outboard boat, came across two rare gold four-*escudo* coins dated 1732. An auction house recently sold one of them for over $30,000!

The recovery work here came to a sudden halt when Kane Fisher brought his salvage vessel *Dauntless* onto the Patch and began dusting the sand with his blowers. A state agent took photographs of the holes made in the bottom, and although the holes disappeared in a matter of days, the photograph didn't. The Marine Sanctuary officials indicated that the reefs and eel grass were being destroyed by the movement of sand, filing a lawsuit against Fisher's company. That lawsuit is in the process of being heard at this time, and the results could affect the entire salvage community.

There remains a mystery to many within the salvage community surrounding the wrecks on Coffins Patch. The question that most often comes up is, "What ship is it that is giving up treasure? Is it the *San Ignacio*, or the *San Fernando*?" I've tried to answer this question based on the facts from translations of documents of the *Archivo General de Indias* in Seville—(Thanks to Jack "Blackjack" Haskins!)—but final decisions have to be made by the salvor.

The *San Ignacio* came apart in several pieces. When the ship first struck the reefs near the old beacon foundation, the hull, second level gun deck and ballast may have remained a few hundred yards from the old beacon. I feel sure this is the *San Ignacio* because of the preponderance of pillar dollars recovered there, and only the 1733 fleet carried these 1732 milled coins. The *San Ignacio* was the only vessel to disintegrate in the manner that the trail of treasure to the southwest suggests. Material recovered over the years along this trail, including dated silver coins and a silver bar, are from a 1733 treasure ship. Both Richard MacAllaster and Art Hartman have located cannon close to shore, in the general direction the trail has taken. This may, or may not, be indicative that only the top gun deck separated from the hull out where the old beacon was. If the "Christmas Tree" wreck is part of the *San Ignacio*, this would explain the pile of *large* cannon on the ballast pile, while the smaller cannon on the top deck were carried nearer shore as the top decks began to come apart. Much of the personal possessions, including jewelry, would have been located in the top decks.

During my Salvage Season 2000 several interesting aspects of the "Christmas Tree" wreck became clear. Along the scatter pattern leading towards Key Colony Beach were recovered many iron axe heads, boxes of iron nails, and building material. These items would not have been *en route* back to Old Spain, which gives this particular wreck a new flavor. It would seem more probable that this is the "Fragata" that was going to St. Augustine. What about the "pillar dollars" that have been recovered in the scatter pattern? Possibly they were part of the soldiers' payroll, transferred from the primary 1733 fleet in Havana. If this is the case, then where is the *San Ignacio*?

The Spanish chart shows the symbol of #19, *San Ignacio*, close to

East Washerwoman Shoal. Within 1-1/2 mile is East Sister Rock where the survivors came ashore. Yet salvors have magged the area relentlessly and have yet to come up with any trace of a ballast pile in this area. Richard MacAllaster reported to me years ago that he located a few cannon near the shoal, but nothing else. Stefan Sykora is a salvor who has recovered many pillar dollars along the scatter pattern, and he is still in the hunt for the *San Ignacio* ballast pile. It would have a fortune in treasure when found, and it has to be somewhere near the west end of Marathon.

Why wouldn't the "Christmas Tree" site be the wreck of the *San Fernando*? I personally don't think so, because only one person lost his life on the *Fernando*, and this site is four miles offshore and scattered. Each salvor would have to make his own decision after reading the chapter on the *Fernando*, but one thing remains clear: Coffins Patch is living up to its reputation as a treasure salvor's dream come true!

*Gold 4-**Escudo** coin recovered by
Geoff Zitver.*

San Ignacio *anchor, located at Key Colony Beach.*

(Above) Silver plate recovered from the Ignacio
scatter trail on Coffins Patch.
(Below) Bronze mortar and pestle recovered from the
Ignacio *scatter trail on Coffins Patch.*

PHOTOS: Seascribe

(Above) Cannon of the **San Ignacio.**

(Below) **Spanish dagger recovered from the San Ignacio** *scatter trail.*

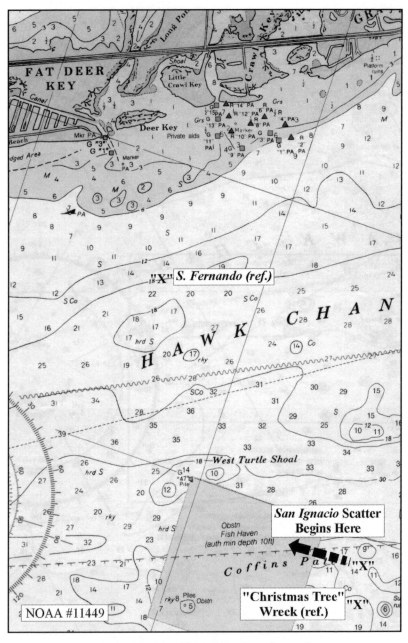

LOCATION CHART: *San Ignacio.*
[Position of "Christmas Tree" Wreck shown as ref.]

CHAPTER 26: *LA BALANDRITA*
Alias: "Balandra That Was Going To Florida"

A *balandra* (Sp. for "by-lander") was generally a fairly small, single-masted sloop and no more than 30 to 45 feet long. A *balandra* of 50 tons was a large vessel of its type. Often they were used as island hoppers, fishing boats, and in diving for sponges. In the early days of the Spanish treasure fleets they were a means of moving small quantities of supplies along the coasts (by-land-er), as they were fast and could move through shallow inlets without grounding because their draft was a matter of inches. So the danger of the "moving" sandbar in the entrance to the harbor at St. Augustine was a reason for selecting a *balandra* to carry flour to the garrison of soldiers located at the fort.

In July 1733, a *balandra* (name unknown) was loaded with 256 barrels of flour and joined Rodrigo de Torres' *Flota de Plata* as it traveled up the Bahama Canal on the way back to Cádiz, Spain. It was to be a five-day journey for *"La Balandrita,"* a nickname the crews of the *flota* had for this little single-masted supply vessel. It was one of two vessels that would accompany the main convoy northward. The other was a *fragata* that was also going to St. Augustine with supplies—and possibly a payroll.

(*Indiferente General* 1987-1733 *Flota.*) In a letter written by Don Francisco de Vara y Valdez to His Excellency Señor Don Joseph Patano:

"They left the expressed Port of La Havana. The Flota was comprised of 19 ships; 5 of his Majesty's named El Rubi, El Gallo, El Infante, El Africa, and El Pinque Populo; 13 Merchant ships, and the Advice ship of the Council."

He did not include the two tag-along ships as being part of Rodrigo's *flota.* As Rodrigo de Torres was assembling his fleet outside the harbor at Havana he stated in his diary, (*Indiferente General* 57 - De Torres' Diary 1733):

"July 13—I crossed over to pick up my boat. I then stowed it within, and by now I saw the 19 ships of my Flota, and the Balandra and one Fragata which were destined for Florida."

The two vessels destined for Florida were apparently not assigned to a particular position within the convoy, because during one of his maneuvers Rodrigo de Torres mentions that the *fragata* came abreast of his *capitana*. When the hurricane struck, the *balandrita* was driven across the shallows shoreward of Hawk Channel, finally holding on an anchor between today's Windley Key and Islamorada. Although she lost her single mast, she remained afloat and lost none of her people on board. Another important aspect of her remaining afloat was that the cargo of 256 barrels of flour remained intact. This became a critical source of food supply for the survivors until rescuers arrived from Havana. Rodrigo very quickly ordered a new mast stepped—and any other repairs required—and then sent her to Havana carrying letters and reports regarding the salvage efforts.

(*Indiferente General* 57- Diary of the *El Infante* 1733):

"July 18—We received notice from the ship of Murgia that it had grounded without taking on water, minus its main mast and some top masts, and that nearby was a Balandra which left in convoy with us from Havana bound for San Agustin loaded with flour. This Balandra was afloat but without mast."

"In Notices of the sites of the grounded ships of the Flota of Rodrigo de Torres: Balandrita—Matecumbe El Grande, remaining afloat."

Alonso de Herrera Barragan, the King's Emissary, wrote a letter that gave the "Places in which are grounded the ships of the Flota under the command of Don Rodrigo de Torres:

#7. Balandra that was going to Florida—Cayo of Old Matecumbe and those before it. They placed the Real [camp] on this Cayo for the bad situation of the horse flies on Tavona"

And finally, the *escribano* at the *real* of Rodrigo de Torres wrote:

"The Balandra sailed in convoy with said Flota. It was dismasted and badly worn, finding shelter between two keys. All of its people were saved, along with 256 barrels of flour which aided in keeping the shipwreck survivors alive. Afterward, the Knight Commander [de Torres] ordered the Florida Balandra repaired and a new mast stepped. In it he sent Don Joseph de San Vicente with orders to La Havana."

In the early years today's salvage community searched for the *balandrita* in the shallows, first near Indian Key, and then later directly off shore of the north end of Islamorada where de Torres had built his *real*. At the time, the historical documentation either was not available or had not been translated. The *balandrita* made it safely back to Havana; it lived to sail another day!

[For the approximate position of the grounding of the *balandrita* see the Location Chart for the *Chavez*, page-133.]

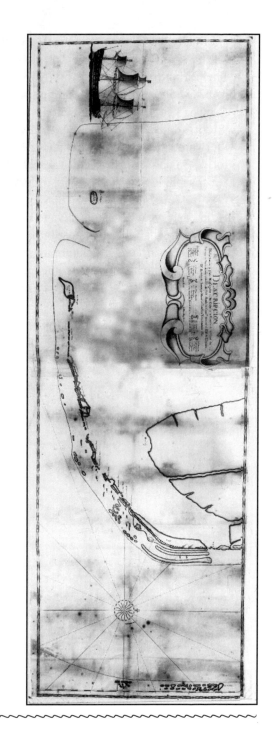

TWO HALVES OF A CONTEMPORARY SPANISH SALVAGE CHART SPLICED TOGETHER list and locate the twenty ships of the Treasure Fleet of 1733 (compare with chart on page 16 for reference.) The "fragata situada" is located, in the legend, with the words "la fragata de la florida esta sumerjida cosa de 6 millas al S.E. del No. 18." — "The Florida frigate is submerged some six miles to the southeast of number 18 [San Fernando]." The Dry Tortugas are shown "east" of the ship and the Marquesas Keys to the right of that, below the legend. The Florida Keys arc upward toward the mainland, and the group of dots at the right are the Bahama Islands.

CHAPTER 27: *FRAGATA SITUADA*
Alias: *"La Floridana"*
Alias: *"Fragata de la Florida"*

Here is a typical case of the "wrong place at the wrong time." The *"Fragata Situada"* (supply/payroll ship) was scheduled to run up the coast of Florida to deliver supplies to St. Augustine. Because the treasure fleet of Don Rodrigo de Torres was in Havana Harbor and scheduled to leave for Cádiz, the captain of the *fragata* (frigate) made the decision to sail along and keep the *flota* company, either for protection or a desire for company during the five-day trip. In any event, had the *fragata* sailed two days earlier, or a few days later, she would have missed the hurricane altogether. Not much is known about this vessel, except that as a frigate it would in all probability be armed with a few cannon. What supplies she was carrying is anyone's guess, but probably sugar, tobacco, citrus products, building material, and food supplies for the military garrison at Fort San Mateo. As a *situada* (payroll vessel) she may have been carrying an amount of cash on board for disbursement to the troops at Fort San Mateo. A good guess would be that the *fragata* was about 140 tons, carrying six to ten cannon and a decent pile of ballast in her hold.

She came up alongside the *capitana* on July 14, which would put her near the head of the fleet the day before the hurricane struck. Yet the reports have the *fragata* "dashed in the surf near Cayo Vaca." In this case, the surf is probably the outer reefs off Grassy Key, based on other reports.

(*Contratación* 5147—1733 *Flota*). In a letter written by the King's Emissary Alonso de Herrera Barragan to Señor Don Francisco de Varas y Valdes—President of Consulado of Cádiz:

"Likewise the sea swallowed a Fragata which was going to Agustin [St. Augustine]."

And under a report:

"Relation of the places on which are grounded the ships of the Flota under the command of Rodrigo de Torres—El Floridano, it was swallowed by the sea according to notice from the one who escaped from it."

(*Indiferente* 57—De Torres Diary—1733):

"July 14—At 6 P.M. the west point of the key of Vaca [Marathon] bore NNW. I tacked with the bow to the ESE and at this time the Florida Fragata arrived off me."

Either the frigate did not leave Havana Harbor at the same time as the convoy, or else she was about to head off by herself towards St. Augustine. The *capitana* was at the head of the fleet, and de Torres' ships would be required to keep position within the security of the four armed *navios* guarding the fleet.

(*Indiferente* 57 —Diary of *El Infante*):

"July 20—We learned that the San Francisco of Urquijo was grounded along with the Almiranta, and that the Fragata going to Florida was in pieces and that only one man escaped from it."

In "Notices of the sites where the ships of the Flota grounded," over a distance of 20 leagues from the Cabeza de los Martires to the Cabeza de las Vacas:

"Fragata de la Florida—submerged, one man escaped to Cayo de Vaca on a spar."

In another report from Matecumbe Grande:

"Escribano Real Don Rodrigo de Torres—19 August 1733— The Fragata Situada going to Florida opened up in the sea and only one man escaped who arrived in the Real of Sanchez Duran on a plank to give this notice."

Sanchez Duran was the owner of the *San Fernando*, and on board his vessel he had Don Juan Feliz de Andrade who was the First Deputy of the *flota*. They had set up a *real* on Crawl Key near where the *San Fernando* was submerged. In a map drawn by Miguel Hurdel de Montellon, it shows the places where the ships of the Spanish silver fleet of 1733 were lost.

On map #M-196 (*Sección Geográfico y Mapas, Biblioteca Nacional*—Madrid) at the bottom of the map he lists the ships' names and locations, and he states:

> "*La Fragata que iva para La Florida esta sumergida cosa de 6 millas al SE del No. 18.*" Translated: "The *fragata* that was going to Florida sank about two leagues [six miles +] southeast of Number 18 [*San Fernando*]."

The Spanish notoriously over-estimated distances, but six miles would certainly put the *fragata* on the reefs at the edge of the Gulf Stream in what is known today as Coffins Patch

About three miles off shore of Crawl Key is East Turtle Shoal. A flashing beacon stands just inshore of the reef today, and across the reef is a trail of ballast stones. Just inshore of the reef is a ballast mound. There is a possibility that this is the *fragata situada*. Cannon were recovered from the site by Dave Wolfner in the 1960s when he lived on Crawl Key adjacent to Grassy Key. The report that she sank six miles from the *San Fernando* is an estimate by the survivor and is not cast in bronze. Hanging on to a spar in fifteen-foot waves does not give the survivor a great opportunity to judge distances. East Turtle Shoal has wreckage of some sort, and in any case the *fragata* might provide a salvage crew with hopes of gold doubloons and pieces-of-eight.

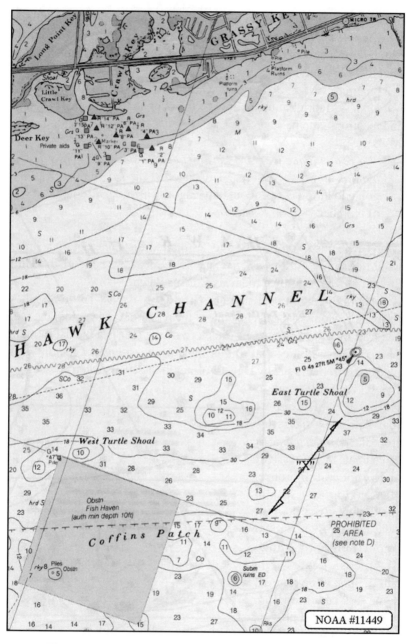

NOAA #11449

**The yet-to-be-salvaged "Fragata Situada" may lie
somewhere between East Turtle Shoal and Coffins Patch!**

EPILOGUE

The Hunt For the *San Fernando*

One of the final chapters of this book is about the ***San Fernando***, possibly one of the last unrecovered galleons from the 1733 Spanish treasure fleet. After finishing the chapter, I had that strange feeling come over me that I am sure many other salvors have had over the years: "Why not finish this book on a positive note by finding the galleon?" Blackjack Haskins made the same statement in a conversation not long after. "Why not find the *San Fernando*!"

I had a good idea where the shipwreck *should* be, but it's a big ocean, and Coffins Patch is a junk yard of shipwrecks and their scatter patterns. Yet it was too good an opportunity to pass up. I applied to the Florida Keys National Marine Sanctuary for a search permit to locate the *San Fernando* and was granted the permit in November 1999.

I had put together a great team of salvors, as well as a 37-foot Striker search boat full of electronics, with the 1708 ***San José*** off Colombia as our objective. The *San José* is the richest unrecovered treasure, both land or sea, in the world. The English commodore, Wager, sank the "*José*" off the coast near Cartagena and, because of the depth of water, no salvage effort was ever carried out by the Spanish. So on the bottom today lies a fortune estimated at between $5 billion and $7 billion, primarily in gold coins, as well as silver coins, bars, 64 bronze cannon, and the personal wealth of over 600 passengers. After seven years of research I have a good idea where it sank. I was joined by John Harkins, Doug Gossage, Bill Brom, Joe Kimbell and Brad Johnson in forming a team that has every potential of locating the galleon. Only new legislation by the Colombian government, yet unsigned, kept this team in training exercises off the coast near Jupiter, Florida during most of the 1999 dive season. In December we made a decision to use our boat and electronic equipment to "go after" the *San Fernando*.

December 1999 found the waters off Grassy Key and Duck Key murky, cold, and full of lobster pots. The surface was dotted with lobster buoys as far as the eye could see. I had applied for a search lease 2.5 miles by five miles, and I was sure that somewhere within that pattern was the sunken galleon *San Fernando*. Joe Kimbell laid out a grid pattern on our navigational software, turned on the autopilot, and we started out. Very quickly we went into a manual mode, as the lobster pots and their umbilical cords with a fancy buoy on the end seemed to create a maze that our autopilot couldn't cope with. At least twice a day we had to stop while Brad Johnson went over the side to cut loose a buoy line that had wrapped around our prop. Trying to spot every buoy in four-foot waves with the sun in your eyes was a real challenge.

For two weeks we ran parallel runs north to south, then south to north, spacing each run 100 feet from the next. At a slow speed of three knots, that took the better part of an hour for each run. We managed to complete twelve runs each day but had only five days of good weather where the runs we logged made any sense. We had recorded a number of anomalies, some moderately significant, while others were potentially "hits" on the underwater telephone cable that lies along Hawk Channel. It had been a long week, and we were on the last pass of the day, with the probability that this was our last day on site. Everyone had settled down to a routine that is best described as boring. As I watched the indicator on the magnetometer, I had on my mind running the Striker boat back up the Intracoastal Waterway to West Palm Beach. It was a long two day trip that I wasn't looking forward to. The sudden swing of the indicator caught me by surprise! "Bingo!!!" The indicator "pegged" full scale, then as we passed over whatever was on the bottom, it pegged full scale in the other direction.

That caught everyone's attention, and suddenly all eyes were fixed on the monitor. Joe put the boat into a slow turn and headed back over the "hit". As we passed over it the second time the indicator seemed to "peg" even further, and faster. "Doug, let's put the side scan sonar over the side and take a better look at the target." With a "Good idea!" Doug and Bill began assembling the side-scan fish and fired up the IBM computer/monitor. We dropped buoys on four sides of the target and, when everything was ready, we put the side-scan fish in the water and headed for the first buoy. The monitor can see the bottom clearly, even though visibility was the color of coffee. As we passed by the target we got an image of something that was about 30 feet long and rose above the bottom several feet. It had good potential of being what we were looking for.

It was getting dark, our weather had gone south somewhere, and we were ready to close up shop. We couldn't check out the "hit" due to zero visibility, it would have to wait until our next visit to the Keys. It did leave us wondering "what was that last hit?" Like a bunch of boys waiting for Christmas to come, we headed our separate ways, Joe back to Tavernier, Brad headed back to Washington, D.C., Doug and Bill to Illinois, and John to Alabama.

It was in February, after everyone had recovered from the effects of celebrating the new millennium, that the team was back on site. The water was clearer, if not a notch warmer, and the first order of business was to check out our previous "hit." It was with some anticipation that I watched Harkins, Johnson, Brom and Gossage head for the bottom on the end of their hookah hoses. Soon a head popped up—I believe it was Johnson's—"It's a large coil of cable with a big metal plate on top." That let the wind out of my sails. As the team climbed back aboard the boat I listened to them describe what had to be disappointment to them. "The fish were stacked over the cable. There were hundreds of them!" "Whoever decided to leave all that cable on the bottom wasn't doing anyone any favors!" "We can cross that anomaly off the record!" It was back to the magnetometer routine, and we still had a lot of work ahead of us.

The weather in February in the Florida Keys isn't considered "tourist friendly." The wind seemed to beat constantly out of the east. The rains swept across the open ocean like isolated tumbleweeds. In spite of the weather we were able to spend five rough days covering the better part of two square miles of our leased area. There were hits, and many of them in the area we consider "primary," but visually checking them out would have to wait until calmer seas prevailed. We did make an attempt. We launched our 12-foot rubber boat with the 50-horsepower engine on the stern, asked for "volunteers," and watched as John Harkins and Bill Brom wobbled around the West Turtle Shoal area. Very quickly we got the "come and get us" signal, and that ended the possibility of sighting any of our magnetometer hits.

As the summer months approached, I put together "Salvage Season 2000," and enlisted the investors necessary to make it happen. I had asked Stefan Sykora if he would be the captain of our salvage boat *Treasure Quest*, and he accepted. He had recovered a number of 1732 and 1733 pillar dollars from the Coffins Patch area and was well qualified for salvage work on any of the Spanish shipwrecks. By 6 May I had both boats, *Treasure Quest* and *Expedition* located in the Florida Keys. The salvage boat *Treasure Quest* was docked behind

Cobra Marina on Windley Key. It was a straight run out to the site of the 1733 *Capitana El Rubí* located about 2/3 mile from the Davis Reef marker buoy that sits on the edge of the Gulf Stream. The Striker search boat *Expedition* was docked behind Bernie Smith's house on Lower Matecumbe Key at Port Antigua. I had hopes of using it to continue the search for the *San Fernando* when the *San José* team got back together.

Our first bit of bad luck happened when both engines on *Treasure Quest* had to be replaced. They had been completely overhauled before leaving the dock in Lantana, and yet within thirty minutes of arriving in the Florida Keys, both engines threw rods through their blocks! The month of May was spent in the bilges of the salvage boat putting everything back in working order, and by 1 June we were ready to begin operations. The weather cooperated, and the seas became flat calm, with underwater visibility ranging from 100 to 200 feet.

The site of the *Capitana El Rubí* lies in twenty feet of water, with a flat white sand bottom and sprinkled with beds of sea grass. When I first worked this wreck site in 1960, the ballast pile rose five feet above the bottom, and Art McKee had stacked several ribs of the wreck back in place so they rose some eight feet above the pile. Even parts of the wooden hull lay exposed. And back in 1960-1961 we recovered some great artifacts from this site. Today the ballast pile has sunk at least seven feet or more below the surface, and little of the wooden hull can be located. I decided not to work close to the ballast pile but chose to work the scatter pattern to the northwest. It would be here that the baggage scattered, and it was here that Jack "Blackjack" Haskins recovered what must be considered the finest artifact from the entire 1733 fleet. It was a solid gold religious medallion with several clear gemstones. There is a lot of bottom to cover, so our method was simple. Stefan had what is known as a "deep scan" metal detector which can "see" a coin the size of a quarter under two feet of sand. Larger objects are found much deeper. We anchored *Treasure Quest* and fired up our Brownie's Third Lung hookah rig with 100 feet of hose on each unit. With this much freedom we were able to cover the bottom for subsurface hits, and mark them with buoys.

I watched Sykora as he decided to uncover one of the hits. He positioned himself about six feet ahead of the hit, braced his hands and arms against the bottom, arched his back and did what later became known as the "Sykora crab knee shuffle." His legs first did a butterfly, then suddenly his knees seemed to become disjointed as they waggled back and forth in all directions. Finally the shuffle came to an end as he lay on each side and finned the sand from the sides of the hole. I have to admit it worked. He soon had a hole at least three feet deep and five to six feet long. It was enough to uncover whatever object the metal detector had spotted. That first object was a flint lock pistol! We moved the salvage boat over to the location, went into a three-point anchorage, and dropped both blowers. Following the DGPS we systematically dusted the bottom to a depth of six feet, each hole having a width of 24 feet. By moving the boat's stern no more than twelve feet on each move, we covered the area very well and in the process uncovered several fire bricks and pottery shards.

As the month progressed we did recover several interesting artifacts. There was a complete bronze powder flask top, including the rotating trap door that allowed the powder to be measured out. One day it was a section of green glass that seemed appropriate for the captain's cabin, glass with air bubbles dating back to the eighteenth century captured in the manufacturing process. Amy Wickliff, on her first dive, recovered a silver piece-of-eight dated 17?? It was her "first coin," and she was allowed to keep it, sending her home to California on Cloud 9. There were also large sections of "Ali Baba" jars, large amphoras used to contain water for the long journey back to Spain. It was like Christmas every day, not knowing what you were going to find, or where.

Individual's schedules kept the *San José* team from coming together until the first week in August. Brad Johnson, Bill Brom, and Doug Gossage arrived about the time hurricane "Alberto" was doing its whirling dervish act out in the Atlantic. The honeymoon with the weatherman seemed to come to an abrupt ending as a constant wind out of the northeast raised white caps on the four-foot waves. The underwater visibility went south somewhere; August weather has always been "iffy." We decided we would brave all the bad weather and at least dive some the hits we had gotten way back in December and February.

We left Bernie Smith's dock about 8:00 o'clock that morning, and after a 30-minute run we had passed under Long Key bridge...and out into the open ocean. My first words were, "Hang on to your hats, this is going to be rough." For the next hour the Striker plowed through waves, rolling side to side, and I tried the best I could to keep from entangling lobster pot lines in the boat's props. If you ever wrap a lobster trap line around your prop, you have a big job on your hands. The season for Florida crawfish had just opened, and there were thousands of lobster pots strung out over every square foot of open ocean.

By 9:30 we were approaching Bone Fish Tower, which sits on the edge of West Turtle Shoal, about two miles off Grassy Key. It was about this time that Stefan Sykora, up on the bow, saw a red flare just off the horizon. He called up to me on the bridge, and a minute later I also saw a red flare go up. I called the Coast Guard and alerted them, gave our position, and picked up speed as we headed towards the flares that now seemed to be going off every minute or so. I counted six before we could spot the small 17-foot outboard boat low in the water about one mile to the west of Bone Fish Tower. As we came up to the boat we could see someone floating about fifty yards away from it, clustered in a pile of *three* life preservers. He was the one firing off the flares. The boat had less than a foot of freeboard, and clinging to the other side of the boat was a rather overweight person…without any life preservers.

We picked up the first person, and once safely on board I maneuvered the *Expedition* around to the downwind side of the boat, and Gossage threw the other man a buoy on the end of a line. "Grab it and we'll pull you in." He answered, "I can't, I'm too tired." We all wondered what would have happened if the boat had decided to take a dive to Davy Jones' locker at that point. Would the other guy have given up one of his three life preservers? We finally got the other man aboard the boat, called the Coast Guard and advised that they were safe, and waited.

It was the better part of an hour before the Coast Guard cutter emerged from the west end of Marathon and made the five-mile trip to take the "survivors" off our hands. In the meantime, while jockeying around to pick up a few things that had floated away from the submerged boat, I managed to wrap a lobster pot line around our prop. Yes, no matter how careful you are, it happens! Brad went over the side, and for the next twenty minutes he clung to the rudder on the stern of our boat bouncing around in four-foot waves and cut the line free. It had almost welded itself to the prop shaft.

It was an interesting day. Our DGPS had decided at the last minute to act up and not function. It was time to call it quits. We headed back to Lower Matecumbe for a well-deserved lobster feast. The weather now definitely had a mind of its own. We had a choice of waiting for several days in the hopes that a few good days of sunshine might happen—or wrapping up the season. The decision was an easy one. I decided to put both boats up on blocks at the Driftwood Marina in Marathon. There they had a better chance of riding out a hurricane, and I wouldn't have to check the bilge pumps every three days or turn the engines over every week. It was a good year, everyone had a great time, and we recovered some interesting artifacts. Thus ended Salvage Season 2000.

What about the *San Fernando*? Everything depends upon the team's schedule. The boat stands ready in Marathon, less than three miles from our lease site. I have requested a one year extension on our state-approved lease and hopefully, after the first of the year, the weather and schedules will cooperate. If Colombia decides to sign the legislation, another schedule will take precedence, one that will have a great deal of excitement attached.

Bob "Frogfoot" Weller

EXPEDITION *CREWMEMBERS AT CROSSED ANCHORS OFFICE. (L. to R.) Joe Kimbell, Brad Johnson, "Frogfoot", Bill Brom, and Doug Gossage.*

CAPTAIN STEFAN SYKORA (L.) tends the magnetometer cable, and Investor/Diver John Harkins (R.) surfaces from inspecting a "hit" on the San Fernando. Photos by: "Frogfoot."

SINKING BOAT and survivor clinging to it...saved by the crew of the Expedition.   Photo by: Bill Brom.

APPENDIX A:
RECOVERY OF THE
1733 *CAPITANA* GOLD MEDALLION
by Jack "Blackjack" Haskins

One of my favorite Florida Keys shipwrecks has to be the 1733 Spanish warship *El Capitana Rubí*. This wreck site lies in 19 to 21 feet of normally warm and clear water, and the bottom around it is pure white sand, interrupted by an occasional grass patch teeming with tropical fish. The main ballast pile disappeared from sight long ago, having been turned over by salvors so many times.

I don't know of a seasoned treasure hunter in the Florida Keys who hasn't fallen in love with "Art McKee's Galleon," as we used to call the *capitana*. In the early 1950s a fisherman named Reggie Roberts told Art about the big cannon-covered pile of rocks out near the edge of the reef off Plantation Key. This intrigued Art, and he persuaded Reggie, accompanied by his two sons Earle and Jack, to take him out and show him the wreck. It was everything they claimed it to be, and more. What none of them knew then was that they had found Lieutenant General Don Rodrigo de Torres' flagship of the ill-fated 1733 New Spain Fleet.

From time to time, when both mood and weather prevailed, I would go out with my underwater metal detector and a couple of 100 cubic-foot dive tanks to play around the scatter pattern of the "Capitana." The wreck lies about 4-1/2 miles off shore, just outside state waters. So, back in 1987, before passage of the Florida Keys National Marine Sanctuary Act, it was fair game for anyone who wanted to work it.

I kept my 16-foot fiberglass skiff, with a 120-horsepower Johnson outboard motor, tied to the dock of my canal-front home off Snake Creek, and it would only take me twenty minutes to be over the *capitana*'s remains. I vividly remember that fateful day, 25 April 1987, when the ocean was flat calm, the wind light, and the sea beckoning. So I gathered up my dive gear and loaded the boat that morning.

On my way out to the wreck the water raced beneath me like a transparent rug. It was one of those rare days in the Keys when the water was crystal clear. As the ocean floor streaked past I could see waving gorgonia fans, grass patches, and sponges, and needle-nosed balao tail-walked playfully in front of the boat. As I passed Hen and Chickens Light, about two miles from the "Capitana," I spotted a flock of resident cormorants perched on the white dung-splattered iron framework, holding their wings spread wide to take advantage of the light breeze to dry their feathers.

About a quarter-mile before reaching the "Capitana" the boat raced across a long black reef. I glanced over my shoulder and lined Hen & Chickens Light up with a group of trees on Windley Key. This was the range which I would follow out to the main site. Once there, I worked my way to the north past a few grass patches and dropped the anchor in a sand hole about 250 yards from the main pile. I switched off the motor and let the boat settle back gently on the anchor line.

It was an ordinary day in paradise, and I had repeated this scenario many times before. Another day in the fabulous Florida Keys treasure hunting for a living. It's a tough job, but somebody's got to do it! A pair of pelicans came swooping in and landed about fifty feet behind the skiff. They were looking for a handout. "Sorry guys," I said, "no fishing today, but you're welcome to watch."

The water temperature in late April was edging toward 78 degrees, and a wetsuit jacket still felt comfortable, so I struggled into my well-worn and patched 3/16-inch neoprene top and proceeded to tank-up for the first dive. Finally, all suited up and with my underwater metal detector in hand, I stepped off into history.

When the bubbles ceased I gave my mask a final clearing and headed for the bottom. It was a good day, and visibility was about eighty feet in all directions. A three-foot long resident barracuda came gliding over to see what all the commotion was about. It hung there suspended about thirty feet away, almost transparent and watching me with a large baleful eye. I looked around to get my bearings, turned on my detector, and started methodically searching the sandy bottom next to a grass patch.

My mind drifted back to 1733...

On the morning of 13 July there was an air of great excitement throughout Havana; the *Nueva España Flota* was leaving for Spain! A rosy sunrise greeted the ships as they worked their way out of the harbor, past stark-white Morro Castle, and into the open sea, where a fair southeast wind met them. Don Rodrigo de Torres' flagship *El Rubí*, newly painted bright red and with cross-emblazoned sails, led the *flota* up the Bahama Channel. This swift north-flowing waterway, known today as the Gulf Stream, would give the ships an extra three to 3-1/2 knots boost and drive them up to the 34th parallel, where the predominant westerly winds would carry them home to Spain.

That was the plan. However, a fast building tropical cyclonic weather system 300 miles to the southeast had other plans for them.

A brown stained, wrinkled and worm-eaten letter I found at the Archive of the Indies in Seville, Spain best describes what happened next. It was written by the Spanish Naval Commissioner, Don Alonso de Herrera, to the President of the Council of Trade in Cádiz, Spain.

"On the 14th of July we discovered the islands of the Florida Keys. By 9:00 that night the wind began to rise out of the north. It continued to freshen to the point where we all knew a hurricane was imminent. We found ourselves close to the expressed keys, with the wind and sea so strong we were unable to properly govern ourselves, and each new gust came upon us with renewed major force.

"On the 15th signs were made among the ships of the fleet to try and arrive back to La Havana. But we were unable to do so for the wind went around to the south without slacking in force or lessening the height of the seas. By 10:30 that night we had all grounded on the expressed keys at a distance of 28 leagues in length.

"This Capitana grounded off the one called Cayo Largo, two and one half leagues from shore. I make assurance to Your Lordship that it was fortunate we grounded for if the contrary had occurred we would have all drowned because the hold was full of water and we were unable to pump it out faster than it was coming in...."

The ships of the New Spain Fleet numbered 21, counting the two supply ships going along in convoy to Saint Augustine. One of the ships, *El Africa* of Captain Daniel Huboni, managed to save itself by deploying two huge storm anchors in 200 feet of water east of the north Key Largo reef line. The rest grounded on top of the reefs and shallows of the Florida Keys, from north Key Largo to Marathon. Several were refloated and taken back to Havana, but the remains of the bulk still lie here awaiting the persistent treasure diver.

In 1974 I worked the "Capitana" under contract with the State of Florida (S-14-A), with a company called Peninsular Exploration & Salvage, Inc., which was operated by Richard MacAllaster and Rex DeRosay. We worked the wreck with an ancient 50-foot fishing boat, equipped with a mailbox-type dredging device that swung down over the ship's lone propeller. When the ship was tied off with anchors and placed in gear in twenty feet of water, the propwash would create a hole 35 feet in diameter and eight feet deep. We found lots of artifacts with this old contraption.

We were always accompanied by a State Agent who catalogued and tagged everything that was brought up. There was this one thing I found which will always stay burned indelibly in my memory. It was an ivory, hand-carved combination sundial and magnetic compass, about three inches tall by one inch in diameter. This piece, along with many other "Capitana" artifacts, can still be seen in the State of Florida's shipwreck display in Tallahassee, Florida.

So when I went out diving that day in April of 1987 I was visiting a wreck which was no stranger to me. I worked around the grass patch for about an hour, picking up several encrusted ship's nails, which I placed in a pile at the base of the grass patch. My thoughts went back to one particular day on the *capitana* when I had spotted what looked like a flintlock pistol, about thirty feet away. It was lying on the surface, partially camouflaged by virtue of nature. I flippered over and placed my detector loop over it. The resulting loud squeal confirmed my suspicions; the object *was* a 1733 vintage flintlock pistol! It is amazing what you can find on the bottom if you know what you're looking for.

As I continued to methodically search the bottom, I was easing away from the grass patch and now was searching an area of open sand about fifty feet east of it. Suddenly my underwater detector let out a squeal. I laid the detector down and proceeded to hand-fan away the sand and coral debris. When I had a hole about six inches deep I placed the loop into the depression.

"Squeeeeeal!" This time much louder.

Knowing I had to be close to the buried object, I gave a couple of more fast sweeps with my hand, stirring up a big cloud of brown sand and rotted grass debris. When it cleared, a grayish object appeared in the center of the hole.

I reached down and carefully felt the object. It was loose, so I brought it up out of the hole and examined it carefully. It appeared to be an iron lock hasp of sorts, the type which would have been used to secure someone's personal baggage or trunk. I reached into my wetsuit and dragged out a net "goodie" bag, carefully placing the hasp inside. This was a "keeper," and I intended to preserve it.

When detecting, there is an unwritten law: Whenever you find something in a hole you always check again to see if anything else is in there. So I placed the loop down in the hole and it gave off another squeal.

Carefully, and now with a hint of excitement since I knew the lock hasp was a sign of someone's valuable baggage, I hand-fanned the hole deeper. After a couple of minutes I was down to about twelve inches, exposing large hunks of coral rubble.

Then I saw it...

The unmistakable color of gold lying on the bottom, with the mid-day sun glittering off it. My fingers trembled as I retrieved the object. Then I lay there, oblivious to the rest of the world, looking at the most beautiful encrusted gold medallion I had ever seen. Even though it was heavily coated with dead coral, I could still make out the jewels around the central figure of Our Lady of Guadalupe. I turned it over and realized the other side was crafted as well. It was a two-sided medallion, which made it even more desirable.

Instinctively, I swung the loop over the hole, hoping for the impossible. Nothing. The area was clean.

I unbuckled my weight belt, which had a surface buoy tied to it, dropped it into the hole and swam my golden prize back to the boat. I reached over the boat's gunwale and carefully placed the medallion on the seat before scrambling back aboard. I shucked off the air tank, kicked off my fins, and sat down on the seat. Carefully I peered at the golden Madonna, knowing I was the first person to do so in over 250 years.

It was even more beautiful on the surface, and I knew I had found something of indeterminable worth. It was the day of all days for me, and the beginning of a lifelong struggle to try and top it.

Life has a way of turning sweet or sour in a heartbeat, so to speak. On 25 April 1987 I found the greatest artifact of my shipwreck salvage diving career. On 27 April I had to commit my best friend to eternity. My buddy of ten years through thick and thin, Henry the Cat, had terminal cancer, and my last kindness to him was to have Dr. Foley put him to sleep. They say this is the ultimate act of love between an animal and its human companion. Maybe so, but it was the hardest damned decision I've ever had to make.

A lot of water has gone under my boat since that day on the "Capitana," and I confess I have yet to recall a day like it. But a word to the wise for the aspiring treasure seeker: *Persistence!* The secret to finding treasure isn't some mystical acumen, possessed only by a certain select few, it's a measure of the time spent on the bottom picking up a million myriad mediocre things, punctuated by the one moment of glory when you find the Holy Grail!

=Jack=

NOTE: Please see photos on pages 158—159.

Haskins' Capitana Medallion
1733 Treasure Fleet
Florida Keys
Drawing by: Cindy Gilbert King—1990

APPENDIX B:
THE "CLASS" OF '33 (1733)

The salvage divers who researched, located, and salvaged the 1733 Spanish Treasure Fleet ships did more than romanticize sunken treasure. They began an era that will be known later in history as "The Treasure Salvage Years." It continues today as this book is being published, but the days are numbered! The constant battle with archeologists, paid by their respective state budgets, is bringing an end to the euphoria of finding one's own "gold doubloon."

In the beginning, these salvors dedicated their time, money, and energy to innovate methods of salvage on a personal basis, something the private sector became involved in only on a commercial level. They were successful. Because of their successes, the public was able to enjoy what had been hidden under the sands of time and the ocean for over 200 years.

In this book, one of the major considerations has been to give credit to those divers who brought the 1733 Spanish Treasure Fleet to life. I hope that I have done that. To the "Class of '33": *¡MAS ORO!*

PHOTO: *"Seascribe"*   PHOTO: *Pat Clyne*

John Berrier   *Mel Fisher*

PHOTO: "Seascribe"

Carl Frederick

Art Hartman

PHOTO: "Frogfoot"

Jack "Blackjack" Haskins

Bobby Jordan

PHOTO: "Seascribe"

"Whitey" Keevan

PHOTO: "Seascribe"

Duke Long

PHOTO: "Seascribe"

Richard MacAllaster

McKee Family Album

Art McKee

Chuck Mitchell

William "Pat" Patterson

C. "Kip" Porter

PHOTO: *"Frogfoot"*

Bernie Smith

PHOTO: *"Frogfoot"*

Henry C. Taylor III

PHOTO: *"Seascribe"*

Roy Volker

Carl Ward

PHOTO: "Seascribe"

Don Washington

Bob "Frogfoot" Weller

Some salvager portraits (other than those in the text) were not available. It was not intentional to exclude anyone—they all helped to make the "Treasure Salvage Years" memorable.

Mention must be made of the following divers as being members of **"The 'Class' of '33"**: Don Gurgiola (no photo); Tom Gurr (photos, page 87, 115); Craig Hamilton (photo, page 47); George Hosford (photo, page 112); Jimmy Jones (photo, page 228); Jim King (photo, page 112); Marty Meylach (photo, page 58); Art Sapp (photo, page 174); Bobby Savage (photo, page 174); and Dr. Bobby Welberry (no photo).

APPENDIX C:
1733 SALVAGE CHART WRECK LOCATIONS
AND G.P.S. CO-ORDINATES

"Parajes Donde Vararon Los Navios de la Flota del Año 1733." —
"Places where the ships of the 1733 Fleet ran aground."

All four contemporary salvage charts agree, by number, as to each vessel's identity and its position:

1. **El Pinque Populo**
   LAT. 25 degrees, 21.833 minutes
   LONG. 80 degrees, 09.676 minutes.

2. **El Aviso (Ref.)**

3. **El Infante**
   LAT. 24 degrees, 56.556 minutes
   LONG. 80 degrees, 28.531 minutes.

4. **San José (San Joseph)**
   LAT. 24 degrees, 56.919 minutes
   LONG. 80 degrees, 29.334 minutes.

5. **La Capitana (El Rubí)**
   LAT. 24 degrees, 55.460 minutes
   LONG. 80 degrees, 30.900 minutes.

6. **Chavez**
   LAT. 24 degrees, 56.171 minutes
   LONG. 80 degrees, 34.985 minutes.

7. **La Balandra (Ref.)**

8. **Herrera**
   LAT. 24 degrees, 54.330 minutes
   LONG. 80 degrees, 35.530 minutes.

9.   ***Tres Puentes***
LAT. 24 degrees, 53.607 minutes
LONG. 80 degrees, 35.011 minutes.

10.   ***Murguia (Ref.)***

11.   ***San Pedro***
LAT. 24 degrees, 51.802 minutes
LONG. 80 degrees, 40.780 minutes.

12.   ***El Lerri (El Terri)***
LAT. 24 degrees, 50.755 minutes
LONG. 80 degrees, 42.850 minutes.

13.   ***El Poder de Dios (Ref.)***

14.   ***San Francisco***
LAT. 24 degrees, 49.185 minutes
LONG. 80 degrees, 45.35 minutes.

15.   ***La Almiranta***
LAT. 24 degrees, 48.10 minutes
LONG. 80 degrees, 45.418 minutes.

16.   ***Las Angustias (Charanguero Grande)***
LAT. 24 degrees, 47.455 minutes
LONG. 80 degrees, 51.738 minutes.

17.   ***El Sueco de Arizón***
LAT. 24 degrees, 46.380 minutes
LONG. 80 degrees, 53.478 minutes.

18.   ***San Fernando (Ref., Not Yet Located)***

19.   ***San Ignacio***
LAT. 24 degrees, 41.550 minutes (old beacon remains)
LONG. 80 degrees, 56.310 minutes.

GLOSSARY OF A 1733 CARGO MANIFEST

Achiote	Annatto seeds used as a spice in cooking
Añil	Indigo, blue dye (English: anil)
Azúcar	Sugar
Azúcar terziado	Brown sugar
Bálsamo	Balsam
Bateas	Wooden trays
Bucaros	Earthenware vessels, possibly olive jars
Cacao	Cocoa bean or nut
Chocolate	Chocolate
Colgadura	Tapestry
Copal	Copal (transparent resin)
Cosas de regalo	Gifts, keepsakes
Crudos medias	Linen stockings
Cueros	Hides
Cueros curtidos	Tanned hides
Escritorios	Writing desks, or chests of drawers
Grana	Cochineal (insects, source of red dye)
Grana fina	Refined cochineal
Grana silvestre	Uncultivated or wild cochineal
(H)arina	Flour
Herramientas de zapatos	Cobbler's tools.
Jarros	Jars, pitchers
Libros	Books
Lienzo de pintura	Painting on linen or canvas
Losa de China	Porcelain tiles
Mechoacan	Bindweed, sarsaparilla used as a medicine
Medias de Paris	Stockings
Oro	Gold
Oro labrado	Worked gold
Piedras de fusil	Musket flints
Pipetas de covalonga	Small bottles of "covalonga," substitute for quinine
Plata	Silver
Plata labrada	Worked silver
Plomo	Lead musket balls

Purga	Molasses
Regalos	Gifts, keepsakes
Tarros de Gada	Glazed earthen pans
Tibores de Loza de China	Porcelain jars
Tinaja	Large earthen jar
Tinta	Dyestuff, logwood
Trigo	Wheat
Vainillas	Vanilla beans

Weights and Measures

Arroba	A unit of weight equal to 25.356 dry pounds (Avoir.) Of oil, 3.32 gallons Of wine, 4.26 gallons
Bocado	Assayers "bite"
Braza	5.5 feet of depth
Cable (English)	1/10th of a sea mile
Carga	6.3 bushels of grain, or 250 pounds of ore
Castellano	1/50th of a Mark
Caxita	Small Box or Chest
Caxones (*Cagones*)	Chests, Crates
Codo (1/2 *Vara*)	16.5 inches
Codo de Ribera	23.37 inches
Cuartilla (quarter part)	1.07 gallons (1/4 arroba) 1.57 bushels (1/4 fanega) 1.05 dry quarts (1/4 celemin) 1.07 quarts (1/4 azumbre)
Fanega	Quintal (101.44 pounds)
Gramo	15.432 grains
Grano	2.0609 grains, 1/12 *tomín*
Grains (1,187)	(1) ounce
Guacales	Hampers
League (British)	3.0 Nautical Miles
Legua (Sp. league)	3.4 Nautical Miles
Mark (*Marco*)	Equals 1/2 pound = 230 Grams = 67 *Reales*

Milla	.866 mile
Onza (oz.) Pre-1728	27.4680 grams (Gold Doubloon)
Onza (oz.) Post-1728	27.0642 grams (Gold Doubloon)
Palmo	8.23 inches
Quilate	Quality, in carats
Quintal	A unit of weight equal to 101.44 pounds
Quinto	20% Royal Tax (one-fifth)
Requa	A train of 50 mules
Sacas	Sacks or Bags
Talago, Talega	Sailcloth Sack for money
Tercios	Bales
Tomín	24.731 grains
Vara	32.9 inches
Zurrones	Leather bags

Official markings on ingots of precious metals

The Spanish method of numbering, particularly on silver bars, can be difficult to understand because it varies from the English in a backward sort of way:

A bar over a letter multiplies it by 1000; thus, $\overline{X}$ equals 10,000. There are two rules when writing integers: If a letter is immediately followed by one of equal or lesser value, the two values are added; thus XX equals 20, XV equals 15, VI equals 6. However, if a letter is immediately followed by one of *greater* value, the first is subtracted from the second; thus IV equals 4, XL equals 40, CM equals 900, XLVII equals 47. Otherwise follow the English rule: CXVI equals 116, MCXX equals 1,120, and MCMXIV equals 1,914.

Spanish symbols for a few of the important words:

Ounce   ⨍

Peso (National Money)

6 Pesos 2 1/2 Reales	$6 \pounds \, 2 \tfrac{1}{2} \, \overline{r}$
8 Pesos	$8\pounds$
11 Pesos, 3 Reales, 5 granos	$11 \,,\, 3 \, {}^{5}\!/\!g$
20 Pesos	$20\pounds$
1,000	$\mathbb{D}$ OR $\ominus$ OR $\bigcup$
Gold	$22G$ OR $\mathcal{CXC}$

Reference Library Information

Archivo General de Indias (AGI)—Seville, Spain
Archivo de Protocolos de Sevilla—Seville
Archivo de Protocolos de Cádiz—Cádiz, Spain
Archivo Histórico de Protocolos—Madrid, Spain
Real Academia de la Historia—Madrid
Biblioteca Nacional—Madrid
Archivo del Catedral de Barbastro—Barbastro, Spain

REFERENCES:
(In order cited)

Shipwrecks of Florida. Singer, Steven D. Pineapple Press. Sarasota, FL. 1992.

Spanish Treasure in Florida Waters. Marx, Robert F. Mariners Press. Boston. 1979.

History of Castillo de San Marcos & Fort Matanzas. Manucy, Albert. National Park Service. Washington. 1955.

Shipwrecks Near Wabasso Beach. Weller, Robert "Frogfoot", and Ernie "Seascribe" Richards. EN RADA Publications. W. Palm Beach. 1996.

The Dreamweaver. Bob "Frogfoot" Weller. Fletcher & Fletcher. Charleston, SC. 1996.

Tragedy on the High Seas: A History of Shipwrecks. Hudson, Kenneth and Ann Nicholls. A & W Publishers. New York. 1979.

Sunken Treasure on Florida Reefs. Weller, Robert "Frogfoot." Crossed Anchors. Lake Worth. 1997, 1993.

Pieces of Eight. Wagner, Kip, and L. B. Taylor, Jr. Dutton. New York. 1966.

Hurricanes of the Caribbean and Adjacent Regions, 1492-1800. Millás, José Carlos. Academy of the Arts & Sciences of the Americas. Miami. 1968.

Deadliest Atlantic Tropical Cyclones, 1492-1994. NOAA Technical Memo NWS NHC-47.

Yesterday's Florida Keys. Windhorn, Stan, and Wright Langley. Seeman. Miami. 1974.

Shipwrecks of the Western Hemisphere 1492-1825. Marx, Robert F. World. NY. 1971.

Treasure Diver's Guide. John S. Potter, Jr. Doubleday. NY. 1960.

In Search of the Golden Madonna. Tippen, G. Lee, and Herbert Humphreys, Jr. Daring Books. Canton, OH. 1989.

"Triaca Producida de un Veneno." Toca Velasco, José Ignacio de. Poem contained in *Naufragios de la Flota Española*, Jaochin Sanchez. Spain. 1734.

Galleon Hunt. Weller, Robert "Frogfoot." Crossed Anchors. Lake Worth, FL. 1992.

(Further Reading)

Diving To a Flash of Gold. Meylach, Martin. Doubleday. Garden City, NY. 1971.

The Funnel of Gold. Peterson, Mendel. Little, Brown. Boston. 1975.

The Spanish Treasure Fleet. Walton, Timothy R. Pineapple Press. Sarasota. 1994.

Famous Shipwrecks of the Florida Keys. Weller, Bob "Frogfoot." Crossed Anchors. Lake Worth. 1990.

(Libraries, Archives)

References in the Public Library, Islamorada, FL.

Biblioteca Nacional—Madrid, Sección Geográfica y Mapas.

British Museum—MSS Room, London, England.

Archivo General de Indias (AGI)—Seville, Spain:
Contratación 5147, 5102.
Indiferente General 2300, 1987, 57, 2021.

Archivo General de Indias (AGI)—Mexico:
Contratación 2977.

(Original Research by Others)

Translation of Spanish documents by Jack Haskins.

Translation of Spanish documents by Jim Clupper.

Translation of Spanish documents by Dr. Alan Craig.

(Newspapers, Periodicals)

Keynoter, various newspaper articles 1965-72.

Miami Herald, various newspaper articles 1960-72.

National Geographic, numerous articles 1888-present.

PLVS VLTRA Newsletter, numerous articles by author.

(Miscellaneous)

Personal discussions with salvors Art Hartman, Don Gurgiola, Bobby Klein, Marty Meylach, Bernie Smith, Kip Porter.

Diving log entries of *Frogfoot*, and "Royal Fifth."

"Underwater Archeological Survey of the 1733 Fleet." Smith, Roger C. and James Dunbar. State of Florida Division of Archives, History and Records Management. Tallahassee.

HAULING IN THE ANCHOR! This was quite a common sight along "Galleon Alley" (U. S. Hwy. #1) in the Florida Keys during the glory days of treasure diving in the 1960s and 1970s! Here a salvage diver is bringing ashore a 10-foot anchor from a ballast mound which marks the wreck site of a ship of the ill-fated 1733 Spanish fleet. Enterprising tourist guides would excite their fares by stopping nearby these scenes—or in view of one of the salvage vessels at work—and announcing over the bullhorn that "This anchor was from...or this boat was salvaging...a rich Spanish galleon which sank nearby 2-1/2 centuries earlier!"

SPANISH SALVAGE CHARTS AND *"RAZON Y CUENTA"*

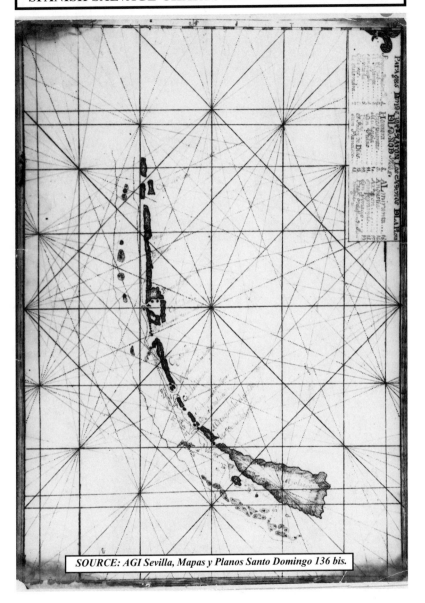

SOURCE: AGI Sevilla, Mapas y Planos Santo Domingo 136 bis.

1733-ERA SALVAGERS' CHART. Cayo Largo is located at upper right.
Wrecks are numbered on THE chart, tabulated at upper left.

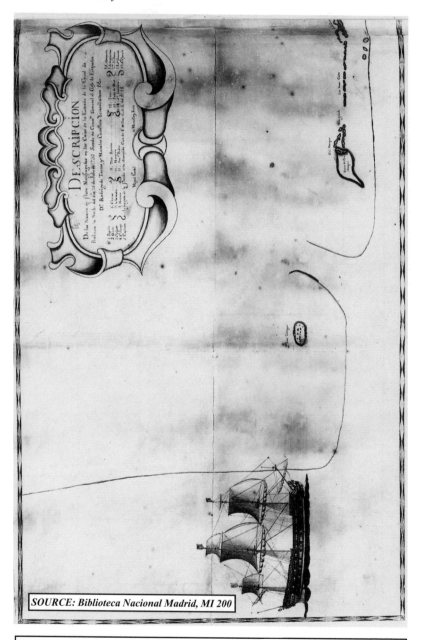

SOURCE: *Biblioteca Nacional Madrid, MI 200*

***1733-ERA SALVAGERS' CHART. Dry Tortugas at lower center. Wrecks
are numbered on the chart, tabulated under Description. (Cont'd >)***

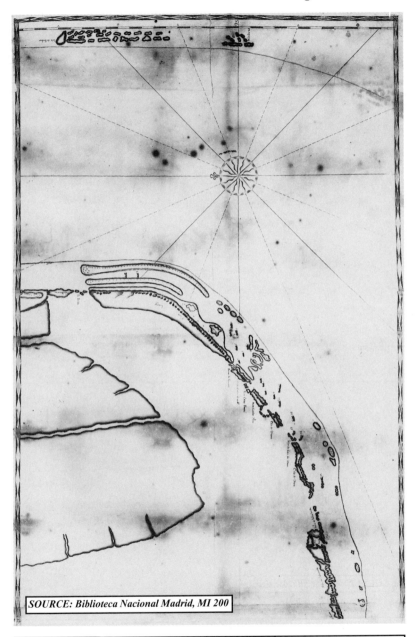

SOURCE: *Biblioteca Nacional Madrid, MI 200*

1733-ERA SALVAGERS' CHART. Continued from previous page, bottom of this chart connects to top of previous. Mainland Florida at top.

SOURCE: AGI Sevilla, Mexico 2977

REFERRED TO AS THE "RAZON Y CUENTA," this is the "spread sheet" of 1733, accounting for the major valuable cargoes carried from Vera Cruz to Havana by the silver fleet of that year. The ships are listed down the left side, the commodities across the top. (Cont'd. next page.)

SOURCE: AGI Sevilla, Mexico 2977

Continued from previous page. The heading reads: "Map of the wealth and assets, that from the port of Vera Cruz are being conveyed registered for Castilla, by the fleet under the command of the Chief of the Squadron Don Rodrigo de Torres y Morales with the following distinction."

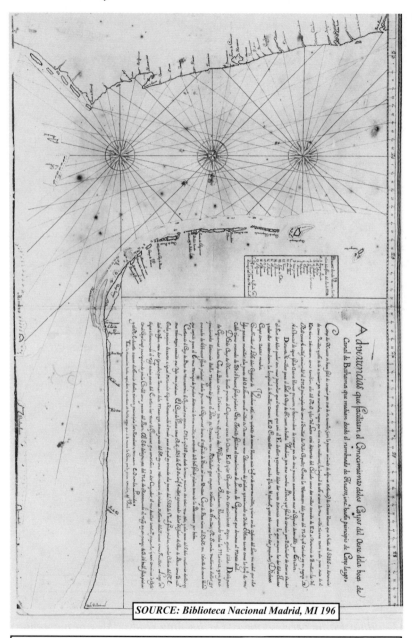

SOURCE: *Biblioteca Nacional Madrid, MI 196*

1733-ERA SALVAGERS' CHART. *Cuba is shown at left of chart, Bahamas at bottom. Wrecks are numbered on the chart, tabulated left of legend.*

INDEX

Y, Z